AIR COMMANDO FIGHTERS OF WORLD WAR II

By

EDWARD YOUNG

ISBN: 1-58007-022-1

Library of Congress Catalog Card Number: 98-60157

Text by Edward Young

Published by:
Specialty Press Publishers and Wholesalers
11605 Kost Dam Road
North Branch, MN 55056
1-800-895-4585

Book Trade Distribution by:
Voyageur Press
123 North Second Street
Stillwater, MN 55082
Phone: 800-888-9653
Fax: 651-430-2211

ACKNOWLEDGMENTS

This history simply could not have been written without the assistance of many former members of the Air Commando fighter squadrons. Four men proved invaluable. I would like to express my sincere thanks to Olin B. Carter (Fighter Section and 6th Fighter Squadron, 1st Air Commando Group), William Burghardt (5th Fighter Squadron, 1st Air Commando Group), W.R. Eason (1st Fighter Squadron, 2nd Air Commando Group), and Ray Lahmeyer (4th Fighter Squadron, 3rd Air Commando Group). Their constant support and encouragement made this history possible.

I would also like to thank the following members of the three Air Commando groups who were kind and patient enough to submit to interviews, to answer correspondence, or who provided photographs:

1st Air Commando Group: Benton Hall, Jack Klarr, Hubert Krug, Roland Lynn, Rudy Melichar, Franklin Misfeldt, Daniel Mitchell, Eugene Piester, Walter Radovich, and Aurele Van De Weghe.

2nd Air Commando Group: Albert Abraham, Donald Branyon, William Buxton, Hadley Dixon, Walter Dzubella, George Eagling, William Gadow, Robert Grace, Dale Grastorf, Harold Hettema, Charles LeFan, Kevin Mallen, Boniface Mayer, Robert Smith, and Bob Spann.

3rd Air Commando Group: Vincent Clark, Kenneth Heller, Vincent Krout, Robert LaCroix, Wilfred McCabe, Rex Pealer, Joe Singletary, Donald Songer, Ray Van Order, and Jacques Young.

I am grateful for permission that was granted to copy original maps created subsequent to World War II for official history works and archives. Maps utilized with this book came from documents from Her Majesty's Public Records Office; *The War Against Japan*, a document commissioned by Great Britain; and *The Army Air Forces in World War II*, a document commissioned by the U.S. Air Force. While some clarity may have been lost in the copy process, these maps are the most accurate depiction of military situations that existed half a century ago and utilize place names that correspond to the history. With the passage of time the names of towns and even nations have changed, i.e. Formosa is now Taiwan.

I would also like to express my thanks to Osamu Tagaya who provided valuable information on Japanese Army Air Force activities in Burma and details of combats involving the Air Commandos; to Thomas Y'Blood of the Office of Air Force History; to the editors of Air Enthusiast for permission to use material that appeared in Air Enthusiast Number 53; and to my editor John Lambert for his support, encouragement, and his patience.

I owe a special debt of gratitude to my family for their understanding of my wish to record a unique time in history.

The reader should be aware that, like the maps, all of the photographs in this volume date from the 1940s. Some were taken by professionals but many are candid shots made by unit members. Most were created under less than favorable conditions and have suffered the ravages of the tropics and time. Despite some obvious flaws in focus or lack of lighting, they were selected because of their uniqueness and historic value as the best visual record of the gallant service of the Air Commandos.

TABLE OF CONTENTS

List of Maps

I

THE ORIGIN OF THE AIR COMMANDOS

Of all the units the United States Army Air Force created during World War II the Air Commandos were the most unique in concept. Designed for the movement and support of large bodies of troops deep behind enemy lines, Air Commando groups combined the roles of troop and supply transport, casualty evacuation, liaison, air superiority, and close air support in a single unit. This multi-faceted application of air power in a lean, flexible, and highly mobile unit was the source of the Air Commando's uniqueness. As their name implies, they were intended to be the aerial equivalent of the army commandos and to add an aerial dimension to commando operations. The Air Commando concept evolved from the interplay of three factors: the nature of the war in Burma, the conflict between divergent American and British interests in Southeast Asia, and the genius and drive of Orde Wingate, pioneer in long-range penetration operations.

The Japanese conquest of Burma in 1942 left British and American military leaders with conflicting objectives and strategies. In capturing Burma, the Japanese cut the Burma road, China's last lifeline. America was committed to supporting China and ensuring that China remained in the war. American war planners were convinced that re-establishing land communications with China through the reconquest of Burma was crucial to sustaining China's war effort. The Americans wanted an offensive that would, at the very least, recapture northern Burma and allow a new overland supply route to China to be built. The British held a very different view. They did not put as great a premium on China's continued participation in the war. More critically, the thought of waging a campaign through the deep jungles of Assam and northern Burma against a fiercely determined foe, using a logistical network that was barely able to support travel in peacetime, was an anathema to Winston Churchill and the British Chiefs of Staff in London. In 1942, the geographic and logistical barriers to Burma's reconquest seemed insurmountable, and the resources required were far in excess of what Britain could make available. Far better, in their eyes, to skip Burma altogether and concentrate on retaking Malaya and Singapore by sea-borne invasion.[1]

The debate between the American and British military leaders over the correct strategy in Burma continued, with the American side increasingly frustrated at what the Americans perceived as a reluctance to pursue an aggressive campaign against the Japanese in Burma. At the QUADRANT Conference held at Quebec in September 1943, Churchill, Roosevelt, and the Combined Chiefs of Staff debated a plan for the defeat of Japan. Despite a number of disagreements on longer term strategy, the Conference did reach agreement on a more limited plan for an offensive to clear the Japanese from northern Burma. At the Conference the Combined Chiefs approved, as part of this campaign, a proposal from a young British General, Brigadier Orde Wingate, to form a long-range penetration group of division strength for operations behind enemy lines.[2]

Orde Wingate was a career officer in the British Army with experience in unorthodox warfare. He combined a brilliant mind with an almost messianic belief in the correctness of his ideas. From his experience fighting the Italians in Ethiopia, Wingate believed that a trained force, if supplied by air, could operate behind enemy lines and wreak havoc on enemy supplies and lines of communication, thereby creating opportunities for the army's main force to advance.

In early 1943, Wingate successfully led a brigade-sized force, named the Chindits, into Burma. The first Chindit expedition proved the validity of his ideas. Wingate's emphasis on mobility and maneuver, supported and sustained by air supply, freed British forces from their dependence on Burma's almost non-existent road system and appeared to offer a solution to the problems of fighting a war in the jungle. Wingate's audacity and drive won Churchill's admiration. Here, Churchill thought, was a real contribution to the Burma campaign he could offer the Americans. Dissatisfied with the quality of British leadership in Burma up to that time, Churchill insisted Wingate be brought to the QUADRANT Conference to expound his theories of long-range penetration.[3]

Wingate's unorthodox ideas caught the imagination of General H. H. "Hap" Arnold, U.S. Army Air Force commander. Arnold was constantly seeking ways to expand and promote the use of air power. In Wingate's concepts of long-range penetration operations he saw an opportunity to experiment with new applications of air power. What Wingate was proposing was a highly mobile form of warfare where troops, supplied entirely by air, would gain a measure of freedom over terrain and would operate without a complex administrative and logistical support structure. What if that same concept of mobility could be applied to air power? Air forces had traditionally been tied to fixed air bases and needed

The inspiration for the Chindits and the Air Commandos: Major General Orde Wingate, left, talks with Colonel Philip Cochran. The atypical British officer and the typical American fighter pilot formed a great Allied team. (NASM)

elaborate logistical support. The various applications of air power — bombardment, close air support, air superiority, and air transport — were contained in separate organizational structures that limited their flexible application. What if these applications could be combined in a single unit, to create an aerial task force, an air force in miniature, and what if this task force could be run with a minimum of men and equipment and made highly mobile? When Wingate asked for air support for his long-range penetration groups, Arnold promised to provide it.[4]

Wingate had asked for transport planes and light aircraft to evacuate his wounded. Arnold promised him an entire aerial task force. Arnold wanted the Army Air Force to be the spearhead of Wingate's operation. He recruited two young veteran fighter pilots, Lieutenant Colonels Philip Cochran and John Alison, and told them to build such an organization to support Wingate.

Cochran had spent six months in North Africa commanding a fighter squadron in the 33rd Fighter Group while Alison had spent nearly a year in China with the 23rd Fighter Group, becoming an ace with six victories. Arnold gave them a blank check and orders to be creative and to experiment: find out what Wingate needed, organize the unit, figure out the tactics, and make it work.

Under the designation Project Nine, Cochran and Alison set to work. They organized a transport section with Douglas C-47s, a light plane section with C-64s and L-5s for liaison and casualty evacuation, a glider section to land men and equipment behind enemy lines, and a fighter section with North American P-51As to provide air superiority and close air support. Once in India they added a bomber section with half a dozen North American B-25s.[5]

The Air Commandos began operations in support of Wingate's second Chindit expedition in February 1944. By then Wingate had organized and trained his Special Force and prepared to insert it deep within Burma to support an advance by Chinese forces under General Joseph Stillwell against Myitkyina.

The aerial invasion of Burma began on March 5 when Air Commando gliders flew in a force to capture a landing site named "Broadway." Within days the Air Commandos had flown in thousands of troops, mules, and supplies. For the next two and a half months, until the onset of the monsoon flooded their forward bases, the 1st Air Commando Group, as it was officially designated, flew constantly in support of the Chindits. These troops severed the main line of Japanese communications to the Myitkyina area, thereby weakening Japanese resistance to the advancing Chinese. More critically for Allied fortunes, in forcing the Japanese to respond to their invasion the Chindits kept an entire Japanese division from fighting in the decisive battle at Imphal, where the British 14th Army inflicted a crippling defeat on the enemy.

Tragically Wingate was killed in an air crash before the end of the campaign, but his second expedition demonstrated how the Allies could surmount the problems of the Burmese terrain. He had proved that a large force of troops could be sustained entirely by air, countering the arguments that Burma could never be conquered over land due to the lack of an adequate transportation system.[6]

For General Arnold, this success was a vindication of his experiment in this new form of warfare. Arnold believed that long-range penetration, combined with the versatility of air power, was the answer to the question of how Burma could be reconquered. What was now needed were the resources to mount an even larger aerial invasion.

On 24 March 1944, based on the initial success of the aerial invasion, Arnold wrote to Admiral Lord Louis Mountbatten, Commander in Chief of South East Asia Command, that he intended to organize four more Air Commando groups for the Burma theater and four new transport groups, to be called Combat Cargo Groups, each with 100 C-47s. He proposed that the Air Commando groups would be used to help long-range penetration groups seize and defend landing grounds behind enemy lines, maintain air superiority over the landing area, and provide close support to the invasion force. The Combat Cargo groups would then fly in large numbers of troops and supplies to exploit the initial landing. He hoped that this new concept would revolutionize the principles of warfare.

That same month General George Marshall, American Chief of Staff, approved Arnold's request to organize the new air commando and combat cargo groups. Arnold requested that John Alison return to the United States to help establish the new units and authorized the activation of the 2nd and 3rd Air Commando Groups.[7]

Colonel John Alison had previously served as a fighter pilot in China with Gen. Chennault's Fourteenth Air Force. (USAF)

Arnold's aerial invasion force would have amounted to 200 fighters, 460 transports, and 400 liaison planes, but at the time it was unwanted. In April 1944, the British high command in India and London continued to resist any plans for the reconquest of Burma. British strategy in Southeast Asia was still focused on sea-borne operations to retake Malaya and Singapore. An overland campaign through deep jungle over a limited road and rail system against a fiercely determined foe remained anathema to Churchill and the British Chiefs of Staff, who were then unaware of the magnitude of the defeat the British 14th Army was inflicting on the Japanese at Imphal.

With the death of Orde Wingate there was no longer a champion for long-range penetration and thus no support for expanding Special Force which was ultimately disbanded at the end of the year. When Mountbatten was not forthcoming with a plan to utilize Arnold's aerial task force, Arnold went ahead with the formation of the combat cargo groups but canceled activation of additional air commando groups.

While the 1st Air Commandos remained in Burma, ostensibly to continue support for Special Force, Arnold and his planning staff debated where to employ the 2nd and 3rd Air Commando Groups who were then in training. General George Kenny, commander of the Fifth Air Force, asked for the two groups to be assigned to the Southwest Pacific for the planned invasion of the Philippines where the initial island-by-island strategy presented opportunities for Air Commando-type operations in conjunction with Philippine guerrilla forces. Then the strategic situation in Burma turned dramatically in favor of the Allies. At Imphal, the 14th Army inflicted a catastrophic defeat on the Japanese 15th Army. General William Slim, 14th Army Commander, realized that a vigorous pursuit of the retreating Japanese would put his troops across the Chindwin River and into Burma's central plains, where Allied air and tank superiority could prove decisive, before the Japanese had a chance to recover. He proposed to Admiral Mountbatten Operation Capital, an advance across the Chindwin into Burma. Admiral Mountbatten agreed with the plan and developed a further scheme for a sea-borne invasion of Rangoon, to be called Operation Dracula, should Operation Capital prove successful. What had seemed impossible in April was under active consideration in August.[8]

At the OCTAGON Conference in September 1944, the Combined Chiefs of Staff, by now fully aware of the magnitude of the Japanese defeat at Imphal, accepted the plan for Operations Capital and Dracula. To ensure that Mountbatten had sufficient air support for both these operations, the Combined Chiefs agreed to allocate the 2nd Air Commando Group to Burma. The Combined Chiefs then allocated the 3rd Air Commando Group to the Pacific theater for the reconquest of the Philippines.

As it happened, the Air Commando groups never again operated in the manner for which they were created: supporting aerial invasions behind enemy lines. While several air commando-style operations were planned, the rapid advance in Burma following the Japanese defeat at Imphal and the decision to speed up the invasion of the Philippines led to their cancellation. With Arnold's reluctant agreement, the Air Commando groups were instead employed as conventional squadrons. In this role, each made their own contribution to the ultimate victory over Japan. This is the story of the Air Commando fighter squadrons.

Fighter Section pilots and their commanders at the start of the campaign. Front Row (L-R): 1st Lieutenant Ned Schramm, Jr., Captain Paul Forcey, Major Robert Petit, Lieutenant Colonel Robert Smith, Lieutenant Colonel Grant Mahony, Colonel John Alison, Colonel Philip Cochran, Lieutenant Colonel Arvid Olson, 1st Lieutenant Robley Melton, 1st Lieutenant Martin O'Berry, Captain Duke Philips. Back Row (L-R): Captain Craig Jackson, 1st Lieutenant Robert Boyd, Captain John Kelting, Captain Olin Carter, Captain Roland Lynn, Lieutenant Herbert Krug, Captain Holly Keller, Captain Neil Bollum, Captain William Gilhausen (KIA), 1st Lieutenant John Meyer, Captain Mack Mitchell, Captain Lester Murray, Captain Earle Schneider (KIA). (NASM) Names via R.D. Van Wagner, *Any Place, Any Time, Any Where: The 1st Air Commando Group in World War II.*

2

WINGATE'S AIR COMMANDOS

The Fighter Section was designed to be the offensive component of the Air Commandos. It was perhaps not unnatural that Cochran and Alison, two fighter pilots, would want to have fighters as part of their new unit; but, in their analysis of what the Chindits would require, they recognized that an offensive capacity was vital to the success of their mission. They envisioned three roles for fighters:

1. Establishing and maintaining air superiority.
2. Providing close air support to the Chindits.
3. Interdicting enemy lines of communications.

The transports would be operating a regular shuttle service in support of the Chindit columns, which would be totally dependent on air drops for their food and ammunition. Light reconnaissance aircraft were essential for the evacuation of wounded. Without reliable air supply, the Chindits could not operate behind enemy lines. The transports would require absolute air superiority over the area of operations in order to function in daylight and fulfill their vital mission. This meant fighters for escort duty and to defeat any Japanese threat in the air.[1]

Wingate's theory of long-range penetration had as its principle goal the disruption of enemy communications, supplies, and targets of value to weaken the main enemy force. With air power, the long-range penetration columns could multiply the disruption severalfold.[2]

The Chindits would need close air support. Once on the ground, their equipment had to be transported by mules. This limited heavy weapons to machine guns and mortars. The Fighter Section would be the Chindits' artillery.[3]

To lead the Fighter Section, Cochran and Alison chose Major Grant Mahony, who had spent a year and a half in combat in the Philippines, Java, and China. Mahony was soft-spoken and reticent on the ground but an aggressive, determined pilot in the air. His intelligent and disciplined approach to any mission commanded the respect of his fellow pilots.[4]

As deputy commander of the Fighter Section, Cochran and Alison chose Major R. T. Smith, an ace with the American Volunteer Group, who was then a squadron commander with the 329th Fighter Group, a P-38 replacement training unit on the U.S. west coast.[5]

Under the proposed table of organization that Cochran and Alison had drawn up, the Fighter Section would have 30 aircraft. Mahony's first task was to recruit experienced pilots. He and Smith chose several with prior combat experience such as Major Robert L. Petit, who had flown P-38s with the 339th Fighter Squadron on Guadalcanal; Captain Mack Mitchell, who had scored three kills flying in China; and Captain Paul G. Forcey, who had joined the Royal Canadian Air Force and flown as a reconnaissance pilot in North Africa. Cochran and Alison had requested that Project Nine be allocated Lockheed P-38s, and in expectation of receiving them, Smith recruited experienced P-38 pilots from the 329th Fighter Group.[6]

Project Nine rapidly began to coalesce as a unit. In total the force had 523 men assigned, one-fourth the number for a regular organization of its size. The fighter pilots reported to Seymour Johnson Air Force Base in North Carolina in late October and early November for training. In the interim, the Fighter Section had a change of aircraft. Lockheed P-38s were not available, and a request for thirty Republic P-47s was also turned down. Instead, 30 North American P-51A Mustangs were allocated. They were hurriedly gathered from training fields in Florida and flown to the West Coast, cocooned, and placed on escort carriers for shipment to Karachi, India.

Fighter pilots arriving at Seymour Johnson received briefings on the P-51A and, for those unfamiliar with it, briefings on the Allison engine as well. All pilots and ground crew were given small arms training. After two hurried weeks, the men of the Fighter Section began shipping out to Miami where they boarded C-54s for the long flight across Africa and the Middle East to Karachi, arriving during the second half of November 1943.[7]

The pilots and ground crew of the Fighter Section moved into barracks at Landi Field, Karachi, to await the arrival of their P-51s. When the first shipment appeared in mid-December it was found that, despite the cocooning process, salt water corrosion had damaged every airplane. None were operational, and the second shipment was in even worse shape. By the end of December sufficient P-51s had arrived and been repaired to allow a small number to move on to India.[8]

On January 1, 1944, six P-51s flew to central India to begin training with the Chindits who had undertaken large scale maneuvers. Wingate, now a Major General, had 20,000 men under his command, consisting of the 14th, 16th, 23rd, 77th, and 111th Brigades, and the 3rd West African Brigade. Wingate's command was

BURMA THEATRE – 1944-45

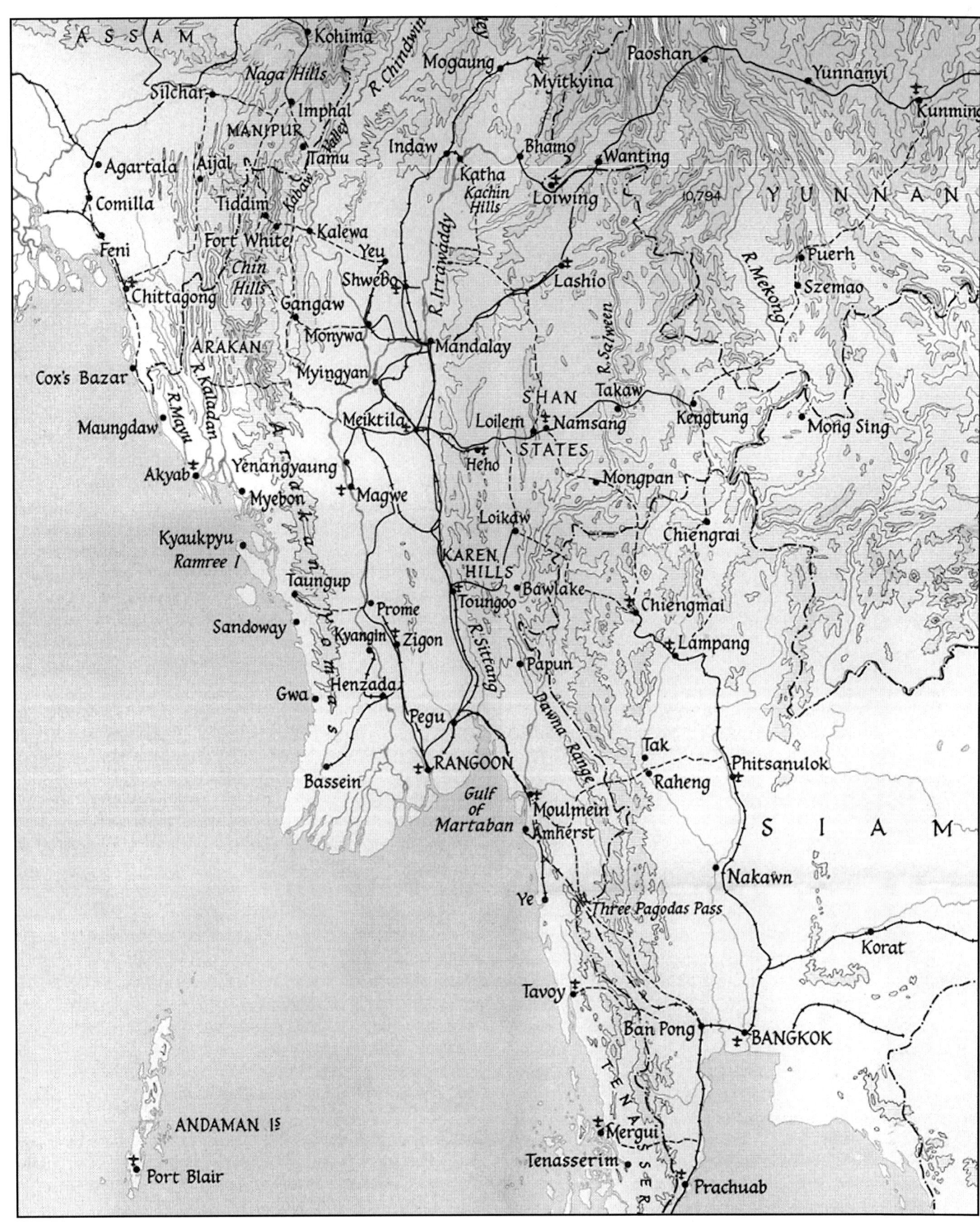

Source: *War Against Japan, Volume III*

designated the 3rd Indian Division and known as Special Force. The Air Commandos received a new designation as well and became the 5318th Provisional Unit (Air). Working closely with the Chindits, the Air Commandos began experimenting and developing a new form of close air support that would become one of their principal contributions to the Burma campaign.[9]

Wingate had requested that Royal Air Force parties be attached to Special Force to control air supply and air support following the success of this practice during the first Chindit operation. In November an RAF component, consisting of 60 officers and 162 enlisted men, joined Special Force at Gwalior. Two officers and three enlisted men were attached to the Headquarters of each Special Force brigade, and an officer and three enlisted men joined each of the several columns that would operate behind Japanese lines. Equipped with portable radios and moving with troops on the march, these RAF parties would coordinate and control air drops of supplies and pass on requests for air support to Special Force headquarters.[10]

The presence of these RAF detachments made possible a new form of close air support that had not yet been attempted in Burma. The most fundamental change was in air-ground communication.[11]

At that point in the war RAF fighters and bombers were equipped with Very High Frequency (VHF) radios, which could not communicate with the Army High Frequency (HF) radio sets. Air strikes in support of ground forces had to be based on the use of coordinates and a thorough briefing before the mission. Once in the air, the pilots could not establish contact with anyone on the ground to guide them to the target. The Army made frequent use of mortar smoke on the target once the RAF airplanes were overhead, but without direct communications, officers on the ground could not give the pilots corrections or new instructions. Finding targets in the jungle was, not surprisingly, extremely difficult and depended to a great extent on a pilot's familiarity with the target area.

In contrast, the Air Commando P-51s were equipped with HF radios, allowing their pilots to communicate directly with the RAF parties on the ground and enabling the RAF control officer to call in air strikes with greater accuracy, and in closer proximity to the ground troops. Senior Royal Air Force officers thought that strikes controlled from the ground were too dangerous, but Cochran and Alison had a strong belief in the capabilities of their pilots and supported the idea.[12]

Working closely with officers from Wingate's staff, Cochran, Alison, Mahony, Smith, and others developed the tactics and procedures to be used for close air support in Burma and then practiced these techniques on maneuvers. What developed was a system combining radio control with target marking. An RAF officer on the ground would direct the fighters to the target area, providing a mortar smoke round just as the Mustangs were ready to attack. Refined with experience, the techniques of close air support employed by the Air Commandos in Burma would prove exceptionally effective.[13]

Cochran and Alison had chosen two forward airfields in Assam, Hailakandi and Lalaghat, as bases for the Air Commandos. These were near to Wingate's for-

Colonel Philip Cochran, left, Colonel John Alison, center, co-commanders of the 1st Air Commando Group, with Lieutenant Colonel Arvid Olson, Group Operations Officer. Olson was a veteran of China's American Volunteer Group (AVG). (NASM)

A flight of P-51As fly over Hailakandi while a Bomber Section B-25H taxis in. (NASM)

ward headquarters at Sylhet. Hailakandi served as Cochran's and Alison's headquarters and as a base for the fighters, while the transports and gliders were based 12 miles away at Lalaghat, commanded by Lieutenant Colonel Clinton Gaty. Both were simple grass strips, little more than a flattened rice paddy, surrounded by jungle. Neither could support operations during the monsoon, which meant that the Air Commandos would have to withdraw sometime in May before the full monsoon broke. While an intensive training program continued without a break in India, the Air Commandos moved in men, equipment, and supplies to the new bases for the coming offensive.

At this juncture Cochran and Alison were called upon to add a fifth section to their unit, a force of medium bombers. In planning for Wingate's operation, it had been assumed that the Royal Air Force would provide some air support to Special Force as a supplement to the Air Commandos. Wingate had asked that more air transport and a squadron of medium bombers be allocated for his use. The RAF's No. 221 Group had assigned No. 84 Squadron, equipped with Vultee Vengeance dive bombers, to support Special Force, but could not provide a force of medium bombers having none available in the theater.

With General Arnold's support, Cochran and Alison went to Major General George Stratemeyer, the newly-appointed American commander of Eastern Air Command, who arranged for 12 North American B-25H Mitchell twin-engine bombers to be assigned to the 5318th. Cochran resorted to the simple expedient of providing his own crews from within the group. They selected R.T. Smith, Deputy CO of the Fighter Section, to lead the new Bomber Section. Major Bob Petit replaced Smith. Armed with four forward-firing .50 caliber machine guns and a 75mm cannon, the B-25s made a potent addition to the Air Commando strike force.[14]

By the end of 1943, it had become clear that the original strategic plan for the recapture of northern Burma, and the role of Wingate's Special Force, would have to be revised with a less ambitious plan. Following the Quadrant Conference in August, Admiral Lord Louis Mountbatten, Commander-in-Chief of the newly-created South East Asia Command, had his staff come up with a comprehensive plan for the dry season offensive involving seven separate, but supporting operations:

1. Three Chinese divisions under General Stillwell would advance from Ledo on the northern front down the Hukwang Valley to capture Myitkyina (Operation Albacore).
2. A separate Chinese force would advance from Yunnan to capture Bhamo and Lashio (Operation Thursday).
3. The British IV Corps on the central front would advance from Imphal to cross the Chindwin River.
4. Wingate's Special Force would land behind Japanese lines to disrupt enemy communications in support of items 1 and 2 above.
5. An airborne attack would seize the Japanese airfield at Indaw, which sat on the railway line from Mandalay to Myitkyina (Operation Tarzan).
6. The British XV Corps would advance down the Arakan Coast to capture Akyab.
7. An amphibious operation "Buccaneer" would be launched to capture the Andaman Islands.

In the original plan Wingate's force would enter Burma over land in three columns to operate in the area of Indaw, a key Japanese communications center, prior to the airborne seizure of the airfield at Indaw itself. Once the airfield had been seized, regular army units would be flown in and Indaw would become the focus for the advance by IV Corps. These attacks would be coordinated with an amphibious operation to seize the Andaman Islands. Generalissimo Chiang Kai-Shek had insisted on the amphibious operation as a prerequisite for Chinese participation in the offensive.[15]

At the Tehran Conference in early December 1943, the Combined Chiefs of Staff determined that the landing craft that had been allocated for Operation Buccaneer would be needed instead for Overlord, the Allied invasion of Europe. Following the cancellation of Buccaneer, Chiang Kai-Shek withdrew his support for a Chinese advance from Yunnan. He then refused to allow any diversion of aircraft from the Hump route, which was the only source of aircraft for the Tarzan airborne operation given the limited number of transport aircraft available in the theater. There was no alternative but to cancel Tarzan.

The plans for an advance by IV Corps were revised as well. IV Corps would now advance up to the Chindwin River but not cross into Burma. The role of Special Force was changed to assisting Stillwell's advance on Myitkyina by disrupting Japanese lines of communication leading north. Any crossing of the Chindwin by IV Corps would be contingent on Wingate's and Stillwell's forces creating a favorable opportunity. There were ominous signs that the Japanese would not remain on the defensive in northern Burma much longer. Allied intelligence was uncovering indications that the Japanese were planning their own offensive into Assam and were moving closer to the Chindwin.[16]

The Japanese were indeed speeding up preparations for Operation U-Go, the invasion of Assam. General Mutaguchi, commanding 15th Army in Burma, had persuaded the Japanese High Command that an advance into Assam would enable them to hold Burma against an Allied offensive, which the Japanese suspected would be launched during the next dry season. Mutaguchi's plan was for the 15th Army to cross the Chindwin and capture Imphal and Kohima and the mountain passes that controlled access between Assam and Burma. Pushing the British Army further back into Assam would give the Japanese a stronger position for the defense of Burma. During December and early January of 1944, the Japanese began bringing troop reinforcements in from Siam and moving supplies up from southern Burma. Mutaguchi hoped to begin his offensive in February or March, as soon as all his troops were in place. While the 15th Army advanced on Imphal, the Japanese 18th Division was instructed to defend the Hukawng Valley and Myitkyina against Stillwell's Chinese force.[17]

The rapidly changing strategic situation presented Wingate with what seemed an insoluble dilemma. The central purpose of Wingate's long-range penetra-

A Fighter Section P-51A undergoing maintenance before going into combat. (NASM)

OPERATION THURSDAY LANDING GROUNDS

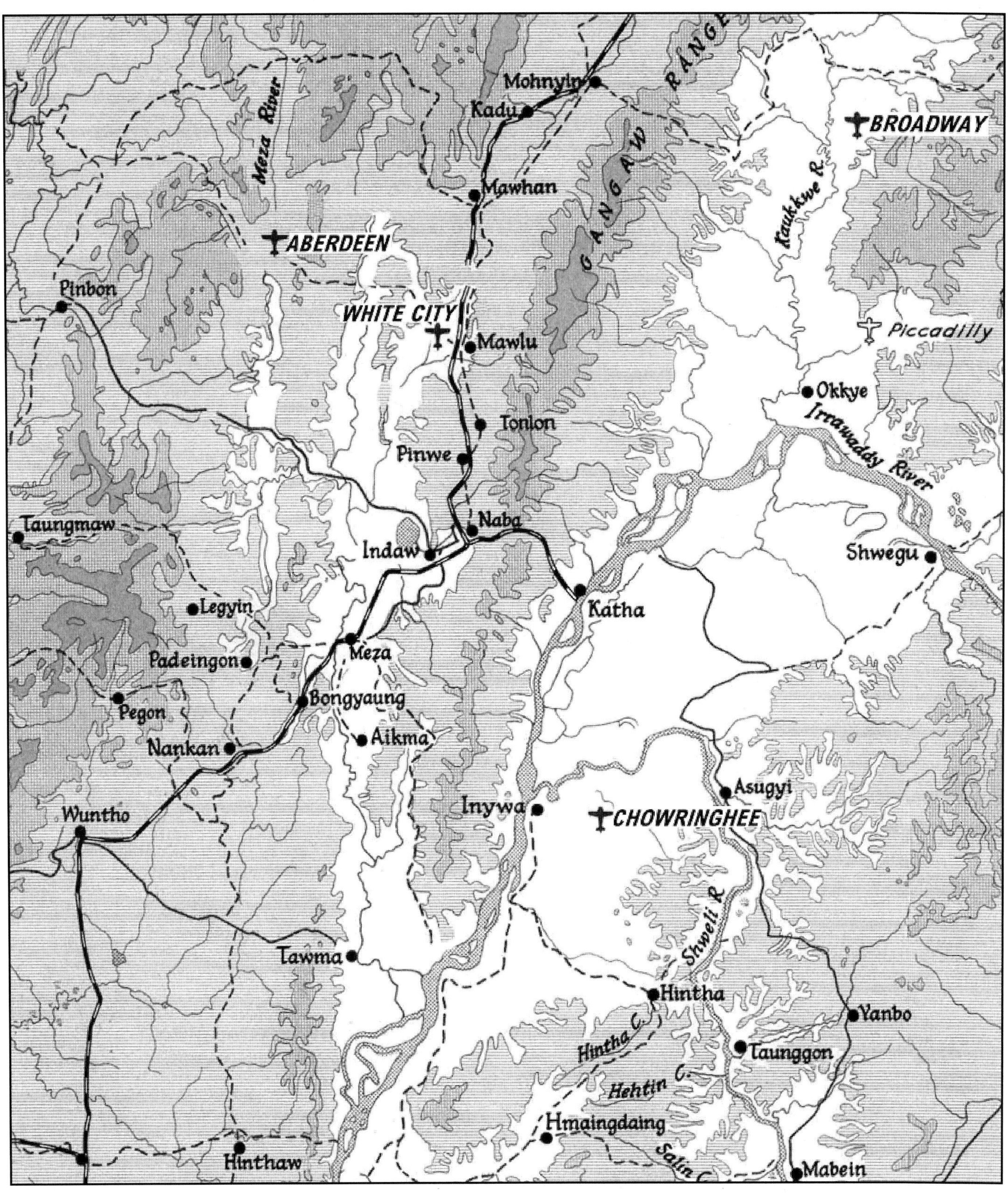

Source: *War Against Japan, Volume III*

tion operation was to create opportunities for the main force to advance into Burma. Now the offensive had been scaled back to advancing down the Hukawng Valley to capture Myitkyina. As in the first Chindit expedition he now faced the potential problem of having to deal with Japanese main force units which would not be drawn off by the advance of the Allied forces. His Chindit columns would be operating well behind enemy lines with no support, to be split up, harassed, and pursued by the Japanese as they had been in 1943.[18]

The Air Commandos provided the solution. Wingate's inventive mind came up with the idea of creating strongholds deep in enemy territory. Wingate realized that he could utilize the air power at his disposal to re-cast his entire operation. The Air Commandos could fly the main force into Burma. The Chindit columns would then set up "strongholds," defensible positions located in areas away from roads and tracks so that Japanese forces could not advance rapidly to counter-attack. The stronghold would overlook an air strip so that supplies could be flown in and wounded troops airlifted out. The stronghold would have a garrison of regular troops equipped with artillery and anti-aircraft guns, and would provide a safe haven for Chindit columns operating in the surrounding area. Wingate also hoped that the fortress-like bases would act as a lure for Japanese troops. With the Fighter Section and the Bomber Section to provide close air support, and with RAF officers on the ground to direct the air strikes, the Chindits now had the capacity not only to defend their strongholds but to inflict severe casualties on any Japanese force that dared attack.[19]

Wingate's final plan was for the 77th Brigade, under Brigadier Michael Calvert, to block the rail line around Mawlu, north of Indaw. The 111th Brigade, under Brigadier W.D.A. Lentaigne, would be flown in to another site south of 77th Brigade a few days later and would operate to the west to cut communications in the Wuntho-Pinlebu area. Meanwhile the 16th Brigade, under Brigadier Bernard Fergusson, would cross the Chindwin and march to the operational area and, taking advantage of the confusion and disruption caused by the other two brigades, attack Indaw and the rail line through it. Wingate chose three landing sites dubbed "Broadway," "Picadilly," and "Chowringhee," for famous roads in New York, London, and Calcutta. The Air Commandos would fly in an assault force with engineers in gliders to prepare rough airstrips for landing the main force in C-47s. The 77th Brigade would fly in on the night of 5/6 March 1944, and 111th Brigade would go in on the night of 9/10 March. The 16th Brigade would begin its march into Burma in early February.[20]

The Fighter Section moved to Hailakandi at the end of January with a total of thirty-three P-51As and twenty-five pilots. They planned to begin operations in early February. Cochran gave the fighters three objectives:

1. Keep a watch on enemy troop movements and concentrations in central Burma.
2. Soften up the area in which Special Force planned to operate, concentrating on Japanese lines of communications leading to the battle area and Japanese supplies.
3. Gain operational experience and familiarity with the terrain, and develop methods of operation.[21]

On 3 February , Cochran took off with six other P-51s on the Fighter Section's first combat mission, an uneventful reconnaissance of central Burma. Two days later, sixteen P-51s armed with 500 lb. bombs sortied to attack the railway junction at Wuntho, a key town along the Mandalay-Myitkyina railroad. They damaged three locomotives and destroyed a dozen freight cars, then flew south to reconnoiter the Japanese airfield at Shwebo, where two Mustangs were slightly damaged by anti-aircraft fire. The next day twelve P-51s returned to Wuntho to bomb warehouses and marshaling yards, destroying four buildings and six freight cars. Again, one airplane was hit by ground fire.[22]

During the following week Grant Mahony led his Mustangs over the area south of Indaw, bombing targets along the rail line as far south as Mandalay. Hitting rail yards at Shwebo and at Monywa, 60 miles west of Mandalay, they destroyed 10 to 20 railroad cars and damaged another ten. A mission on the 10th saw the first use of 325 lb. Navy depth charges, an idea that Major Bob Petit had brought back from Guadalcanal, where the blast effect had proved effective against jungle-covered targets.

On the 12th, the Bomber Section went into action. Six P-51s provided cover for one B-25 that bombed railroad bridges at Meza and Kanni, just south of Indaw. In a demonstration of the versatility and destructive power of its 75mm cannon, the B-25 damaged a temporary bridge at Kanni and blew track out of a roadbed along the railway line.[23]

To date the Fighter Section had not encountered, nor even seen, any Japanese aircraft. That changed on the 14th. At 0820 hours, Cochran led a group of thirteen P-51s on a bombing mission against a railroad station just north of Mandalay. Leaving a few planes above as cover, Cochran and the others dived down on the target. Just after they released their bombs, the high cover shouted out that Japanese fighters were diving on them. Ten Nakajima Ki.43 Oscars of the 50th Fighter Sentai came out of the sun and hit the Mustangs at their most vulnerable point, just as they were beginning their pull out.

The Air Commandos lost two pilots. Captain John Miller bailed out to become a prisoner of war, while Lieutenant Carl Hertzer was posted as missing in action. Three other aircraft were damaged. In the dogfight that followed, Captain Paul Forcey, Major R.T. Smith,

The Meza bridge after Air Commando strikes. The Fighter Section, with the Bomber Section, made regular attacks on Japanese lines of communications. (Courtesy Thomas Y'Blood, Office of Air Force History)

and Captain Duke Phillips each managed to damage an Oscar, one of which crash-landed though the pilot was rescued. In turn, the 50th Sentai claimed eight P-51s destroyed. Following the mission, Wingate put a stop to Cochran's combat flying. He was too valuable to risk losing, and Wingate grounded him.[24]

The Fighter Section's offensive continued without let up. On 15 February, nineteen P-51s set off in the Section's first attempt at destroying a bridge. They bombed a bridge at Ye-u, northwest of Shwebo, destroying it, and then hit another. A group of box cars seen along the way were strafed, leaving eight to ten in flames.

More bridges were attacked over the next few days, in addition to whatever rolling stock could be found. Mahony and Smith developed a form of joint mission where two to three B-25s would have an escort of six P-51s. The bombers ran some risk, though limited, of being intercepted by Japanese fighters, hence the need for a fighter escort. But given the lack of air opposition the fighters also carried bombs. When the bombers had finished their run against the target, the fighters would bomb and then strafe on their own. The combination proved devastating. The B-25s could carry a good load of high explosive, incendiary, or fragmentation bombs, and their 75mm cannon and .50 caliber machine guns gave them a terrific punch as strafers. The Mustangs would carry high explosive bombs or depth charges and could strafe as well with their own four .50 calibers. On 21 February, eight P-51s and three B-25s destroyed a total of ten warehouses in and around the town of Kawlin south of Wuntho.

Cochran's team kept experimenting with new methods and weapons. In an attack on a radio station on February 23, three B-25s dropped high explosive bombs on the target while the 13 escorting P-51s dropped bombs, depth charges, and drop tanks full of aviation fuel. The B-25s then came around and strafed the tanks with their cannon and machine guns, but on

Colonel Cochran flew with the Fighter Section on several early missions until General Wingate grounded him following the mission of February 14, 1944.

this occasion the fuel did not ignite. Still, the experiment had merit and was stored away for future use.

On the 26th, two P-51s took off armed with two 1,000 lb. bombs each to attack the Mu river road bridge at Ye-u. It is believed that this was the first time any Mustang had carried 1,000-pounders on an operational mission. Regarded as a success, the larger bomb joined the Fighter Section's regular armory.[25]

By the end of February the Fighter Section had completed 45 separate or joint offensive and reconnaissance missions. They had attacked most of the primary towns and Japanese supply centers along the main lines of communications heading north from Mandalay. The score included 14 barracks buildings, 45 warehouses, eight railroad or road bridges, a radio station, four locomotives, 63 rolling stock, and three trucks destroyed; and many more damaged. The Fighter Section had adopted, as standard practice, combining fighter sweeps and escorts with bombing missions. The B-25 and P-51 combination had proved its worth and the Fighter and Bomber Sections, sharing both leaders and pilots, worked in close cooperation.[26]

As the date of the aerial invasion approached, the Fighter Section began flying more offensive reconnaissance missions, checking the approaches to the invasion area for signs of Japanese movements while continuing their attacks on Japanese supplies and communications. During the first few days of March, the combined effort of B-25s and P-51s destroyed five locomotives and damaged several others, as well as destroying or damaging a substantial amount of rolling stock bringing supplies north for the planned Japanese offensive.

On 3 March, twelve P-51s bombed the airfield at Shwebo, hitting the runway and buildings on the airfield and then strafing. A few hours later four B-25s followed up the attack, again bombing the runway and aircraft revetments. No Japanese aircraft were seen on the field. [27]

The aerial invasion of Burma began on the night of 5 March 1944. At literally the last minute, reconnaissance photos showed that the landing site at Piccadilly was blocked by logs, and the operation was quickly shifted to Broadway. Despite the losses of several gliders and key equipment, the landings were successful and a rough airstrip was carved out during the next day. By late afternoon, light planes of the Air Commando force were able to land to begin evacuating the wounded. On the night of March 6, Air Commando and RAF C-47s began flying in the main body of the 77th Brigade, as well as tons of stores needed to build Broadway as a stronghold. That first night the transports flew in 900 men, 100 mules, and 20 tons of stores. The remainder of the 77th Brigade and part of the 111th Brigade were flown in over the next several days.[28]

The Fighter Section continued to maintain a close watch on the approaches to Broadway and a constant surveillance over Japanese airfields in the area. On the night of 6 March, a small Air Commando party flew into Chowringhee in gliders to prepare a landing strip for the insertion of the 111th Brigade. On the nights of 8-9 March, transports began landing troops, completing the insertion by 10 March.

A Bomber Section B-25H after striking a target near Wuntho. The Fighter Section's P-51As and the Bomber Section's B-25Hs were a powerful combination. (Courtesy Thomas Y'Blood, Office of Air Force History)

Because of its proximity to Japanese airfields, Wingate wanted Chowringhee abandoned as soon as possible. 111th Brigade formed up into its columns and marched west toward the Irrawaddy and its operational area. On 12 March, under an umbrella of Mustangs, the Brigade crossed the Irrawaddy. Small boats had been brought in the night before by gliders landing on a sandbar in the middle of the river. The noise of the P-51s overhead drowned out the sound of the outboard motors as the troops crossed the river, but fortunately there were no Japanese forces in the area.

The Mustangs carried drop tanks to increase their time over the crossing area, flying in uneventful circles over the river until the crossing was completed at day's end. Wingate's intuition had been correct. On the 12th the Japanese sent a small force to bomb the now abandoned strip at Chowringhee.[29]

On 9 March 1944, Brigadier Calvert began marching the columns of 77th Brigade toward "railway valley," where the rail line and road from Mandalay ran north up to Myitkyina. Prior to the arrival of the 77th Brigade in the area, the Air Commandos launched two heavy raids to knock out Wuntho, where the Japanese held considerable supplies. On 13 March, eight B-25s and sixteen P-51s hit the town with bombs and rockets, destroying a number of warehouses and suspected supply dumps and leaving an inferno. Smoke from the fires rose up to 8,000 feet. The next day, nine B-25s and eight P-51s returned to Wuntho to bomb warehouses and wooded areas west of the town, leaving those targets also in flames.[30]

To keep Japanese troops in the area preoccupied while 77th Brigade closed in, five B-25s and 12 Mustangs bombed Mawlu, some two miles south of the block, on 17 March. The Chindits marked the target area with mortar smoke. The P-51s began the attack, bombing with depth charges, and the B-25s followed, dropping cluster and 500 lb. general purpose bombs from 1,200 feet.

Calvert and his men captured the site for the block after a short, sharp fight and quickly established a defensive position. The British troops soon named the block "White City" after all the supply parachutes that covered the area. It took the Japanese a few days to react, but on 21 March a battalion of the 114th Infantry Regiment from the 18th Division attacked White City in an attempt to oust the British.

That afternoon the Air Commandos conducted their first strike under ground control. The RAF liaison assigned to Calvert's 77th Brigade, Squadron Leader Robert Thompson, whom the Air Commandos called "Tommy," directed three B-25s and eight P-51s, led by Grant Mahony, onto the targets with excellent results.

The next afternoon Calvert called for strikes on Japanese positions 200 yards north of the block. The Vengeances of No. 84 Squadron attacked first, followed by three B-25s and twelve P-51s, the latter dropping depth charges on the Japanese positions that had been marked by mortar smoke. The enemy tried to frustrate the attack by putting their own smoke down on the British positions, but the Mustangs ignored this. These strikes and a spirited defense by Chindit forces broke the back of the Japanese attack. Following this failure the Japanese withdrew and did not attack again for two weeks.[31]

Although a poor photo, this briefing in a bamboo building, where all ranks attended and uniforms were "come as you are," is an interesting contrast with similar well-publicized scenes from England where briefings were held in theatres with officers in ties and uniform attire. The picture is courtesy of Olin Carter, sitting on the floor, third from the left.

JAPANESE AIRFIELDS IN CENTRAL BURMA

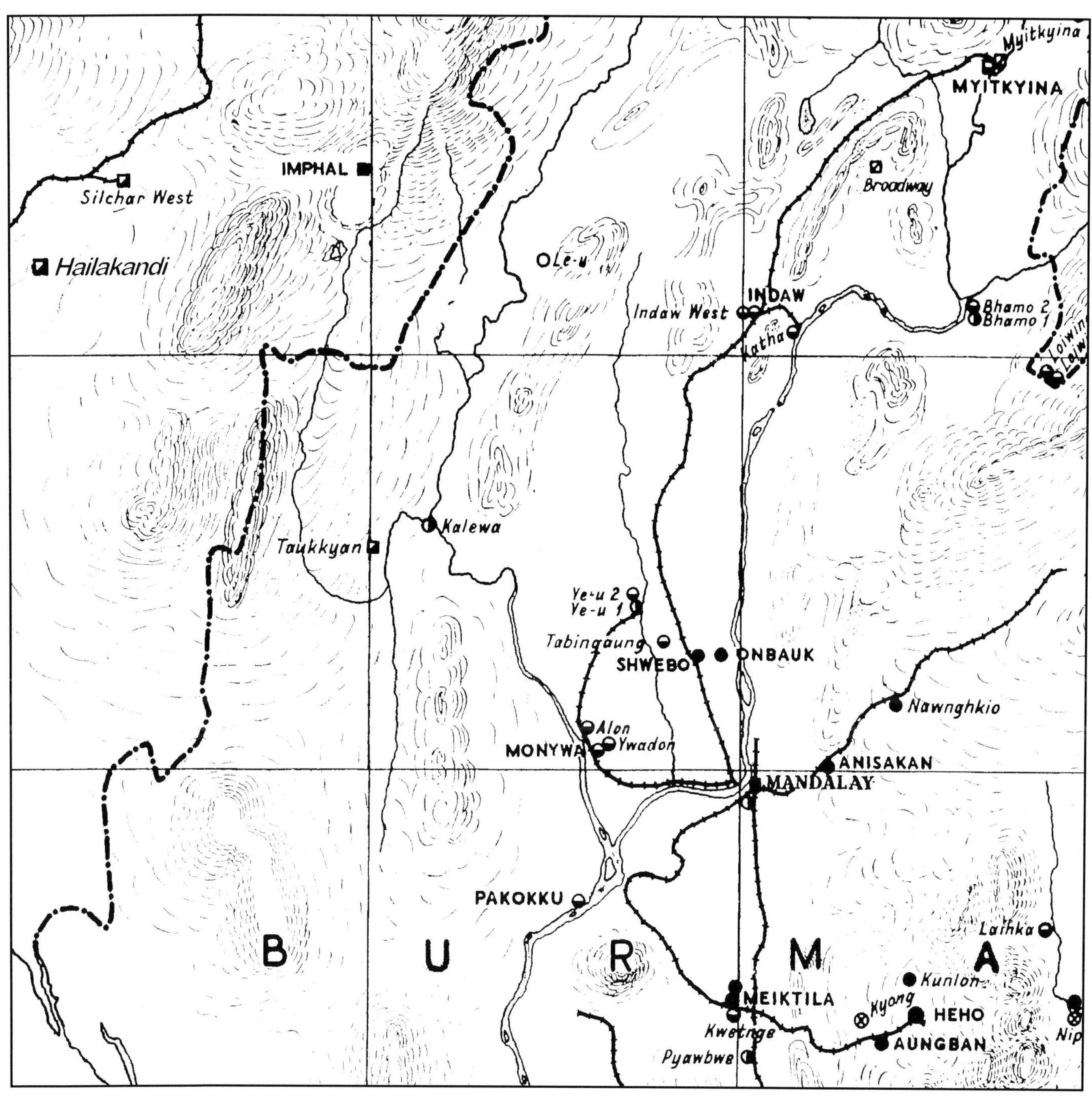

Source: *Public Records Office*

With White City secure, the Air Commandos shifted to supporting the 16th Brigade's attack on Indaw. On 23 March, B-25s and twelve P-51s bombed ammunition and gasoline dumps. The B-25s made three passes, dropping fragmentation bombs and incendiary clusters. Mustangs then dropped twenty-four 1,000 lb. bombs on the target.

The Mitchells and the Mustangs returned in the afternoon to bomb the nearby rail junction at Naba, three miles to the east of Indaw. Nine B-25s and eight P-51s dropped twenty-four 1,000-pounders on rolling stock and warehouses adjacent to the railroad.

Brigadier Fergusson had sent two of his battalions to attack Indaw from the north, and these reached the area on 26 March to find that the Japanese, aware of the approach of the Chindits, had left 2,000 men to defend the airfields. An attack to the west ended in failure, but the 2nd Battalion of the Leicesters reached the village of Inwa, near the edge of Indaw East airfield where they held out for two days and three nights against fierce Japanese counter-attacks.

The Air Commandos supplied, "the most daring and accurate close support with bomb splinters whirring into the Leicesters' forward posts."[32]

When Fergusson called off the attack on Indaw and ordered the Leicesters to withdraw, the Fighter Section flew four missions in support. On the 28th, seven P-51s bombed Inaw village with 500 lb. bombs. When the fighters were four miles from the target, the Leicesters laid out a triangle of mortar smoke to mark the target. Three Mustangs dropped six bombs on the target. The Leicesters sent up more smoke to mark a second target area, which received six more bombs. This pounding broke up a Japanese attack, and the next morning, eight P-51s returned to cover the Leicesters' withdrawal. The Mustangs fired rockets into the target area and returned for repeated strafing runs, lengthening their time over the target area by making dummy runs and by firing only short bursts.[33]

In the midst of the fighting around Indaw, tragedy struck. Returning to Hailakandi on the evening of 24 March from a meeting at Imphal, the Air Commando B-25 carrying Wingate crashed in the hills to the west, killing all on board. The Chindits and the Air Commandos received the news with shock and dismay. Their leader, their inspiration, and the driving force behind the Chindits was gone. General Slim had to fill the gap quickly. At the recommendation of Wingate's chief of staff he chose Brigadier Lentaigne, commander of 111th Brigade, as the new commander of Special Force. It proved to be a poor choice. Lentaigne was a career soldier and a good officer, but he had little sympathy with Wingate's ideas or his methods. He would not champion Special Force, nor would he seek to employ it along the lines of Wingate's own ideas.[34]

These missions closed out an eventful month during which Fighter Section flew 77 missions supporting the Chindits. The fighters and bombers added to their total score 29 motor vehicles, 48 rolling stock, four locomotives, three steam rollers, eight bridges, 38 large warehouses, and 79 other buildings destroyed and many more damaged.[35]

Perhaps most importantly, the technique of ground-controlled close air support had proven a complete success. Combining mortar smoke, to identify the target area, with an RAF officer on the ground to talk the fighters and bombers onto the target, had produced excellent results. In the coming month the Air Commandos would demonstrate increasing accuracy and would achieve a level of close air support unparalleled in the Burma campaign.

By the first week of April the battle for Imphal and Kohima had been well and truly joined. The British IV Corps had withdrawn its various units into defensive positions around Imphal, which was now under siege, while the garrison at Kohima was under attack in what would prove to be one of the most bitter and desperate fights of the entire Burma war.

On 3 April 1944, Admiral Mountbatten called a conference of his generals to assess the strategic situation in light of the Japanese advance. General Slim and his commanders were confident that they could contain the Japanese thrust towards Assam and inflict a punishing defeat on the Japanese forces, but it would take time and hard fighting. Concerned about the battle against his lines of communications, General Stillwell suggested postponing his own offensive, but Mountbatten instructed him to continue his advance on Myitkyina as planned.[36]

Conferences among Mountbatten, Slim, Stillwell, and Lentaigne, and between Lentaigne and his brigade commanders, led to a change in the orders for Special Force. Lentaigne faced a number of immediate problems. He knew the Japanese were preparing a renewed and strengthened offensive against White City with the intention of breaking the block. Lentaigne realized that he could not hold either White City or Broadway unless he could convert one into an all-weather airstrip, which he did not believe would be possible. The monsoon was about six weeks away, and the rains would prevent air supply and air support. Lentaigne had also to consider Wingate's original stipulation that the Chindits spend no more than three months in the field, which gave him until the end of May. In addition the Air Commandos were scheduled, under General Arnold's stipulation, to be pulled out after 90 days. Lentaigne concluded that Special Force should evacuate the Indaw area before the monsoon broke and move north up the railway valley toward Mogaung to be closer to Stillwell's advance. A new block would be set up, and once this was done, White City and Broadway would be abandoned. In the meantime, White City had to be held.[37]

Bob Petit's MRS.VIRGINIA being refueled from 55 gallon drums (flown in by C-47 transports) with a hand pump at Hailakanda. The temperature was probably in the 90's, and the humidity not much different. (Courtesy Thomas Y'Blood, Office of A F History)

Following the initial Chindit landings, General Mutaguchi had organized a force of three battalions to deal with what he first thought was a minor incursion. When the size of the Chindit invasion became clearer, he organized a larger force to deal with it. By the end of March, the Japanese had a body of troops equivalent to a division ready to advance against the Chindits. In the first week of April, this army marched to Mawlu and dug in to prepare for the attack on White City. In the meantime, Lentaigne had reinforced the base, sending in artillery and anti-aircraft guns and the 12th West African Regiment to serve as a defense garrison. This allowed Calvert to take several battalions outside the perimeter of the block to form a mobile striking force.[38]

Chindit patrols made contact with the Japanese at Sepein, two miles south of Mawlu, on 4 April. On the evening of 6 April, the Japanese launched their first attack, beginning with an artillery barrage and then a frontal assault on the Chindit positions. The attack was repulsed with heavy losses. The next morning, Calvert called in the Air Commandos to hit Japanese gun positions and assembly areas around Mawlu.

Cochran sent out a full complement, nine B-25s and twelve P-51s. Over the target the Air Commandos established radio contact with their RAF liaison officer, who ordered the targets marked with mortar smoke. As the B-25s approached the target, the Japanese, who had moved in nine anti-aircraft guns, opened up with every weapon they had, sending up streams of 40mm, 20mm, and small arms fire.

Six B-25s thundered across the area at 200 feet, dropping fragmentation bombs on the artillery positions. When they had passed, eight Mustangs hit the gun positions with 500 lb. bombs, putting them squarely on top of the smoke marking the target. Four more Mustangs followed, dropping eight 325 lb. depth charges. The three remaining B-25s then came in to drop their fragmentation bombs, after which Mustangs returned to strafe the area thoroughly, concentrating on the anti-aircraft positions. Later that afternoon eight Mustangs returned to bomb the gun positions once more. The pilots noticed that the gun batteries bombed earlier in the day were empty and that there was no AA response during the later attack.[39]

With a remarkable lack of originality, the Japanese continued this pattern over the next five days, attacking the British positions at night and retiring to Mawlu during the day where Calvert would direct "the ever-willing Mustangs" on to the Japanese positions.[40]

Left: A close-up of the rocket installations on the P-51A. Lt. Colonel Grant Mahony didn't want to substitute rockets for bombs and insisted that the rocket installation not interfere with the Mustang's bomb racks. Major Frank Fazio, from Eglin Field, and Lieutenant Andrew Postlewait, the Fighter Section's armaments officer, with Corporals Jennings Rader and Milan Urbancic, developed this solution. (NASM)

Below: The Air Commandos were among the first Army Air Force units to utilize rockets in combat. With two 500 lb. bombs, or in this case 1,000 lb. bombs, and six 4.5 inch rockets, the Fighter Section's Mustangs packed a powerful wallop. This photo was taken in the rain, explaining the two ground crewmen sheltering under the wing. (NASM)

The Fighter Section flew six missions in support of White City over a five day period, attacking troop and artillery positions with bombs, depth charges, and strafing. The Mustangs paid particular attention to the Japanese anti-aircraft positions, bombing them just before the B-25s made their runs and then strafing them repeatedly following their own attacks. The amount of flak steadily diminished, and although sometimes accurate, no Air Commando aircraft were lost and only one Mustang was slightly damaged. The Chindits estimated that the Japanese lost over 700 men killed in these repeated but fruitless attacks.[41]

When the West African Brigade arrived on 12 April, Calvert moved several battalions out of White City to launch his own counterattacks against Japanese positions around Mawlu. On 13 April, with covering strikes from the Air Commandos, he launched an attack on Sepein, the main headquarters of the Take Force, located south of Mawlu. The attack stalled against heavily entrenched Japanese troops, whom even the 500-pounders of the Air Commandos failed to dislodge.

Calvert withdrew and, leaving some forces as a block around Sepein, launched an attack against Mawlu on 17 April. He contacted the Air Commandos and requested a maximum effort strike for 1:00 p.m. the next day. Around noon on 18 April, the Japanese launched a heavy counter-attack, pinning down Calvert and his force under heavy machine gun fire. As he lay on the ground with machine gun bullets flying a foot over his head, Calvert "heard the welcome sound of very many Mustangs."[42]

He radioed for mortar smoke to mark the Japanese positions and urged that the air strikes be accurate, as the British were very close to the Japanese. By this time the Chindits had gained complete confidence in the efficiency of the Air Commandos, and the Fighter Section, after repeated strikes, knew the target area like the back of their hand.

Calvert was not disappointed. "Down went the smoke." he later wrote, "and down went the Mustangs."[43] Ten Mustangs came barreling in to bomb the target, followed by six B-25s disgorging fragmentation bombs. The P-51s then returned to strafe, catching the Japanese as they were forming for a counterattack. The air strikes were accurate and close; the leading British units said the nearest bombs fell within 50 yards of their position. Under cover of the air strike, Calvert and his troops withdrew. The Japanese did not attack White City again.[44]

The defense of White City had been a dramatic vindication of the techniques of close air support jointly developed by the Air Commandos and the Chindits. By controlling air strikes from the ground, last minute adjustments to the target could be given, leaving the Japanese no time to react and preventing them from sending out their own smoke to confuse the attackers. The Air Commando pilots benefited from working regularly with the same RAF liaison officers and from covering the same target area day after day. Reports from Special Force intelligence repeatedly stressed the devastation that Air Commando attacks caused, and how under repeated and accurate attacks the Japanese not only suffered severe casualties but were forced to withdraw their artillery, thereby reducing losses within the block. In their attacks on White City, the Japanese not only failed to break the block but suffered irreplaceable casualties.

In its postwar history of the campaigns in the Far East, the Royal Air Force stated that "the most important single factor molding the progress of all operations on the Burma front was the establishment and continued maintenance of air superiority."[45]

Absent air superiority, the Allied armies could not have relied on air transport for their supplies nor close air support to make up for their lack of artillery. More critically, Wingate could never have launched his expedition and sustained 20,000 men behind Japanese lines without air superiority. With his men totally reliant on air support, Wingate had to be sure that the transports could always get through, the fighters and bombers would be there to break up Japanese attacks, and his own forces would not be subject to crippling air attacks. Air superiority, as the Royal Air Force history states, has to be firmly established and then continuously maintained. In this battle the Fighter Section made a significant contribution.

Japanese Army Air Force units in Burma were under the command of the 5th Hikoshidan at Rangoon consisting of eight Sentais with approximately 270 aircraft. The airfields around Rangoon were the main administrative and logistical bases for Japanese air operations in Burma. The flying units used forward airfields nearer the front line for their operations. There were several airfields around the Mandalay area and a second complex around the administrative and communications center at Meiktila. The Japanese also maintained some rough airstrips up along the Irrawaddy corridor toward Myitkyina. By early March 1944, the 5th Hikoshidan had the following units available to support the Imphal offensive:

4th Hikodan (HQ Heho)
50th Sentai: Nakajima Ki-43 Oscar (20 operational aircraft)
81st Sentai: Mitsubishi Ki-46 Dinah (detachment)
8th Sentai: Kawasaki Ki-48 Lily (eight aircraft at Loilem)
7th Hikodan (HQ Hlegu)
12th Sentai: Mitsubishi Ki-21 Sally (15 aircraft)
81st Sentai: Mitsubishi Ki-46 Dinah (10 aircraft)
64th Sentai: Nakajima Ki-43 Oscar (20 aircraft at Mingaladon)
204th Sentai: Nakajima Ki-43 Oscar (20 aircraft at Mingaladon)
62nd Sentai: Nakajima Ki-49-IIa Helen (15 aircraft at Mingaladon and Hwambi).

The 62nd Sentai had recently arrived in Burma from Malaya where they had transitioned from Ki-21 Sallys to the Nakajima Ki-49-IIa Helen heavy bomber.[46]

From the invasion of Burma in early 1942 till the end of 1943, the Japanese had been more or less successful in maintaining air superiority over British and American air forces in Burma. The introduction of Spitfires in Burma in November 1943 spelled the beginning of the end. The Spitfire Mark V, and later Mark VIII, demonstrated a clear ascendancy over the Nakajima Ki-43 Oscar. But with Spitfires, the struggle for air superiority was limited to a defensive battle. The Spits did not have the range to take the air supremacy contest deep into enemy territory.

The Allied air forces had found that bombing advance airfields had minimal affect on enemy air units. The Japanese were masters at the rapid repair of damaged runways, so that the effect of bomb craters was at best temporary. The solution lay in a vigorous and sustained fighter offensive against Japanese air units and their air bases deep in enemy territory, where Japanese aircraft could be destroyed in the air or on the ground. The air superiority battle thus became primarily a fighter battle, and with the arrival of American long-range fighters in early 1944 in the form of the Fighter Section of the Air Commandos, the 459th Fighter Squadron with P-38s, and the 530th Fighter Squadron also with P-51As, the Allies finally had the ability to conduct long-range offensive fighter operations. Beginning in February 1944 Allied strategic and medium bombers launched a series of raids on the main Japanese airfields in Burma.[47]

For Fighter Section, the air superiority campaign began on 3 March 1944 when 12 Mustangs bombed Shwebo airfield hitting the runway, revetments, and anti-aircraft gun positions. Following the bombing they strafed a collection of buildings at the north end of the strip, leaving many in flames. No aircraft were seen on the field.

Four days later ten Mustangs and ten B-25s attacked the Japanese airfield at Bhamo early in the morning, planting 33 bombs on the runway but again seeing no enemy aircraft. Later that day Grant Mahony took off with Captain Mack Mitchell on a reconnaissance of the airfields at Mandalay, Heho, and Anisakan, south of the invasion area. As they passed Anisakan, Mahony saw six enemy aircraft, which he identified as Oscars, taking off from the field. These probably were from the 50th Sentai, which was temporarily based at Anisakan. Four were in the air heading east at 2,000 feet, one had just taken off, and the sixth was at the end of the strip beginning his takeoff roll.

Lieutenant Colonel Grant Mahony, veteran of the Philippines, Java, and China, became commander of the Fighter Section. (NASM)

Mahony dove on the four Oscars and damaged one, but either his or Mitchell's guns jammed and they broke off the fight. The Oscars used their maneuverability to evade and disappeared.

Early in the morning of 8 March, a large force of nine B-25s and 16 Mustangs bombed the airstrips at Indaw and Katha, the P-51s carrying 1,000 lb. bombs. No Japanese aircraft were seen, but that afternoon the Fighter Section would hit the jackpot.[48]

The 5th Hikoshidan had planned a major raid against the Allied airfield complex in northern Assam in support of the Japanese invasion which was scheduled to begin around that day. On the morning of 8 March the 64th, 204th, and 62nd Sentais staged from their base at Mingaladon near Rangoon to the airfields at Shwebo. On arrival over the area, the 62nd Sentai went to the wrong airstrip and mistakenly landed among the 64th Sentai's Oscars, much to the fury of 5th Hikoshidan's staff officers present. Shwebo West was a small field and it now became completely congested. They decided to cancel the afternoon mission and instructed the 62nd Sentai to fly to its assigned field. Meanwhile, the 50th Sentai arrived over Shwebo in the afternoon at the appointed time to learn that the mission had been canceled. When they arrived back over their airfield at Anisakan, they found that the Air Commands had preceded them.[49]

Following his brush with the Oscars on the 7th, Mahony had received permission for a major strike on Anisakan airfield. He led 22 Mustangs from Hailakandi, each armed with one 500 lb. bomb and a belly tank. Arriving over Anisakan at 1350, Mahony saw numerous Japanese fighters on the ground. Leaving four aircraft overhead as cover, he led the others down to bomb runways and revetments. The Mustangs then returned to strafe, shooting up every Oscar they could locate.

In the midst of this attack, the top cover called out approaching aircraft. These were 50th Sentai fighters returning to their base. The Oscars dove down on the P-51s, and in the melee that followed Captain Holly Keller claimed one Oscar destroyed, possibly 1st Lieutenant Takemi Takagi. 1st Lieutenant Roland Lynn claimed a damaged. Captain Erle H. Schneider hit one Oscar, flown by Corporal Harumi Watanabe, but tragically crashed directly into his victim. The pilots of the 50th Sentai claimed three P-51s destroyed and two probables.[50]

Leaving Anisakan in flames, Mahony took the remaining fighters back to Hailakandi via Shwebo and Onbauk, where they found both airfields covered with airplanes. Coming in on Onbauk, 1st Lieutenant Hubert Krug wrecked havoc on the unfortunate 62nd Sentai. In repeated passes, Krug destroyed five Helen bombers and damaged a sixth. Krug recalled how he and Roland Lynn teamed up:

> "We sort of got together at the rendezvous point, and then we headed back towards Hailakandi. Going back, we came across this airfield [Onbauk] that had been deserted earlier, and it was just covered with airplanes. So that's when we started, and I don't know how many of us there were there. I thought that I counted six airplanes that I had shot, but it wasn't my plane I was flying, it was one of the flight leader's, and it had a gun camera in it. There weren't many that had gun cameras in them. I didn't know I even had a camera. When we were being interrogated, the crew chief came in and handed me my film. I was as surprised as anybody. Well, they developed them real quick and saw exactly what kind of planes were on the ground. I think at the time I told them I thought they were Betty bombers. It showed five destroyed. So that was quite exciting. No one was shooting back. I didn't see anybody on the ground, just the airplanes."[51]

Oscars of the 204th Sentai were also hit hard. At Shwebo, the 64th Sentai was unable to scramble its fighters immediately to intercept, giving the Air Commandos time to strafe Onbauk and Shwebo without interference. When the pilots of the 64th did get off, they attacked where they could. 1st Lieutenant Goichi Sumino, a leading 64th Sentai ace, claimed one Mustang shot down. This may have been 1st Lieutenant Martin O'Berry, who was listed as missing from the mission. In turn, Captain Lester Murray claimed two Oscars destroyed over Onbauk, and 1st Lieutenant Robert Boyd claimed an Oscar damaged.[52]

On his way back to Hailakandi, Mahony reported the results of the strike by radio and requested that B-25s be bombed up for a second attack on the airfields. The fighters landed, were hurriedly rearmed and refueled, and took off again for another strike.

The bombers found the target and hit Shwebo airfield, starting numerous fires. Fifteen Mustangs sortied, but only two could find their way to Onbauk in the smoke and haze of the early evening. Unable to find the target the remaining Mustangs turned back to Hailakandi, but by that time it was dark, and they knew that finding their own field would be difficult

Radio brought them back to the vicinity, but they couldn't see the airfield in the dark. Ground crews quickly rolled out drums of gasoline, emptied them into a drainage ditch that ran around the perimeter, and then set the gas alight. Suddenly the pilots could see the outline of the field and were able to land. But for this quick thinking, the Fighter Section might have lost all the airplanes on the mission.[53]

At the end of the day the Fighter Section totaled up the score. The pilots had claimed 27 Oscars, six Dinahs (in actuality the Helens of the 62nd Sentai), one Sally, and one unidentified transport destroyed on the ground. In the air, they claimed one Oscar destroyed, two probables, and two damaged. Japanese records indicate that at Onbauk the 62nd Sentai lost six Helen bombers destroyed and the 204th five Oscars destroyed, while at Anisakan the 50th Sentai also lost five Oscars destroyed, in addition to two fighters shot down. The 64th Sentai appears to have gotten off fairly lightly, recording a number of its fighters damaged but none destroyed. The total number of damaged aircraft was not recorded. It appears that there was some over-claiming on the part of the Fighter Section, with multiple claims for the same aircraft. This is not surprising given the number of pilots involved strafing the same airfield.[54]

Regardless of the actual numbers, the Air Commando initiative had stopped the Japanese Army Air Force's air offensive from getting off the ground and by doing so, helped establish air superiority over the Chindit landing grounds. The Fighter Section destroyed or damaged more than a quarter of the airplanes that 5th Hikoshidan had sent forward to begin the offensive. The 62nd Sentai was forced to withdraw back to Malaya to re-equip. The Japanese were unable to launch strikes against the Chindits or support the Imphal battle until four days later. By that time the entire Chindit force had already been flown into Burma.

On the afternoon of 12 March, the 5th Hikoshidan launched a major sweep of the Silchar area, near the Air Commando's field at Hailakandi, with the remaining full strength (sixty Oscars) of the 50th, 64th, and 204th Sentais and a small force of bombers from the 8th Sentai. On the way to Silchar the Japanese force encountered a squadron of RAF Hurricanes and, in the ensuing combat, claimed 14 shot down, the RAF suffering just two Hurricanes damaged. British radar had tracked the approaching Japanese formation and had warned Hailakandi.

At the time nearly the entire Fighter Section was gone, covering the 111th Brigade's crossing of the Irrawaddy. The only pilots available were 1st Lieutenants Neil Bollum and Olin B. Carter who were both in the dispensary recovering from dysentery. They received the scramble call and ran for their airplanes, though Carter's plane had not been fully serviced and had an oxygen leak. Without waiting for Bollum, who got off shortly afterwards, Carter took off and climbed to 25,000 feet, following British radar vectors. When he reached the intercept point, he couldn't find the Japanese.[55]

As Carter recalled, "I couldn't see the Japs even though radar said I was right in their area. Radar didn't have altitude capability, but suggested I could be on top of them, so I rolled up on a wing and there they were, several thousand feet directly below, my first sight of Japs in the air. My first impression was that they looked like a bunch of butterflies loosely surrounding a twin-engine Betty reconnaissance plane in the middle [this may have been a Kawasaki Ki-48 light bomber from the 8th Sentai]. I wasn't tracking mentally very well due to the lack of oxygen, so I rolled over and dove straight down on them. I went through the middle of their formation like a shot without once firing my guns!"[56]

Using his speed advantage, Carter climbed to the right ahead of the Japanese formation to make another pass. This time he rolled to the left and dove head-on into the formation. As he closed with the Japanese he opened fire, but several of the Oscars simply raised their noses and opened fire on him. Fortunately Carter wasn't hit, but neither had he hit any of the enemy aircraft. Using his speed advantage, he again climbed up above and to the right rear of the Japanese formation. Two Oscars broke off and made a feint towards him, but then rejoined their formation. Carter gave more thought to his next pass and this time came in from the rear for a straight stern shot, selecting a fighter on the right rear of the formation.

"I fired a long burst and saw many pieces fly off (one of which looked like the canopy) and smoke started to trail off the aircraft."

The Oscar slowly rolled off to the right and started down. Carter climbed back up to a position on the right rear of the formation and attacked, damaging another Oscar. He climbed and made a fourth pass, damaging a second fighter then ran out of ammunition. Breaking off the attack, he returned to Hailakandi.

Although Carter did not see him, Neil Bollum attacked the enemy formation around the same time, damaging one Oscar.On his return to the field, Colonels Cochran and Alison interrogated Carter:

"I clearly remember Colonel Cochran saying finally, 'Why did you break off and come home when you still had gas?' I explained that I had run out of ammo, and he very seriously said, 'but you were over friendly ground and still had gas. Why didn't you ram one of them from the rear, bail out, and walk home?' I was shocked and dejected because I was convinced I had not done my job as I was supposed to. Exhilaration rapidly turned to depression and dejection. I was convinced then that Cochran was serious and I still think so."[57]

Since no one had seen the first Oscar crash, Carter was awarded a probable as well as a credit for one Oscar damaged. However, the 64th Sentai reported that one of its pilots, Corporal Shigeo Ishiyama, had been lost that day, apparently Carter's victim.[58]

Captain Olin Carter and his crew chief, Sergeant Albert Piester, with LITTLE KITTEN. Piester, like all the Fighter Section crew chiefs and maintenance staff, worked incredibly hard under difficult conditions to ensure that the Fighter Section's Mustangs were kept in shape. (Courtesy Olin Carter)

In their next encounter, the Fighter Section was on the receiving end of Japanese attention. On 12 March, Cochran sent Grant Mahony and three other pilots (Capt. Roland Lynn, Lieutenant Hubert Krug, and a third, name not recorded) to the airstrip at Broadway to provide close support for the Chindits.

Independently, and apparently without Cochran's knowledge and much to his annoyance, the RAF had sent eight Spitfires from No. 81 Squadron to Broadway to provide air defense for the base. They were accompanied by a radar set and anti-aircraft battery. The radar could provide some early warning, but due to the proximity of the hills, the set was not fully effective, as events would prove. It took nearly a week for the Japanese to realize that the Chindits were well-established at Broadway, but on13 March fifteen Oscars attacked the landing ground. The Spitfires received a warning in just enough time to scramble before the arrival of the Japanese. In the ensuing combat they claimed three destroyed and six damaged.[59]

Mahony and his three pilots operated out of Broadway for four days, attacking targets in the surrounding area. They were due to pull out on the afternoon of 16 March, when they received an urgent warning that a Japanese raid was approaching. Lieutenant Hubert Krug thought they would be ordered to head to the dugouts but Mahony, with characteristic aggressiveness and eagerness, ran to his own airplane, shouting to the other pilots, "Come on, guys, let's go!" Krug was fourth in line when three Sally medium bombers, escorted by six Oscars, unloaded a salvo of fragmentation bombs right onto the airstrip.

> "I had just closed the windows," Krug remembered, "and put my hand on the throttle. I was going to take off, and that's all I remember. There was evidently an explosion. I came to, I must have been knocked out for a little bit, and the cockpit was on fire, and with the torque of the prop going to the right I was going around in a big circle. Of course I didn't know what had happened, and I started worrying about it. We had fifty-five gallon drums of gas and bombs lying all over the field, so I was concerned about those. And then I was trying to get out of my plane. The fire was coming from the right and the latch on the cockpit was on the left, so I was trying to keep the fire out of my face with my right hand, and trying to open the cockpit with my left hand. Seemed like forever, and man, it was hot. I finally got the cockpit opened and was going to get out, but I couldn't. Everything seemed like slow motion. I couldn't get out, and in desperation I dropped my hands, and hit my safety belt. So I thought, 'Oh yeah, my safety belt' I flipped it, and rolled out of the airplane."[60]

Krug ran stumbling from the flaming Mustang to a dugout where he was met by the Air Commando doctor, Captain Cortez Enloe, who happened to be present. Enloe worked on Krug's burns and that night had him evacuated to India. With one Mustang destroyed, Mahony took his small team back to Hailakandi. The next day a dozen Oscars caught the airstrip by surprise, shooting down one Spitfire that managed to get off and destroying three more on the ground, as well as the early-warning radar. Absent adequate warning it became impossible to base fighters at Broadway and the remaining Spitfires were withdrawn. Thereafter, the defense of Broadway would depend on routine patrols and the ability of the Fighter Section to maintain its aggressive campaign against the Japanese airfields.[61]

On 19 March twelve Mustangs set off to bomb Shwebo and Onbauk airfields but, seeing no aircraft on either field diverted to the secondary target, the airfield at Meiktila. In the face of intense light anti-aircraft fire, they bombed several buildings on the perimeter, starting large fires.

On the 30th, six P-51s returned to Anisakan, dropping 500 lb. bombs on the dispersal area and setting one twin-engine bomber on fire.

Six Mustangs returned to Anisakan again on 3 April, dropping six 500-pounders and rocketing bashas around the airfield. The Mustangs then went down to strafe several well-camouflaged aircraft, setting one fighter on fire and damaging three more. Another heavily camouflaged aircraft was also seen burning after the strafing pass. This strike proved to be a mere warm-up for a major success the next day.[62]

That afternoon the Fighter Section received a report from RAF intelligence that a large force of Japanese aircraft might be moving north from the Rangoon airfields. The British had intercepted radio traffic from fighter units in the Rangoon area and ground controllers at an airfield believed to be Heho, headquarters of the 4th Hikodan, or the nearby satellite field, Aungban. Early that morning the Fighter Section received intelligence that there were approximately 21 aircraft at Aungban, and another 17 at the main airfield at Heho. They resolved to attack Aungban.[63]

Grant Mahony set off at 0800 hours with nineteen P-51s equipped with long-range tanks and armed with bazooka rockets. One aborted. The formation first took a look at Shwebo and Onbauk fields and, finding no worthy targets, continued south for Aungban. When about six miles north of the field Mahony ordered that auxiliary tanks be jettisoned and, leaving seven aircraft under Captain Paul Forcey as top cover, took the remaining 11 Mustangs down on the airfield.

Captain Olin Carter's North American P-51A, LITTLE KITTEN, with two 500 lb. bombs under the wings. The "A" Model Mustang carried two .50 cal. machine guns in each wing. (Courtesy Olin Carter)

Once again the Fighter Section achieved complete surprise. About an hour and a half before they arrived over Aungban, eight P-38s of the 459th squadron had strafed the nearby Heho airfield, destroying a number of Sally and Lily bombers belonging to the 8th Sentai and damaging several 50th Sentai fighters. Japanese fighters that had scrambled to intercept the P-38s had been ordered to land at Aungban, so the field was full but not expecting another attack. Airplanes were taxing around the perimeter of the airfield and mechanics were servicing others. Mahony and Lieutenants Gilhausen and Boyd pulled ahead of the other Mustangs and rocketed several anti-aircraft gun positions that had been identified from reconnaissance photos.[64]

The Air Commandos had a field day. In the space of a few minutes, most completed at least four separate strafing passes across the airdrome. Mahony destroyed one twin-engine bomber and set two fighters on fire in six strafing passes, damaging another fighter with bazooka rockets.

Lieutenant Younger Pitts submitted claims for one bomber and three fighters destroyed, while Major Bob Petit, Neil Bollum, and William Gilhausen claimed three fighters each, Bollum and Petit sharing a fourth. Lieutenant John Meyer strafed one fighter that he reported as having an in-line engine. This may well have been a Kawasaki Ki-61 Tony which was undergoing an operational evaluation with the 50th Sentai at the time. In this first attack, the unit claimed three bombers and 19 fighters destroyed, and another nine fighters damaged.[65]

Mahony summoned Captain Forcey to bring down the top cover and led his own force up to altitude to provide cover. Forcey scored a direct hit with his bazooka rockets on a twin-engine bomber, which he identified as a Sally, causing it to explode. He then strafed a fighter identified as a Tony, which may have been the same fighter strafed by John Meyer. Roland Lynn had similar success, blowing up a fighter with his rockets. Olin Carter set one fighter on fire, but the other pilots in the flight had less success as by now most of the airplanes on the field were already damaged or in flames. On the return flight Carter found a Sally bomber at Anisakan and set it on fire.

The Japanese at Aungban had radioed for support, and several 50th Sentai Oscars that had remained at Heho took off hurriedly to intercept the attacking Mustangs. Someone called out to Forcey to break off his attack as enemy fighters were approaching. As he began to gain altitude, Forcey noticed a P-51 flying off to the west with an Oscar approaching from the rear. Flying slightly higher, Forcey dove down on the Oscar and opened fire from 300 yards away, closing to 200 yards. The Japanese fighter pulled up gently, and Forcey fired another long burst, sending it straight down to explode violently as it hit the ground.[66]

After a review by the unit's intelligence officer, the Fighter Section received credit for four Sally bombers, 19 Oscars, and one Tony destroyed, one Oscar and one Tony probably destroyed, and eight Oscars damaged. Once again, the speed of the action and the numerous passes made on the same targets appear to have caused some over claiming. Nevertheless, the Air Commandos had dealt the Japanese a crippling blow. The 50th Fighter Sentai lost at least 15 aircraft destroyed or severely damaged, nearly three-quarters of its strength.

The 50th was withdrawn from Burma and sent to Saigon in French Indochina to re-equip, returning to the front a week or so later. The number of bombers destroyed may well be accurate, but are not included in postwar Japanese records. The 50th Sentai claimed one P-51 shot down in the interception, but the only damage to the Fighter Section was a single hit to the wing of one fighter from a 7.7mm machine gun round. This was attrition in its worst form. The Japanese Army Air Force could not replace these aircraft at the pace they were being lost to the marauding American fighters, while the number of damaged aircraft put an enormous burden on their already strained logistical system.[67]

The Air Commando's counter air sweeps continued with regular reconnaissance flights over Japanese airfields. While never again hitting the jackpot as they had on 8 March and 4 April, they did have additional successes which maintained pressure on the 5th Hikoshidan.

On 16 April, two Mustangs on a reconnaissance to Shwebo and Anisakan came upon several fighters at the latter field. Sweeping down, they made repeated attacks in the face of only meager anti-aircraft fire, leaving two Oscars in flames.

Six days later Grant Mahony led Major Bob Petit, William Gilhausen, and an unknown fourth pilot to bomb a viaduct with 1,000-pounders. Following the attack, Mahony took the flight on a sweep over the airstrip at Naungkhio, northeast of Anisakan. Here they found two Oscars which had apparently just landed. Petit strafed one as it was taxing off the runway, setting it on fire. Gilhausen strafed the second Oscar, forcing the pilot to quickly abandon his aircraft. Mahony followed and set this second aircraft on fire. On 9 May, the Fighter Section scored its last ground victory when three Mustangs on another sweep of Shwebo and Anisakan found an Oscar at Anisakan, which was promptly strafed and torched.[68]

The Air Commandos encountered Japanese aircraft on three more occasions. On 17 April 1944 the 5th Hikoshidan launched a major attack on the Imphal area, part of a series of raids intended to damage British airfields at Imphal. While twenty Oscars from the 50th Sentai carried out a sweep nearby, 50 Oscars from the 64th and 204th Sentais escorted six Sally bombers from the 12th Sentai to bomb Pale Field at Imphal. Spitfires of No. 81 and No. 607 Squadrons intercepted this force and pilots of No. 81 Squadron claimed one Oscar shot down and several more damaged. The Japanese fighters escorted the bombers back toward Japanese lines and then one group of 64th Sentai fighters turned back toward Pale.[69]

At the time of the Imphal raid Grant Mahony was leading twelve P-51s on a bombing mission to Mawlu. He received an urgent message to abandon the mission and divert toward Imphal to intercept the Japanese force. Jettisoning their bombs, the Mustangs headed west, soon encountering 14 eastbound Oscars traveling at 14,000 feet.

Mahony led his force underneath, turned, and began climbing after the enemy. Both formations were soon engaged in individual dogfights. Mahony got behind one and opened fire at 400 yards, closing to 200 yards. The Oscar broke away and Mahony followed, firing a 20-degree deflection shot. Fatally hit, the Japanese went straight down and crashed, a kill confirmed by Captain Mack Mitchell.

Mitchell attacked two Oscars, firing on one from 500 to 200 yards and getting a deflection shot on another, damaging both. Captain William Gilhausen attacked an Oscar from astern and fired an eight-second burst, hitting the Oscar in the fuselage. The Japanese pilot began a slow turn away, but Gilhausen was unable to follow up the attack as two Oscars bounced him in turn.

Captain Paul Forcey was attacked by four Oscars. Managing to get on the tail of one, he gave it a burst, blowing off the canopy and apparently killing the pilot. Passing alongside, he saw the Japanese pilot's head and arm over the side of the cockpit. The Oscar spun down and crashed.

Forcey then found that he had an Oscar right on his tail. He dove, building up speed rapidly, heading straight for a cliff. At the last minute he pulled up violently. The Oscar tried to follow the maneuver, but as it did so the fighter's left wing ripped off and it crashed and exploded. All three kills were photographed and confirmed. That day the 64th Sentai lost four pilots, and it appears that the Fighter Section shot down Lieutenants Motoyuki Inagaki and Taro Kubodera, and Corporal Koji Nakasone.[70]

A month later, on 16 May 1944, two Mustangs providing close air support to the Chindits came across 12 Oscars strafing damaged transport aircraft on the

Captain Paul Forcey's P-51A, BOBBIE, showing his claims for three Japanese aircraft. Forcey shot down an Oscar over Aungban on April 4, and claimed two Oscars over Imphal on April 17. (Courtesy 1st Air Commando Association)

airstrip at Blackpool, the new block established near Mogaung. Four Oscars attacked the two Mustangs, and in the ensuing combat one Oscar was damaged before both formations withdrew.

Three days later the 8th Sentai sent out eight Lily bombers, with an escort of around 20 Oscars from the 50th and 64th Sentais, to bomb Chindit positions at the new Blackpool stronghold. In what proved to be the Fighter Section's last day in air-to-air combat, seven Mustangs had been sent out on a similar mission to attack Japanese positions around Blackpool. They were approaching their target at 0828 hours when they sighted the Japanese formation, which was returning to base having been unable to locate the target due to poor weather. The P-51s jettisoned their bombs and turned to attack. The bombers were flying at around 7,000 feet, with one formation of ten Oscars 2,000 feet above on the right and another group of four at the same altitude on the left side of the formation. When the Japanese detected the approaching Mustangs, they split into two flights, six fighters sticking with the bombers while the others turned to do battle. The Air Commandos also split into two flights, Captain Olin Carter going after the fighters and Captain Mack Mitchell leading his flight against the bombers.[71] Lieutenant Jack Klarr was flying Carter's wing.

> "We made a pass at the Japanese formation and Carter went after one Oscar," recalled Klarr, "That Oscar's wingman peeled off to the left and I followed him. I got fairly close and gave him a burst. He pulled up very sharply and fire was coming out all underneath the plane and then he fell over. At the time I saw a couple of other Oscars above, so I had to dive out. Then I looked around and rejoined the formation and it was confirmed that I had shot down an Oscar, which was a big thrill for me."[72]

The second Mustang flight simultaneously made a diving attack from the rear of the bomber formation, closing to 100 yards before breaking off. Rear gunners put up a determined defense but Mitchell set one bomber on fire, receiving credit for one Lily bomber destroyed, while Lieutenants Newman and Wilkinson damaged two others.

Carter's flight then made a second pass on the Oscars, forcing one into a split-S at only a few hundred feet altitude. The Japanese failed to recover and crashed. This claim appears to have been awarded to Lieutenant Robley Melton. Another Oscar, approaching underneath the Mustangs, was in turn attacked and when last seen was diving down with its forward fuselage on fire. Captains Holly Keller and John Meyer were given credits for damaging two Oscars.[73]

In two-and-a-half months the Fighter Section of the 1st Air Commandos had claimed 68 Japanese aircraft destroyed on the ground and a further ten destroyed in the air. This was second only to the 459th Fighter Squadron's 126 aircraft destroyed over the same period. Between them, the two American units claimed 83% of the Japanese aircraft destroyed during March, April, and May.[74]

The 5th Hikoshidan never fully recovered from this blow. By the end of May 1944, Allied air forces had established a clear dominance over central Burma. The long-range fighter sweeps over forward Japanese airfields and the constant surveillance of same made it difficult and dangerous for the Japanese to launch sorties against the Chindits or against the main British bases around Imphal. Denied the ability to operate regularly from their forward airfields, the number of actual and potential sorties the 5th Hikoshidan could mount was sharply reduced.[75]

Air superiority thus established made the Chindit invasion possible. Remarkably, not one transport or light aircraft was shot down during the course of the operation, although a few were destroyed on the ground from strafing. The constant flow of supplies and the evacuation of the wounded continued without interruption. Japanese air attacks on Chindit positions were limited, and for the most part, ineffectual. In this respect, the impact of the Fighter Section's contribution to the campaign for air superiority was far greater than simply the number of enemy airplanes destroyed.

When not providing close air support to the Chindits or seeking out the Japanese at their forward airfields, the pilots of the Fighter Section devoted their time to destroying Japanese supplies and disrupting Japanese lines of communication. Cochran's objective was straightforward and in line with the overall goal of the Chindit operation: to use his air power to inflict the maximum damage possible against the Japanese army contesting against Stillwell's forces.

In attacking suspected supply dumps or known supply centers, the Fighter Section most often worked in concert with the Bomber Section's B-25s in the pattern worked out during the first few weeks of operations. The P-51s would go in first, bombing the target with 500 or 1,000 lb. bombs. The B-25s followed, sweeping across the target area at 1,500 feet or below to drop fragmentation and incendiary clusters, or 500-pounders. Then both the Mitchells and the Mustangs would return to strafe the target area repeatedly. This proved particularly effective against warehouses and bamboo bashas. The fighters and bombers would usually leave the target area in flames, with smoke rising several thousand feet in the air. During March, the Fighter Section flew 11 of these combined missions, hitting supply dumps, warehouses, and motor transport pools at Wuntho, Indaw, and Mohynin, and making several attacks on the rail facilities and a railroad bridge at Meza.

These attacks continued in April with a new innovation. During March the practice of marking nearby targets with mortar smoke had proved to be successful. However, many targets lay outside the line of sight or radio range of the RAF liaison officers on the ground. A new method of marking arose quite by chance. In early April, an RAF liaison officer with 16 Brigade found a Japanese gasoline and supply dump south of Indaw, near the Aberdeen block. He reported his find to Brigadier Fergusson, the Brigade commander, who requested an air strike. Unable to locate the target on the available maps, Lieutenant Colonel Clinton Gaty, who was now commander of the Light Plane Force, flew the liaison officer over the area in a Stinson L-5 so that he could pinpoint the location.

On 9 April, six B-25s and eight P-51s rendezvoused with Gaty over the target. While Gaty piloted the L-5, the liaison officer leaned out and dropped smoke mortar shells on the supply dump, effectively identifying it. Fighters and bombers proceeded to savage the base with 500 lb. high explosive bombs, 325 lb. depth charges, fragmentary and incendiary clusters and a dose of .50 caliber machine gun fire. This turned out to be a major supply dump along the route of Japanese forces assaulting Imphal, and its destruction forced the use of a more circuitous route.

This technique was employed again on 21 April, when a light plane dropped smoke shells on a suspected supply dump just north of Indaw, marking the target for the B-25s and P-51s.[76]

When not occupied with more critical missions, Fighter Section pilots went out regularly in pairs or in flights of four on offensive reconnaissance missions over central Burma. They paid particular attention to the road and rail network leading north to Myitkyina, often flying south to pick up the road or rail line, then following it north towards White City and Broadway, strafing trucks or any other type of transport encountered. Locomotives were considered "great sport," as they often erupted in clouds of steam when hit.[77]

The most outstanding attack against the Japanese communications network was the destruction of the suspension bridge over the Shweli River at the small village of Shweli, southwest of Bhamo. The bridge had defied repeated raids by Allied bombers and fighter-bombers. On 17 March, a combined force of 10th Air Force B-25s, A-36s, and P-51s attacked the bridge without success.

In the second week of April, the Fighter Section received five P-51Bs as replacements for aircraft lost in combat. With the greater range of the P-51B, a mission to dive bomb the Shweli bridge with more powerful 1,000 lb. bombs became possible. Major Bob Petit led two other pilots in the first attempt. The three managed to score near misses. Petit returned the next day with three other pilots and this time succeeded. Petit's own two 1,000-pounders scored a direct hit on the bridge towers. The center span collapsed, and as the pilots withdrew, the bridge span and its supporting cables lay in the Shweli River.[78]

In their attacks on enemy supplies and lines of communications, the Fighter Section had the distinction of being one of the first American fighter units to utilize rockets in combat. In early 1944, the Army Air Force was experimenting with 4.5-inch rocket projectiles at the Air Force armament proving ground at Eglin Air Force Base in Florida. To test the rockets under combat conditions it was suggested that the Fighter Section would be an appropriate unit for operational trials, given the Air Commando's general brief to experiment with new applications for air power. Accordingly, in March Major Frank Fazio, who had been working on the project at Eglin, was dispatched to Hailakandi with a shipment of 1,000 rockets. The rockets were inadvertently diverted to the 14th Air Force in China, and Major Fazio had to part with three precious bottles of Scotch to persuade the 14th Air Force's logistics chief to get them shipped back to Hailakandi.[79]

Major Fazio's first task was to devise a new aircraft installation. The 4.5-inch rockets were carried in long bazooka tubes, which imparted a small measure of directional stability, grouped in threes with one tube on top and two on the bottom. The top rocket tube was attached to the wing in place of the standard bomb rack. However, Grant Mahony insisted that the rocket installation not interfere with the bomb rack. Since the P-51s had to carry bombs or drop tanks on nearly every mission, the bomb racks were constantly in use. Replacing the bomb racks with rocket tubes not only reduced the Fighter Section's flexibility on ground support missions, but would take valuable time and result in delays while

Loading 4.5 inch rockets into their tubes. Although not always accurate, against large targets like a warehouse the rockets could be devastating. (NASM)

racks were changed. If rockets could be carried in addition to the regular load, mission flexibility and fire power would be greatly enhanced.

Technical manuals insisted that this could not be done, but Fazio decided to throw away the book. Working with the Fighter Section's armament officer, 1st Lieutenant Andrew Postlewait, and Corporals Jennings Rader and Milan Urbancic, Fazio developed a new attachment 23 inches further out on the wing, leaving the bomb rack free to carry bombs or drop tanks. Test flights proved the installation to be sound, and soon the Fighter Section Mustangs were carrying rockets as a normal part of their operations.[80]

The first significant use of rockets appears to have been on the mission to bomb Wuntho on 13 March 1944. Four Mustangs fired off 24 rockets at warehouses and bashas, which proved to be excellent targets. The 4.5-inch projectile was not particularly accurate and would sometimes spiral off in the wrong direction but against a large target like a warehouse, accuracy was less of a problem. One or two rockets could demolish a warehouse. Smaller targets, like locomotives or airplanes, were harder to hit, and the pilots found with experience that the best approach was to volley all their rockets at once. If just one rocket hit, the results were devastating. In the 4 April strafing raid on Aungban, several Japanese aircraft simply disintegrated when hit with a rocket.

An unidentified Air Commando pilot looks at the damaged wing of a P-51A. This photo may have been taken following the combat with Oscars of the 50th Sentai over Aungban on April 4, 1944, during which one Mustang was hit in the wing. (NASM)

Rockets proved invaluable in ground support missions, helping prolong both the time over the target and the damage that could be inflicted. The rocket tube installations did not interfere with the Mustang's ability to bomb a target and were not affected by the high speeds built up in the dive nor the strain of the recovery. Once contact had been made with the ground controller and the target identified with smoke, the Mustangs would roll in and drop their bombs or depth charges. As the last man in the flight completed his bomb run, the flight leader would come over the target to lose two rockets, followed by other members of the flight in turn. Three passes would dispose of the rockets, and then the Mustangs would return for repeated strafing runs. Each rocket hit with the force of a 105mm artillery shell. This pattern was particularly effective when the Fighter Section was covering the withdrawal of British troops and trying to keep the Japanese tied to their positions.[81]

In committing the Air Commandos to support the Chindit invasion, General Arnold had specified that they should be withdrawn from combat after 90 days, which was the limit General Wingate's experience had set as the ideal length of deployment for special forces. The original commitment had been up to May 1, but with the planned withdrawal of the Chindit force up the railroad corridor towards Mogaung to the north and the need to build a new stronghold to support this offensive, Special Force asked the Air Commandos to extend their support for a few weeks more. This was agreed to, though the approach of the monsoon season was evident with the daily build up of heavy cloud formations and, once the rains began, both Hailakandi and Lalaghat would be inoperable.

By the beginning of May the strain on the Air Commando force was beginning to take its toll. Pilots and ground crew had been operating continuously under difficult conditions for nearly three months. The pilots flew nearly every day, weather permitting, and were averaging around 50 missions each, though some were approaching 70 missions. Apart from the unrelenting heat, the Air Commandos had to put up with a monotonous diet and frequent bouts of dysentery. But as long as they were committed to supporting the Chindits, operations proceeded without letup.

The Chindits were set to abandon their strongholds at Aberdeen, Broadway, and White City, and withdraw north. A new stronghold, code named Blackpool, was to be established by the 111th Brigade near Pinbaw, approximately 40 miles north of White City, while Brigadier Calvert's 77th Brigade moved on Mogaung to put added pressure on the Japanese forces facing Stillwell and the Chinese. The plan was for the Air Commandos to fly in the 111th Brigade and supporting equipment for the stronghold, while Calvert and his men marched over land to the Mogaung area. Sixteenth Brigade was to be flown out to India as they had been on operations for the longest period and their strength was seriously de-

Lieutenant Colonel Grant Mahony in his weathered P-51A. The two white stripes on the tail were his command markings. (Courtesy James F. Lansdale)

pleted. Fourteenth Brigade was to move towards White City to cover the withdrawal of 77th Brigade and the garrison force, 3rd West African Brigade. These moves were scheduled for the first week in May.[82]

Prior to 111th Brigade's occupation of its new stronghold, the Fighter Section flew several missions against suspected Japanese supply dumps around Pinbaw to soften up the area. At the same time, the Air Commandos kept up the pressure on the Japanese forces around White City, which had been remarkably quiet after their previous thrashing. 111th Brigade reached Blackpool on 7 May and immediately started preparing a landing strip, but it took several days before the landing ground could be used safely. The West Africans withdrew from White City on 9 May under cover of repeated strikes by the Fighter Section without interference from the Japanese. Following the withdrawal, the Fighter Section devoted its efforts to supporting Blackpool. Being closer to Japanese forces near Mogaung, Blackpool soon came under attack from Japanese troops and artillery.

On the night of 14/15 May, two Japanese battalions launched a heavy attack on the stronghold which was repulsed. Three Mustangs took off at 0730 hours on the morning of the 15th to bomb nearby Japanese positions which the Chindits had marked with smoke. A few hours later eight Mustangs returned with six B-25s for a more thorough saturation. The next day they flew five missions to Blackpool, bombing Japanese gun positions with 500 and 1,000 lb. bombs. Weather prevented any operations on the 17th, but on the 18th the Air Commandos returned to Blackpool four times.[83]

19 May was the Fighter Section's last day in combat and it proved to be eventful. Early in the morning they suffered one final loss. At 0600 hours, Captain William Gilhausen took off alone on a weather reconnaissance. As he approached the Japanese airstrip at Kawlin, he radioed that he saw fighters on the strip. His next call stated that he had strafed and burned two grounded aircraft, but that his own plane had been hit. He was planning to fly further north closer to Allied lines and then bail out. He was not heard from again and a search mission flown after his last transmission failed to find any sign of Gilhausen or his airplane. After the war, it was learned that Gilhausen was captured and died of malnutrition in a Japanese prison in Rangoon. He had been renowned for flying missions in a paratroop jacket with the pockets full of hand grenades, in case he had to bail out and encountered Japanese troops. Ironically, on his last mission he had taken off in a T-shirt and slippers.[84]

Shortly after Gilhausen's flight, seven Mustangs left for Blackpool on a ground support mission where they encountered Japanese airplanes, as previously related. At 1545 hours, eight more Mustangs sortied on the Fighter Section's last mission. Fittingly, this too was a ground support mission. They bombed the Pinbaw railway station with 500-pounders, then strafed Japanese troop positions in the area, returning without incident. This was the last of 230 missions.

With their assignment to the Chindits completed and the monsoon holding sway, the Fighter Section withdrew from the now waterlogged field at Hailakandi and returned to India. A former RAF base at Asansol, roughly 100 miles northwest of Calcutta, was chosen as a base for the Air Commandos to rest and recuperate.

With typical initiative and energy, they set about repairing facilities and building officer and NCO clubs for recreation. Many were sent on leave, while others were reassigned to the United States.

General Arnold had summoned Colonel John Alison back to Washington at the end of March to report on the lessons learned and to help form new air commando units. When the move to Asansol was completed, Colonels Phil Cochran and Arvid Olson left for the States as well, and leadership of the Air Commandos shifted to Colonel Clinton B. Gaty, an experienced pilot and engineer who had been deputy to John Alison on the initial landings at Broadway.

A close-up of shark-mouth P-51B, which also has a cartoon figure of Popeye's girlfriend, Olive Oyl, beneath the cockpit. It was a replacement aircraft and arrived with the art work. (Courtesy A.R. Van De Weghe)

Lieutenant Colonel Grant Mahony departed, as did the other combat veterans. Captain Duke Philips, now promoted to Major, replaced Mahony as head of the Fighter Section. After nearly four months of hard combat, the Section's remaining P-51As and P-51Bs were badly in need of maintenance and were temporarily withdrawn.[85]

The Chindits continued fighting. In mid-May control of Special Force shifted, as planned, to General Stillwell who used the Chindits cruelly. Nearing the limit of their endurance, they were ordered to fight on. Blackpool proved to be untenable. The stronghold was abandoned on 27 May 1944 and a weakened 111th Brigade moved north to counter Japanese movement against Mogaung. Stillwell assigned the capture of Mogaung to Calvert's 77th Brigade. Employed as regular infantry, but with no tanks or artillery in support, Calvert's men hurled themselves at the entrenched garrison. After vicious fighting Mogaung fell on 26 June. In its five weeks under Stillwell's command, 77th Brigade lost half its strength. Completely exhausted, and down to an effective strength of only a few hundred men each, the 77th and 111th Brigades were finally withdrawn in July. Over the course of its operations in Burma, Special Force had lost 3,628 men killed, wounded, and missing.[86]

Myitkyina's capture in the first week of August signaled the successful end of a campaign that had begun six months earlier. Special Force's contribution to the campaign on the Northern Front was substantial. In severing the Japanese main line of communications to the Myitkyina area, and destroying supplies intended for its defense, the Chindits weakened the ability of the Japanese to resist the steady advance of Stillwell's Chinese force. More critically for Allied fortunes, in forcing an enemy response, the Chindits kept an entire Japanese division from participating in the decisive battle at Imphal.[87]

Wingate's theories and the contribution of Special Force to the Burma campaign have remained controversial. While Special Force's impact on the Northern Front is undoubted, the Chindits did not create the paralysis in Japanese capabilities in Burma that Wingate had hoped for. Wingate's greatest achievement lay in his "seeing and contributing a way whereby the Japanese could be made to fail."[88]

Above all he had demonstrated that air power could surmount the problems of terrain which had stymied the British Army for much of the Burma campaign. The second Chindit expedition proved that a large force of troops could be sustained for a considerable period of time entirely by air, disproving the arguments that Burma could never be conquered over land due to the lack of an adequate road system.

The Air Commandos were vital to Chindit success. The achievement of the Fighter Section was more than simply the amount of Japanese airplanes, supplies, and troops destroyed, although the total was considerable. The long-range of the Fighter Section's Mustangs enabled them to attack the Japanese forward airfields and inflict extensive damage on Japanese air units that could ill afford the losses in men and airplanes.

Fighter Section's greatest contribution to the Burma campaign was in pioneering, perfecting, and proving the effectiveness of ground-controlled close air support. The RAF squadrons that provided close air support to the Chindits insisted that their targets be indicated well in advance so that the pilots could be thoroughly briefed. The Fighter Section's method of having targets marked by mortar smoke and the attacks directed from RAF officers on the ground proved far more timely, effective, and more flexible. When the advance into Burma resumed later in the year, Visual Control Posts (VCPs) staffed with RAF officers became standard operating procedure.

3

THE 5TH AND 6TH FIGHTER SQUADRONS IN THE BURMA CAMPAIGN

While higher command debated future deployment, the men of the 1st Air Commando Fighter Section spent the intervening months in training at Asansol or sitting alert. At the end of May 1944 they received a batch of war-weary Curtiss P-40Ns to supplement the tired Mustangs while the latter underwent maintenance. The Fighter Section received several replacement pilots as well to make up for the combat veterans transferred back to the States.

As most of the replacements had trained on the P-40, they began conversion training when the Mustangs returned from overhaul. To keep the pilots occupied during the monsoon season, the Fighter Section was assigned the task of providing a standby alert flight at two bases west of Calcutta where the newly arrived Boeing B-29 Superfort groups were based. The assignment was hot, wet, and boring. The monsoon season was in full force with frequent heavy rains. Through June, July, and much of August, the pilots of the Fighter Section sat and waited, flying training missions and alternating alert duty with a mixture of P-40s and P-51s, wondering what the future would hold.[1]

In early August, the 1st Air Commando Group underwent a reorganization to bring it in conformity with the structure the U.S. Army Air Forces had established for air commando units. On 9 August 1944, the various sections —fighter, transport, light aircraft — were reconstituted as numbered squadrons. Because it was established several months after the 2nd and 3rd Air Commando Groups, the Fighter Section became the 5th Fighter Squadron (Commando). On September 1, the 5th Fighter Squadron (Commando) was activated with an authorized strength of 25 aircraft.

Major Duke Philips returned to the United States, and Captain Roland Lynn, the Fighter Section's operations officer, became the 5th Fighter Squadron's first commander.[2]

Lynn had hoped to obtain new P-51Cs, as replacements for the Fighter Section's older P-51A and B models, but was informed that all P-51Cs were going to China where their range and greater fuel efficiency made them the preferred fighter. Instead the 5th Squadron was allotted Republic P-47 Thunderbolts, brand new P-47D-23s arriving at Asansol toward the end of August. Another batch of replacement pilots, fresh from P-47 training units in the United States, arrived around the same time. The veteran Mustang pilots were unhappy with the switch to the heavier and less maneuverable Thunderbolt, but began transition training straight away and soon accepted their new mounts.[3]

In September Major General Stratemeyer authorized the formation of a second fighter squadron for the 1st Air Commando Group to make the Group equivalent to the 2nd Air Commando Group that had just been allocated to the Burma theater. Constituted on 22 September 1944, the 6th Fighter Squadron (Commando) was activated on September 30 with Captain Olin B. Carter as commanding officer. The 6th also had an authorized strength of twenty-five P-47D-23 aircraft.

A few Fighter Section veterans transferred from the 5th to the 6th Fighter Squadron and new P-47-trained replacement pilots joined them from the States. Captain Carter immediately began an intensive training schedule to get his new squadron into shape. Both squadrons would shortly return to combat, but not in the way they envisioned.[4]

At the completion of the Chindit operation, the men of Special Force were evacuated to rest camps in India. Kept in combat well beyond their allotted time, Special Force had suffered heavily and was now under strength. Although the initial plans for Operation Capital envisioned using Special Force for long-range penetration operations, manpower shortages among British troops and the lack of transport aircraft to support the advance into Burma and a large long-range penetration operation, led to Mountbatten's decision to disband Special Force in January. For the remainder of their time in Burma, the 5th and 6th Fighter Squadrons would serve more as regular tactical fighter units.[5]

Little more than two weeks after the 6th Fighter Squadron's activation, the 5th and 6th Squadrons went back into combat. In the Pacific, General MacArthur had scheduled the invasion of Leyte, the first step in the reconquest of the Philippines, for 20 October 1944. To support the Leyte invasion, the Allied air command in Burma organized a large joint fighter sweep of Japanese airfields in the Rangoon area for 18 and 20 October in the hope of destroying a quantity of what might have been reinforcement aircraft for the Philippines. The 5th and 6th Fighter Squadrons received orders to form a composite unit for the planned sweep.

Twelve P-47s from each squadron flew from Asansol to the RAF base at Cox's Bazar on the Bay of Bengal south of Chittagong, a staging base for the raid on Rangoon. The mission was to sweep the main Japanese airfields at Mingaladon, Hmawbi, and Zayatkwin, destroying any aircraft encountered in the air or on the ground. Allied intelligence estimated that the 5th Hikoshidan had somewhere between 45 and 55 aircraft in that area, including fighters of the 50th and 64th Sentais. The allied attack force included 12 Beaufighters and 9Mosquitos of the RAF, the 459th Fighter Squadron with P-38s, one squadron of P-47s from the American Tenth Air Force (58th Fighter Squadron, 33rd Fighter Group); one from the RAF (261 Squadron); and the Air Commando composite squadron, a total of 93 fighters.[6]

Early on the morning of 18 October Roland Lynn led off the 5th and 6th Squadrons' P-47s from Cox's Bazar for the first of the two sweeps. Each P-47 carried two 165-gallon drop tanks for the mission, a round-trip of nearly 900 miles. While the flight leaders were all veterans, for many of the others it was their first combat mission. The Air Commandos were assigned Mingaladon, located some six miles north of Rangoon, as their target, and were scheduled to be the third group of fighters over the airfield. At 0930 hours, nine RAF Mosquitos swept over the airdrome without encountering any opposition and claimed one Dinah (Mitsubishi Ki-46) damaged. Then at 1015 hours, twenty-four P-47s from the 10th Air Force's 58th Fighter Squadron attacked, encountering a small group of Oscars over the airfield. The squadron claimed two victories, and four more aircraft destroyed on the ground.[7]

Lynn had staggered the composite squadron so that the 12 aircraft from the 6th Squadron were in the front of the formation, with the 12 aircraft of the 5th flying above and behind. The plan was for the 6th Squadron to dive down and strafe, then pull up and act as top cover while the 5th took a turn. Nearing the target area, Lynn spotted a formation of single-engine fighters approaching his formation head-on, at their same level. Quickly alerting his pilots to get ready to drop their external tanks, at the last second Lynn recognized the fighters as Thunderbolts, the 58th Fighter Squadron coming off the target and on their way back to base.[8]

As the formation approached Mingaladon, Olin Carter brought the 6th Squadron down to 2,000 feet in preparation to strafe the airfield, leaving the 5th at 20,000 feet as top cover. Just as he was about to begin his strafing run, Carter heard someone call out, "Bogies at 6 o'clock high!"

A flight of eight Oscars had flown between the two Air Commando formations. Realizing that Lynn's formation was in a perfect defensive position, Carter called for his pilots to drop their tanks and commence their strafing runs. The speed of their dive quickly carried them away from the Oscars, which immediately ran into the high cover Thunderbolts.

Closing on the Japanese formation, one Oscar turned toward Lynn who sent a stream of bullets toward the Oscar until the two planes almost collided. The Oscar fell off into a spin, through 4,000 feet, and was still descending when Lynn looked up and saw two more Oscars directly above him.

He closed in on the pair and opened fire as one started to turn. The enemy pilot then tried to change direction. Lynn had to break off firing, and passed beneath him, pulling up to the side. When the Japanese pilot saw Lynn above him, he immediately climbed onto Lynn's tail. In his more powerful fighter Lynn slowly outdistanced the Oscar, and both aircraft then peeled off. Lynn tried to set up another pass but was unable to get a bead on the Oscar. As he noted in his combat report, "We played tag for 20 minutes between the clouds." None of the other Oscars reacted as aggressively as the pilot in Lynn's second encounter. Flying his first combat mission, 2nd Lieutenant Marion Ball managed to damage another Oscar.[9]

A line of P-47D "Razorback" Thunderbolts from the 5th or 6th Squadron at Cox's Bazar on November 3, 1944, preparing for Operation "Eruption." (Courtesy NASM)

THE RAGOON AIRFIELDS

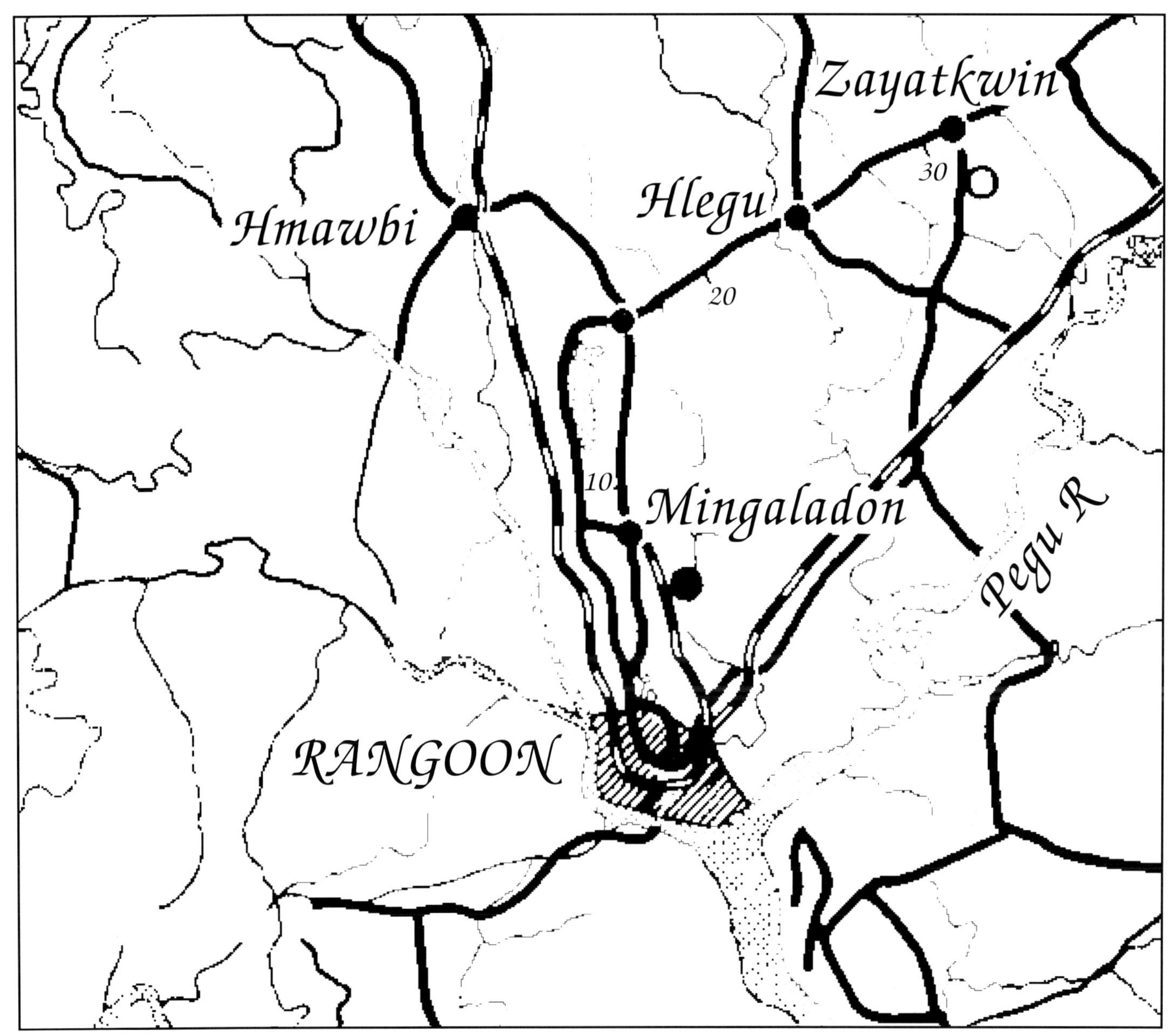

Source: *War Against Japan, Volume IV*

Lt. "Moon" Mullins taxis past in his Thunderbolt with South East Asia Command theater markings consisting of a blue cowl and blue bands on the wings and tail surfaces. (Courtesy NASM)

While the aerial dogfight swirled above him, Carter concentrated on the strafing attack. As the Air Commandos came in over the field, Japanese anti-aircraft guns opened fire, sending a stream of tracers at the approaching Thunderbolts. On his first pass, Carter fired at an Oscar and watched it explode. He and the other pilots made several more passes, damaging several additional aircraft, but there were few targets. As they pulled off from their final run, Carter gave the order to return to base since they had consumed too much fuel to act as top cover for the 5th Squadron.

Coming off the airfield toward the west Lieutenant Everett Kelly, an element leader on his first combat mission, heard his wingman shouting that a Japanese fighter was on his tail at 5 o'clock, and asking for aid. Kelly pulled up and swerved to the right, cutting inside the Oscar. Opening fire, he saw smoke. As the fighter descended it burst into flames, and the pilot bailed out. Kelly had achieved the rare feat of shooting down an enemy airplane on his first mission.[10]

The encore mission on the 20th found Roland Lynn leading 17 fighters to attack Mingaladon, while Olin Carter took seven to strafe the airfields at Hmawbi and Zayatkwin. Unprepared for the first attack on the 18th, the Japanese had flown in reinforcements from Bangkok the next day. Thus on the arrival of the P-47s over Mingaladon, the Air Commando pilots found 16 enemy fighters in the air over the field. On this day the Japanese pilots were noticeably more aggressive and demonstrated improved tactics and organization. The 64th Sentai sent up several flights of Oscar fighters to intercept the Thunderbolts, and stayed to fight.

Flying above the field Roland Lynn saw Captain Younger Pitts below with an Oscar in pursuit. Lynn told Pitts to continue on a straight course, then dove down on the Oscar, waiting until the wings of the Oscar filled his gun sight. Lynn opened fire from about 100 yards away. However, he was going too fast to get in more than one quick burst, damaging the Japanese fighter, before he swept past.

Marion Ball, on just his second combat mission, had the good fortune to find himself above and behind an inattentive Japanese pilot. Ball turned inside the Oscar, opened fire, and the aircraft burst into flames. 2nd Lieutenant Lee "Moon" Mullins managed to damage a third Oscar. The Air Commandos then dropped down to strafe, destroying several aircraft on the ground. In combats with Thunderbolts that afternoon, one pilot from the 64th Sentai was shot down and killed, possibly Sergeant Major Rokuro Nagai, who may have been Marion Ball's victim.[11]

Racing across Mingaladon on the deck, "Moon" Mullins ran into a stream of fire from a Japanese machine gun mounted on one of the hangars. The P-47 was flying so low that the Japanese were firing down at it. One of the bullets hit Mullins' windshield directly head-on, cracked the armored plate glass in front of him, and ricocheted around the cockpit before dropping, spent, into his lap. Unable to see straight ahead, Mullins immediately pulled up and set course for Cox's Bazar. After landing he got out on the wing of his aircraft and stood there cursing the damage to his airplane, ignoring the questions from an inquiring bystander, who turned out to be Major General Stratemeyer.[12]

Olin Carter's flight met no enemy airplanes over Hmawbi or Zayatkwin, but had some success strafing. Carter destroyed a Dinah and an Oscar at Zayatkwin, giving him a total of 11 claims against Japanese aircraft (two in the air and nine on the ground), and damaged an Oscar at Hmawbi. Lieutenants Malcom Wilkins and Hilton Weesner of the 5th Squadron each claimed one aircraft destroyed on the ground, while from the 6th Squadron 1st Lieutenants Jack Klarr and Joe Setnor, and 2nd Lieutenants Edward Bayne and Allen Vanderyeck submitted similar claims. The Air Commando composite squadron emerged as the high scorer for the

Rangoon sweeps, with a total of 11 airplanes destroyed in the air and on the ground, one probably destroyed, and seven damaged.[13]

The day after the second Rangoon sweep the composite squadron returned to Asansol where the Thunderbolts underwent needed maintenance. Towards the end of the month both squadrons set to work painting their aircraft with the standard South East Asia Command markings, broad dark blue bands on the wings, tail, and horizontal stabilizers; and Air Commando unit markings, five stripes representing the Group's five original sections. The 5th Squadron painted an aircraft number under the cockpit, while the 6th Squadron chose to paint their numbers in the blue band on the tail.

Olin Carter ended his long tour of Air Commando duty at the end of October, and Younger A. Pitts replaced him as 6th Squadron CO.[14]

At the beginning of November, the 5th and 6th Squadrons were alerted for another long-range mission to Rangoon. Eastern Air Command had planned two days of combined bomber and fighter strikes on targets in the Rangoon area. Designated Operation Eruption, the raids employed Boeing B-29 Superforts from Twentieth Bomber Command, RAF and AAF B-24s from the Strategic Air Force, and a mixed fighter force. It was destined to be the largest air strike carried out in the Burma theater. The first day's mission, planned for 3 November, would begin with a fighter sweep of the Rangoon airfields, followed by a B-29 attack on marshaling yards in Rangoon, followed by a second fighter sweep. The plan for the second day was for the B-24s to bomb the Insein locomotive shops with fighter escort, while other fighter squadrons swept Rangoon airfields for the third time. This time the 5th and 6th Squadrons sent a full complement of 20 aircraft each to Cox's Bazar, where they joined the Lightnings of the American 459th Fighter Squadron and RAF No. 30 and 135 Thunderbolt Squadrons.[15]

On this occasion there were fewer Japanese aircraft to be seen in the air or on the ground. Following the invasion of the Philippines the Japanese Army Air Force had begun a systematic withdrawal from Southeast Asia to reinforce the Philippines, where they were locked in an unequal struggle with the U.S. Army Air Force and Navy. With little hope of replacements given the demands from the Philippines, the 5th Hikoshidan had to conserve its aircraft as best it could. By the end of 1944, the Japanese Air Force had built nearly 4,000 aircraft shelters on its various airfields in Burma. They were on the defensive and were henceforth obliged to conserve remaining aircraft.

The 5th and 6th Squadrons were assigned to the second airfield sweep on the first day of Eruption, with the 5th taking Mingaladon and the 6th Zayatkwin and Hmawbi. Nineteen 5th Squadron aircraft (one aborted the mission) arrived over Mingaladon at 1030 hours on 3 November 1944 to find no Japanese aircraft defending the airfield. Leaving eleven airplanes as top cover, the remaining eight descended to strafe. Three lost sight of the field descending through clouds, one failed to find a target on the field, and the other four ended up strafing empty hangarettes.[16]

The 6th Squadron had more success, although three aircraft had to abort and one crash-landed on takeoff. The remaining seventeen first attacked Zayatkwin. Four airplanes remained at altitude as top cover while the remainder dove down to strafe the airfield. They found no aircraft on the field, but on their way to strafe Hmawbi nearby they encountered two Oscars flying on the deck, most likely from the 50th Sentai. Two pilots (whose names are not recorded) got off quick bursts and claimed to have damaged both aircraft. At Hmawbi airfield the P-47s observed several aircraft on the ground, Lieutenant Joe Setnor blowing up a Ki-21 Sally, while other pilots damaged another Sally and a Ki-61 Tony.[17]

The next day the two squadrons switched targets and remarkably had the same experiences. Twelve aircraft from the 6th Squadron hit Mingaladon at 1220 hours and found nothing. After setting several hangarettes on fire, the flight went on to Hmawbi and found it barren as well.

Nineteen aircraft from the 5th Squadron attacked Zayatkwin and Hmawbi. Leaving four aircraft as top cover, the remainder strafed hangarettes and bashas at Zayatkwin and found one Oscar which was claimed as damaged. The squadron then flew on to Hmawbi, where two Oscars jumped one flight at 4,000 feet. Captain P.K. Oram closed on one Oscar riding the tail of another P-47 and sent the Oscar crash-landing into a rice paddy. The second Japanese escaped. Honors that day went to the 459th Fighter Squadron, which ran into a group of Oscars and Tojos, claiming three probables and five damaged.[18]

For the two missions, the 5th and 6th Squadrons submitted combined claims of two aircraft destroyed and five damaged.

In the months that followed, neither squadron had much of an opportunity to increase its score. With the Japanese on the defensive and avoiding combat whenever possible, the chances of encountering enemy aircraft in the air or on the ground were few and far between. While both squadrons would destroy several more Japanese aircraft, this would be a rare occurrence. The pilots would meet Japanese airplanes in air combat on only three more occasions before the end of the campaign. For the rest of their time in Burma the 5th and 6th Squadrons would be fully engaged in the less glamorous, but vitally necessary work of supporting the ground campaign.

By early November Operation Capital, 14th Army's advance to the Chindwin River and beyond, was well under way. Advance units were pushing Japanese rearguard forces back towards Kalewa, the first major crossing point on the Chindwin, as the Army's main body followed. Relentless pressure through the monsoon rains had not given the Japanese 15th Army time to recover or prepare a defense. General Slim looked set to begin getting his forces across the Chindwin and on their way into Burma in mid-December 1944 as planned.

Following the debacle at Imphal, the Japanese Burma Area Army had little choice but to go on the defensive. A change of command in September brought in Lieutenant General Hyotaro Kimura, a shrewd and skillful tactician. Recognizing that they had lost control of northern Burma, the Japanese Imperial General Staff ordered a defense of southern Burma. Kimura decided to maintain a line across central Burma, roughly the same as the objective for Operation Capital, running from Lashio to Mandalay and covering the area of the Irrawaddy River south of Mandalay. He hoped that, at best, his forces could stall an Allied offensive until the onset of the monsoon in May 1945.[19]

Eastern Air Command, responsible for all Allied air units in eastern India and Burma, now had considerable force available in the theater to support Operation Capital. The RAF's No. 221 Group, with 13 fighter squadrons, was responsible for supporting the main advance of 14th Army. No. 224 Group had 12 RAF fighter squadrons, the USAAF's 12th Bombardment Group and 459th Fighter Squadron to support the advance of the British XV Corps down the Arakan coast.[20]

These Allied air units, including 5th and 6th Air Commando Squadrons, had four operational tasks:

1. Destruction of the Japanese air force in Burma in order to maintain air superiority.
2. Provision of adequate direct support for the ground forces.
3. Destruction of enemy defenses in advance of the Allied ground forces.
4. Isolation of the main enemy force by disrupting rear lines of communication, destruction of the enemy's installations and supplies both in the immediate battle area and on his lines of communications, and repeated bombing of Japanese headquarters to foster confusion and disorganization.[21]

The Combat Cargo Task Force (CCTF), organized the previous June, had responsibility for all transport squadrons and all air supply operations and would, therefore, be responsible for supporting any airborne or long-range penetration operations. CCTF assumed responsibility for the 1st Air Commando Group and any other Air Commando groups that would be assigned to the theater. Although CCTF in theory exercised operational control over the Air Commandos, no air commando-type operations were then under consideration, so 5th and 6th Fighter Squadrons were available for other tasks.

In early November Eastern Air Command decided to second the two squadrons to No. 224 Group to work alongside the B-25 equipped 12th Bombardment Group based at Feni, roughly 100 miles north of Cox's Bazar. The Air Commandos were tasked with providing escort to the bombers, conducting their own independent sweeps over Burma to attack the Japanese line of communications, and to assist in maintaining air superiority through regular sweeps over Japanese airfields. Because facilities at Feni were somewhat limited, the two squadrons would serve in rotation.

Two 6th Fighter Squadron Thunderbolts taking off, display the individual and unit markings. Aircraft in the foreground is a P-47D-23-RA. (Courtesy NASM).

On 8 November, twenty-three P-47s of the 5th Squadron flew into Feni, while six C-47s and four gliders brought in additional pilots and ground crews, supplies, and equipment. The 12th Bomb Group made the 5th Squadron welcome, and provided a building to use as an operational headquarters with revetments for the P-47s nearby. The 6th Squadron remained at Asansol conducting training missions.[22]

The 5th Squadron's first mission, a sweep of the Japanese airfield at Meiktila, was scheduled for 10 November 1944. It proved uneventful as there were no enemy aircraft at Meiktila. Sweeps over the Japanese airfields in central Burma continued over the next two days, but few worthwhile targets could be found.

The Air Commandos found and destroyed an Oscar at Nawnghkio airfield on the 11th and a Sally bomber out in the open at Laihka airfield the next day. However, while strafing Meiktila, 2nd Lieutenant Hilton D. Weesner was hit by anti-aircraft fire and crash landed close to the field, where he was taken prisoner. Imprisoned in Rangoon, Weesner was freed in May 1945.

A return visit to Nawnghkio on 15 November resulted in the possible destruction of another Oscar. The only other claims against Japanese aircraft for the month was for an Oscar damaged at Hmawbi airfield during an escort mission to Rangoon.[23]

The 5th began escorting the 12th Bomb Group on 13 November, the first of 19 such missions. Several flights of P-47s would escort 12 to 36 bombers to targets in central Burma and shepherd them back to the Chindwin River. Once the B-25s were west of the Chindwin, the Air Commandos would return to strafe targets of opportunity along the many roads, rivers, and rail lines the Japanese used as supply conduits. Air Commandos hit locomotives and rolling stock, sampans on the rivers, and bullock carts, on one occasion destroying some 20 carts found to be carrying gasoline.[24]

Throughout November the many units of Eastern Air Command concentrated on disrupting Japanese lines of communication. The 5th Fighter Squadron contributed to this effort through a bombing campaign against railroad bridges, beginning with a mission against a bypass bridge on the Mu River on 16 November. The absence of Japanese fighters meant that small flights of Thunderbolts could be used against bridges, which often required repeated strikes to inflict serious damage and to undo Japanese repairs. Usually three to six planes would go on a bombing mission, armed with 500-pounders, and often a morning strike would be followed by one in the afternoon. As soon as photo intelligence indicated that a bridge had been repaired, it would be struck again.[25]

The Mu River railroad bypass bridge, located west of Mandalay, provides a good example of the constant interdiction effort. The rail line from Rangoon to Mandalay went west to the Chindwin River area with one line going north to Shwebo while a second fork went to Ye-u, crossing the Mu River where the Japanese had built a bypass bridge next to the original bridge. Cutting the Mu River bypass bridge would severely limit supplies to Japanese troops in the Chindwin area.

During the month the Air Commandos hit the Mu River bypass bridge five times. On 16 November, three planes bombed the bridge in the morning and five in the afternoon, resulting in two hits on the tracks approaching the bridge, but none on the bridge itself. Four aircraft returned the next morning and had more success, scoring two direct hits on the bridge. Six days later, when intelligence reported the connection once again serviceable, three Thunderbolts bombed the bridge in the morning and nine attacked in the afternoon, scoring six near misses and several hits on the railroad tracks just off the bridge. On the 24th, five aircraft returned and knocked out one span with two direct hits. A few days later the Japanese had the structure functioning once more.

Captain Lynn decided to use the 5th Squadron's last day of operations to concentrate on the bridge. Five planes struck in the morning, but missed. That afternoon, Lynn took one other pilot to the bridge, this time carrying 1,000-pounders. He managed two direct hits, knocking 25 feet out of the central span.[26]

The next day the 5th flew back to Asansol, exchanging places with the 6th Fighter Squadron. During their time at Feni the 5th Squadron's pilots had flown 51 missions and 355 sorties, averaging 17 sorties per day. During the month they had dropped 84 tons of bombs, claiming seven bridges destroyed. While the escort missions proved uneventful, the 12th Bomb Group noted that their bombing accuracy improved when they didn't have to worry about possible interceptions.

In addition to the loss of 2nd Lieutenant Weesner, 2nd Lieutenant Walter C. Lair had been shot down on a mission against the Mu River bypass bridge on 22 November. Coming out of his dive Lair smelled gas fumes in the cockpit and saw that his fuel gauge was heading towards empty. He turned west, but ten minutes later his engine ran out of fuel, and he elected to crash land rather than bail out. Overshooting the clearing, he plowed through a stand of small trees, shedding his plane's wings in the process. Fortunately, the Thunderbolt's immense strength protected him. Lair managed to walk out from behind Japanese lines with the help of friendly Karen tribes, who hid him from the enemy for weeks and put him in touch with British patrols. He arrived back at Feni in January 1945.[27]

Soon after their arrival 6th Squadron carried out a sweep of Meiktila, Heho, and Kangaung airfields, while eight aircraft escorted thirty-six B-25s from the 12th Bomb Group to bomb Yamethin to the south of

A poor photo, but S/Sgt. Cebrelli graphically demonstrates the comparative size of a 1,000 lb. bomb on SOUTHERN BELLE. (Courtesy Wm. Burghardt)

1st Lieutenant Jack Klarr, 6th Fighter Squadron, with the insignia of the 1st Air Commando Group on his flight jacket. Klarr claimed a probable Oscar on December 13, 1944. (Courtesy 1st Air Commando Association).

Meiktila. The first flight found no aircraft, but did come across a row of boxcars on a rail line north of town which they strafed. 2nd Lieutenant Brents A. Lowry, on his first combat mission, was on his strafing run when an explosion engulfed his P-47 sending it crashing to the ground. Lowry had either flown over an exploding boxcar or had possibly flown too low and crashed into a tree. It was the squadron's first combat loss.[28]

Early in the month they joined Thunderbolt squadrons from the Tenth Air Force in large sweeps of the Burmese railroad system, bombing rail yards and stations and then following the lines to strafe any locomotives and rolling stock that they encountered. After every bombing or escort mission the Thunderbolts hunted targets of opportunity to strafe.

Although the 6th Squadron encountered few really lucrative targets, the score of rolling stock, trucks, sampans, and bullock carts destroyed mounted steadily. On one occasion a flight encountered over 100 river craft, which the squadron proceeded to bomb and strafe, leaving at least 22 destroyed.

One choice target was gasoline supplies. For protection and easy access the Japanese would store drums of gasoline in small valleys off the main roads, covering the drums with camouflage netting. The Air Commandos would stay up above a road while a flight leader went down the road at low level, peering up valleys on each side. Jack Klarr remembers when the flight leader found a gasoline cache. "He'd come back and give it a squirt and then the rest of the flight would come in and strafe. That was always a lot of fun, when you'd find one of those. They'd go up with a big bang."[29]

The vital and often-repaired Mu River bypass bridge was attacked on six missions. It became such a regular target that the pilots began calling it "old faithful."

Japanese anti-aircraft fire varied from target to target. Some were undefended, which allowed a more leisurely attack. Others, such as the bridge at Myitnge, put up enough fire to preclude a second pass. Lieutenant Allen Abrahams had a lucky escape while attacking the Myitnge bridge. Pulling out of his bomb run, a huge explosion flipped his Thunderbolt over vertically so hard that Abrahams hit his head on the side of his canopy. Remarkably, the plane was undamaged, despite what had seemed to be a direct hit.

As a precaution, the pilots would often fire several bursts at a bridge in their dive, just to keep heads down. Some of the stronger structures proved to be difficult targets. The bridge at Sinthegon, which had heavy concrete abutments, withstood three attacks during which the fighters dropped fifty-six 500 lb. bombs.[30]

The 6th Squadron encountered Japanese aircraft on only one occasion. On 13 December 1944, they joined the 5th Fighter and two RAF Thunderbolt squadrons to provide cover for 12 RAF Liberators bombing bridges in southern Burma. Approaching the target,

Younger Pitts, who was leading that day, called out a flight of ten Oscars to the left of the bombers. Jack Klarr, who had a flight on that formation, saw the enemy and waited to determine their intent. When the Japanese fighters made a half-hearted feint at the bombers, Pitts told Klarr to go get them.

Klarr pulled up alongside the leader of the Japanese formation and gave the Oscar a burst, causing the Japanese fighter to emit a stream of smoke. The Oscar rolled over and dived for the deck with smoke pouring out. Klarr's wingman, Lieutenant A.E. Haunt, attacked the Japanese leader's wingman at the same time, knocking pieces off. Klarr received credit for a probable, and Haunt for a damaged.[31]

Allied air forces maintained constant pressure on enemy airfields in central Burma, particularly as intelligence found indications that the Japanese were trying to strengthen their forces in upper Burma by flying in aircraft for a few quick operations. Flights of Oscars made several sweeps over British forward positions, doing little damage but gaining valuable intelligence on British movements. The 6th Squadron contributed to this effort with weekly strafing sweeps over the airfields around Meiktila, Magwe, and the old battle grounds of Anisakan, Heho, and Aungban. No aircraft were encountered on any of these sweeps, as the Japanese Army Air Force had less than 20 based in upper Burma and these were kept well hidden by day. The best that could be achieved was to damage facilities around the airfield perimeter. On these sweeps, the pilots usually set fire to the small bamboo and palm frond hangarettes that lay about the field and strafed whatever buildings lay in their path. In a new tactic, to frustrate temporary use of these airfields, the 6th Squadron began bombing the runways, pitting the runway at Magwe on 16 and 21 December.[32]

The 6th Squadron flew its last missions from Feni on 22 December 1944 and then made preparations to return to Asansol for Christmas, rotating again with the 5th Fighter Squadron. During its three weeks in combat the 6th Squadron had flown 440 sorties, with only 15 aircraft failing to complete missions. This averaged out to 22.4 sorties per day for the 23 aircraft available, a testament to the hard work and devotion of the squadron's ground crews and maintenance staff. The pace of operations meant that the P-47s often had to be re-fueled and re-armed at night, putting added burdens on the hard-working ground crews. Although the 12th Bomb Group gave the Air Commando fighter squadrons all the assistance they could, the Air Commandos had to make do with limited facilities and a constant shortage of transport.[33]

The 5th Fighter Squadron returned to Feni on 28 December to begin its second period of combat. On the Squadron's arrival Roland Lynn, recently promoted to Major, declared that the 5th Squadron would out-fly the 6th and would better its impressive tally of sorties per day.

The 5th Squadron flew 47 sorties in five missions, escorting the 12th Bomb Group's B-25s to the Arakan area and conducting its own bombing attacks on the Japanese-held towns of Myingyan and Pakokku along the Irrawaddy River. The next day 24 aircraft flew to the Arakan to attack road bridges, followed by a combined road and river sweep with 25 aircraft which destroyed a number of river craft, trucks, and a locomotive, and damaged six railcars. The following day 18 aircraft went out again to bomb bridges. In its first three days the Squadron flew 114 sorties, an average of 38 per day.[34]

The new year began with a considerable bang. For some time, Roland Lynn had wanted to develop a method for inflicting greater damage on the more substantial Burmese bridges, those with abutments, piers, and foundations of heavy metal beams, concrete, or stone. He felt that the 500 lb. bombs previously employed weren't doing the job, and wanted to try placing heavier bombs as close as possible in the hope that the blast effect would cause structural weakness, and possibly collapse piers or abutments. On one or two occasions the Air Commandos had used two 1,000 lb. bombs on a bridge; Lynn now wanted to try three. But would the P-47 have enough ground clearance for a 1,000-pounder, mounted in place of the belly drop tank? And would the takeoff roll, with such an ordnance load, be excessive, using too much of the runway?

Lynn contacted Younger Pitts (who had also been promoted to Major) back at Asansol. Pitts agreed to test fly a Thunderbolt with two 1,000 lb. bombs under the wings and one under the belly. On 30 December he lined up at the end of the Asansol runway, ran his airplane up to full power, set ten degrees of flaps, and then released the brakes. The Thunderbolt trundled off without undue complaint, and when he reached 135 mph, Pitts pulled the airplane off the ground. At no time did the fins of the belly bomb scrape the runway. He had taken off in 4,800 feet, a bit more than normal, but had 1,200 feet of runway remaining. Climbing to altitude Pitts found that the plane flew normally, except that it was a bit sluggish in a turn. He then dove down and dropped the bombs using the standard glide-bombing pattern common to the two squadrons, encountering no problems.[35]

On the afternoon of 1 January 1945, Lynn and his operations officer, Lieutenant Malcom Wilkins, sortied each armed with three 1,000-pounders. They headed for the important railroad bridge at Taungdwingyi, on the main Mandalay-Rangoon rail line south of Meiktila, roughly 350 miles from Feni. The Thunderbolts had first to transit the Chin Hills, reaching to 10,000 feet in some cases, before letting down over the Burmese central plain.

Major Roland Lynn's Thunderbolt armed with three 1,000 lb. bombs. On January 1, 1945, Lynn, 5th Fighter Squadron commander, and 1st Lieutenant Malcolm Wilkins, his operations officer, each carried three 1,000 lb. bombs to dive bomb a railroad bridge at Taungdwingyi. This is believed to be a record bomb load for the P-47. (Courtesy NASM)

Once at the bridge, Lynn dove down first and dropped his two wing bombs, then made a second dive to drop his belly bomb. Wilkins dropped all three of his bombs on his first dive. Lynn scored a direct hit on the center span with his bombs, knocking it out. The return flight was uneventful. On landing each plane was found to have sufficient gas for another 30 minutes of flight. This mission is believed to be a record for the P-47. Three 1,000 lb. bombs were equal to the bomb load of a twin-engine B-25 Mitchell. While Lynn and Wilkins proved that a P-47 could carry the load and deliver it with accuracy, the experiment was not repeated. The sacrifice in range was too great for the targets the Air Commandos needed to hit.[36]

During the first two weeks of January 1945 the 5th Squadron flew missions on every day but one, continuing to concentrate on rail and road bridges. On January 2, they returned to "old faithful," the Mu River bypass bridge, and in a successful strike knocked out the bridge's three central spans. The next day the Kyaukse railroad bridge was hit hard, with three direct hits knocking out ten to 15 feet of the southern end. That same day thirteen aircraft dove through intense anti-aircraft fire to bomb the oil refineries at Yenangyaung, starting fires that sent up a huge column of smoke over 7,000 feet. On 4 January, thirteen aircraft knocked out a span on the Sinthegon railroad bridge, which the Air Commandos had attacked on several previous occasions without success, while four aircraft destroyed 100 feet on the Sinthe bypass bridge.

For a change of pace the squadron spent two days bombing Japanese troop concentrations, then went back to bombing bridges. On the 12th, nineteen aircraft again hit the Sinthe bypass bridge and an oil pipeline bridge, sending smoke up to 14,000 feet. Coming off their bombing runs, the Air Commandos found a long line of rolling stock on a nearby rail line and strafed, damaging 40 cars and destroying three tank cars. On the 13th twenty-one aircraft bombed anti-aircraft positions near Mandalay in advance of a B-24 strike. One P-47 flown by Lieutenant Price was hit by anti-aircraft fire. Price made it as far as the Chin Hills where he was forced to parachute. He made his way back to the squadron the following month.[37]

The British advance had made rapid progress and by 11 January 1945, units of 19 Division stood on the west bank of the Irrawaddy River preparing to cross and establish bridgeheads north of Mandalay. Crossing the broad river in daylight the assault craft and motorized rafts carrying men and vehicles made easy targets, as did the lines of troops waiting to cross. Eighteen Oscars from the 64th Sentai attacked British forward positions, and 16 Oscars returned again the next day to bomb the first British bridgehead on the east bank. To stop these attacks, the British Army wanted Japanese airfields within range of the Mandalay area neutralized. Eastern Air Command responded by ordering RAF and USAAF fighter and bomber squadrons to launch daily strikes on each field.

On 15 January, Roland Lynn led 18 Thunderbolts to attack the airfield at Heho. After cratering the runway with bombs, they dropped down to strafe. Lynn set fire to one hangarette, and the other pilots flamed another six.

An escort for B-24s bombing Mingaladon airfield on the 16th proved uneventful, but the next day while escorting 12th Bomb Group B-25s to airfields at Hsumhsai and Nawnghkio, the 5th Squadron encountered heavy anti-aircraft fire. After shepherding the B-25s, the Thunderbolts bombed the runways, revetments, and flak batteries, then strafed hangars around the field. Six aircraft were hit by anti-aircraft fire, one seriously, but no pilots were hurt and all returned to base.[38]

The next day, while the 6th Fighter Squadron was escorting RAF and AAF B-24s to bomb the airfields around Meiktila, Roland Lynn led 18 aircraft from the 5th

Squadron as escort for thirty-six B-25s from the 12th Bomb Group to attack Aungban and Heho airfields. At Heho, four aircraft bombed anti-aircraft positions just before the B-25s came over the field. When the bombers had finished their run, the Thunderbolts again hit runways and hangars. Lynn then led four P-47s on a strafing pass. He raked one hangarette and watched it burst into flames. On his second run across the field he saw an Oscar inside this same hangarette surrounded by flames. In the shell of the hangarette he had strafed on the 15th, he spotted the remains of a twin-engine aircraft. On his return he submitted claims for one aircraft destroyed and one probably destroyed.[39]

During the strafing attack, AA fire caught Lieutenant Richard Gilmore's Thunderbolt as he raced across the field. Gilmore pulled up and the other pilots saw him bail out successfully. The next day six P-47s escorted a B-25 from the 12th Bomb Group to search for Gilmore. The formation rendezvoused with two First Air Commando L-5 aircraft in the hope that they could land and effect a rescue. They located Gilmore with what were believed to be friendly Burmese natives, but the L-5s could not land in the surrounding area. The B-25 dropped supplies for him, and the pilots returned to Feni, hoping that Gilmore would be able to walk back to Allied lines. Sadly, he was captured and sent to Rangoon as a POW. He died after the war from the effects of his mistreatment while a prisoner.[40]

That same day, 19 January, eight aircraft escorted a dozen 12th Bomb Group B-25s to Kwetnge airfield. On their return they flight strafed Meiktila airfield where one aircraft was hit by anti-aircraft fire.

On the 20th, the 5th Squadron escorted 12 B-25s to give Toungoo airfield the same treatment, returning the next day to strafe Toungoo and Magwe airfields, where anti-aircraft fire damaged three aircraft. While the 5th Squadron could claim only two Japanese aircraft from these attacks, they nonetheless had the desired effect. These and other strikes by RAF and Tenth Air Force fighters prevented the Japanese from making more than minimal use of their forward air strips. During the six days of Allied strikes, the Japanese mounted only one strafing attack on Allied ground troops in central Burma.[41]

For the remainder of the month the squadron continued attacks on rail and road bridges, but devoted an increasing amount of time to bombing Japanese troop positions in front of the British advance. Japanese oil supplies also became a priority target. From January 22 to 25, the 5th Squadron sent out flights every day to bomb bridges and strafe oil storage tanks, leaving broken spans and huge columns of smoke behind them.

On the 26th, 25 Thunderbolts escorted twenty-five B-25s to attack positions at Kangaw, the P-47s bombing just ahead of the medium bombers. The next day the same force attacked Singu, P-47s bombing gun positions to spot them for the B-25s, which followed close behind and sighted in on the explosions.

Two more combined missions followed then, on the 30th, nineteen P-47s took off on a sweep of the rail line south, dropping two spans of a bridge near Pyawbwe and destroying two freight cars and damaging a further 46. The 5th Squadron's final mission took place on 31 January when eighteen aircraft escorted the full 12th Bomb Group on an uneventful exercise.[42]

The 5th Fighter Squadron at Feni, January 1945. (Standing Back Row) (L-R): Frank Byrne (KIA), Lee "Moon" Mullins, Fred Stevens, Nelson Tewksbury, Randolph Owen, Roland Lynn, Squadron Commander; Malcolm Wilkins, Operations Officer, Francis Wheeler, M.C. Ball, James Knight, William Burghardt, James Hutchinson (KIA), Edward Reimel. (Seated Middle Row) (L-R): William Raynolds, Thomas Brown, Robert Ferguson, Daniel Donovan, Eldon Gandrud, Charles Hess (KIA), William Davison (KIA), Edward Aumann (KIA), James Wheeler, W.R. Gago, Ernest Dornbush; (Seated Front Row) (L-R): Louis Lenz, Ernest Reichardt, Richard Gilmore (POW), Daniel Mitchell, Paul Oram, Carl Townson, Rudy Melichar, Frank Misfeldt, Herbert Hainey, Elmer Wingo. (Courtesy William Burghardt)

The 5th Squadron completed 58 combat missions during the month, flying 702 sorties for an average of 22.6 sorties per day. This was just slightly better than the average the 6th Fighter Squadron had achieved in December, meeting Major Lynn's goal. It had been a busy month, and Lynn was fortunate to have lost only one pilot. On 1 and 2 February the 5th Squadron flew back to join the 6th Squadron at Asansol, where both units set to work preparing for their next operation, supporting the capture of Meiktila, the second decisive battle of the Burma campaign. During the next two months they would fly more missions and suffer more casualties than the 1st Air Commandos had during the Wingate operation.

In planning the advance into central Burma, General Slim had been convinced that the Japanese would defend the approach to the Irrawaddy River with characteristic tenacity, and that the decisive battle he sought would be fought on the Shwebo plain, a triangle-shaped area incorporating the west bank of the Irrawaddy south of Shwebo and west to the Chindwin River. Here he could bring the Japanese Army to battle on his own terms and destroy it. But once across the Chindwin River in early December, Slim's division's made rapid progress. The Japanese made no real attempt to block the British advance, which made Slim suspect that they had no intention of fighting a battle west of the Irrawaddy. In this he was absolutely correct.[43]

General Kimura's instructions were to hold southern Burma, with its oil fields and vital rice production, at all costs. The key to defending southern Burma was to hold the line of the Irrawaddy, but with his armies weakened and with little hope of reinforcements, Kimura ordered the 15th Army to withdraw across the Irrawaddy and defend the Mandalay area from the east bank of the river, thereby forcing the British to make an opposed river crossing. There the Japanese could, hopefully, bring the British advance to a halt and delay it until the onset of the monsoon season.[44]

Slim needed to force the Japanese Army to do battle, preferably on ground and conditions favorable to 14th Army, and to that end he devised a remarkable plan. Slim would convince Kimura that the main weight of 14th Army was aimed at Mandalay, forcing a concentration of Japanese forces on Mandalay's defense. Slim would then send a column farther south, cross the Irrawaddy well below Mandalay, and cut Kimura's lines of communications to southern Burma. Kimura would have to fight to re-open his routes to the south or see his armies trapped around Mandalay.

The key to Slim's plan was the capture of Meiktila, the main administrative center for both the Japanese 15th and 33rd Armies. Surrounding Meiktila, and the nearby town of Thazi, were supply dumps, maintenance centers, hospitals, and airfields which supported the two Japanese armies. Meiktila and Thazi controlled the main road and railway link to Rangoon. Sever this line and Japanese forces would be cut off from the ammunition, rice, and oil that they needed to effectively resist.[45]

In mid-December Slim submitted the plan, which his Japanese opponents would call his "master stroke," to Mountbatten. Slim proposed that his XXXIII Corps would advance to the Irrawaddy, cross the river and encircle Mandalay from the north and the west, bringing the Japanese forces there to battle. Meanwhile, Slim's IV Corps would swing west behind XXXIII Corps and, in total secrecy, advance to Pakokku, near the Irrawaddy River. Once XXXIII Corps had established bridgeheads across the Irrawaddy, IV Corps would cross the river and send an armored force racing across the open countryside to capture Meiktila.

The capture of Meiktila required secrecy, surprise, and speed. Slim had to get his forces to Meiktila and astride Japanese lines of communication before Kimura could block him and withdraw his troops from Mandalay. 14th Army and IV Corps staffs developed a complex, four-part plan to accomplish this, designated Operation Multivite.[46]

7 Corps was composed of 7th and 17th Divisions and 255th Tank Brigade. Once 17th Division and 255th Tank Brigade broke out of the Irrawaddy bridgehead, they would be entirely dependent on air supply. Moreover, while the open central plain gave great scope for mobility and was ideal for a mechanized advance, 14th Army's divisions lacked sufficient motor transport. IV Corps did not have enough trucks and vehicles to carry 17th Division's full strength of three brigades. Borrowing from Orde Wingate's theories, IV Corps came up with a new concept (for Burma) of coordinating operations of a fast-moving mechanized force with an air-transported contingent.

IV Corps proposed that 17th Division's mechanized force, with its supporting armor, seize a landing ground near Meiktila. Its third brigade would be rapidly airlifted there to reinforce the division's defense of the town. The air requirement for the operation would be a transport force to insert the 99th Brigade and maintain a stream of supplies to the captured airfield. Fighter support would be expected for both the mechanized column and defense of the air bridgehead.[47]

The planners immediately recognized that the Air Commandos were ideal for this operation. The CCTF, responsible for all air transport in support of the 14th Army, was accordingly assigned all elements of the 1st Air Commandos and the recently arrived 2nd Air Commando Group for Operation Multivite.

General Slim asked that IV Corps be given more air support for the capture of Meiktila to make up for the lack of adequate artillery and tanks. Accordingly the 5th and 6th Squadrons, and the Mustang-equipped 1st and 2nd Fighter Squadrons from the 2nd Air Commando Group were assigned directly to IV Corps. This gave them a force of 100 fighters and freed RAF No. 221 Group to devote all its efforts to supporting XXXIII Corps' attack on Mandalay.

THE BATTLE FOR MEIKTILA

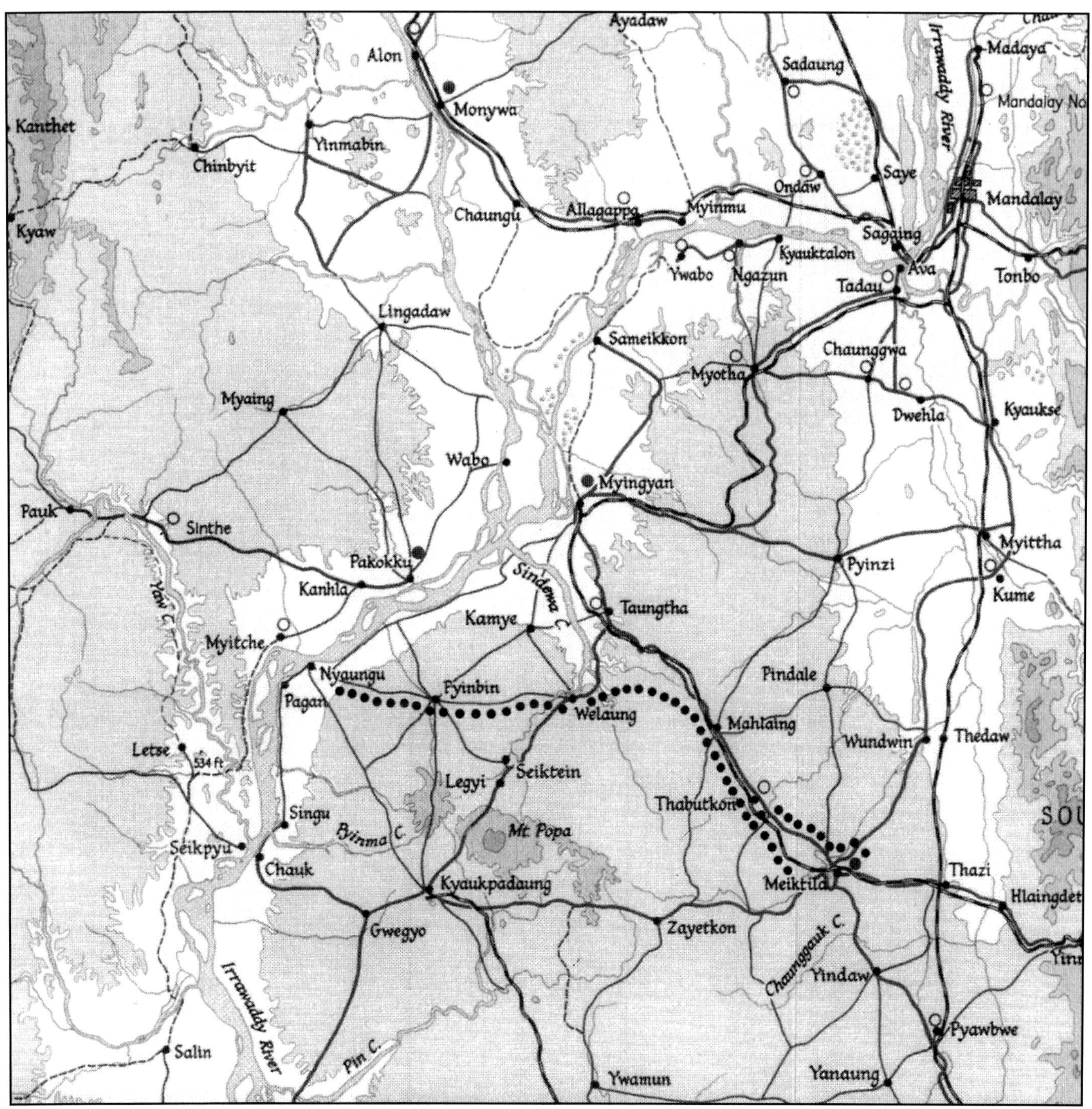

Source: *War Against Japan, Volume IV*

Preparing for Operation Multivite. P-47D Number 00, PITT'S POT, of Captain Younger A. Pitts, commander of the 6th Fighter Squadron, at Cox's Bazar with P-51Ds from the newly arrived 2nd Air Commando Group. The 5th and 6th Fighter Squadrons were combined with the 1st and 2nd Fighter Squadrons from the 2nd Air Commando Group to form the First Provisional Fighter Group. (Courtesy W.R. Eason)

To simplify operations, the different types of aircraft in the Air Commando groups were brought under unified commands. The fighter squadrons were grouped together in a temporary formation, the First Provisional Fighter Group, under the command of the 2nd Air Commando's head of fighter operations, Lieutenant Colonel Levi Chase. (See Chapter IV.) The four fighter squadrons moved closer to the front, the 1st and 2nd Fighter Squadrons going to Cox's Bazar, and the 5th and 6th Fighter Squadrons moving to Hay Field a few miles away.[48]

For the advance into central Burma, and particularly for the capture of Meiktila, the RAF put into practice the lessons in close air support learned the year before by the Chindits. 14th Army's divisions would advance with Visual Control Posts (VCPs), consisting of an RAF controller (an RAF officer with flying experience) and a radio crew traveling in a jeep. The VCPs had the responsibility of directing aircraft flying in close support of the ground troops. The RAF controller could call in air support, help identify ground targets, (usually through directing mortar smoke onto the target), and assign aircraft to new missions as needed. IV Corps arranged for three VCP teams to accompany 17th Division and 255th Tank Brigade on the advance to Meiktila.[49]

The close air support role under VCP control fell to the 5th and 6th Fighter Squadrons because of the commonality of radio equipment. During January the 6th Squadron had replaced the high frequency (HF) radios in the Squadron's Thunderbolts with very high frequency (VHF) radios, except for flight leaders, who retained their HF sets. On their return to Asansol at the end of January, the 5th Fighter Squadron did the same. The Mustangs of the 1st and 2nd Fighter Squadrons were equipped with VHF sets, which meant that they could not contact the VCP teams, who had only HF radios. Using HF, the VCP controller could contact a 5th or 6th Squadron flight leader and give him directions to the target, and the flight leader could then relay instructions to the rest of his flight (or the 1st and 2nd Squadrons' Mustangs) on his VHF set. Although seemingly cumbersome, the system worked quite well.[50]

During the planning sessions between IV Corps staff, CCTF, and the two Air Commando groups, it became clear that the 5th and 6th Squadrons would have to maintain a standby patrol, what the British called a "cab rank," over the advancing column to ensure that any enemy strong points in the way were promptly dealt with. A "cab rank" consisted of a flight or two of fighters orbiting near the line of advance, which could be rapidly called into action by one of the VCP teams. Hay Field and Cox's Bazar were approximately 250 miles from the battle area. Lieutenant Colonel Chase estimated it would take about two hours from the time a request for air support was submitted until the fighters were over the target, with an hour needed to bomb up the aircraft and brief the pilots, and another hour to fly to the target. Delays in communications could extend the time to three or more hours. To ensure that the columns encountered no delays, the 5th and 6th Squadrons agreed to maintain at least one flight of four aircraft over the lead columns at all times.

They worked out a plan to send out one flight of four aircraft every hour. The flights would take an hour to reach the forward column, spend an hour on call, and then take an hour to fly back to base. The VCP teams would assign targets to the flights overhead based on specific map references. If the flight was not called on, at the end of its assigned hour the flight would hit a secondary target. The fighters would take off as soon as it was light, and would continue throughout the day, leaving the target area with adequate time to return to base before dark.

Eastern Air Command arranged for squadrons from No. 221 Group based at advanced airfields to cover the target area during the crucial dawn and dusk periods before the Thunderbolts arrived, and after they had to depart at the end of the day. It was accepted that there would be times when the cab rank flights would encounter no worthwhile targets, but the absolute need to maintain the speed of the advance meant there was little alternative to providing the close support standby system. In addition, Air Commando fighter squadrons would also be required to carry out regular strikes on Japanese lines of communication, supply dumps, and troop positions ahead of and on the flanks of the advancing columns.[51]

The first week of February 1945 found the 5th and 6th Squadrons at Asansol, preparing for their move to Hay Field. In expectation of the number of sorties that would need to be flown, additional P-47D-23s were acquired bringing each squadron to 30 assigned aircraft. While the 5th Squadron's pilots got a brief rest, the ground crews and engineering staff in both squadrons carried out needed maintenance, checked the installation of the new VHF and HF radios, and packed equipment for the move. At the end of the week the pilots flew the P-47s down to Hay while Air Commando transport aircraft carried the ground crews, other staff, and supplies.

Hay Field was a grass strip 200 feet wide and roughly 6,000 feet long. The squadrons were housed in bamboo bashas about a mile from the field. Other bashas around the field itself served as operations and maintenance buildings. Rations were pretty basic, and for the first few weeks a shortage of water meant that washing and bathing facilities were practically nonexistent. But the two squadrons quickly settled in and in a few days, were ready for operations.[52]

Thanks to Allied air superiority, the Japanese had failed to detect IV Corps' approach to the Irrawaddy. Units of 7th Division were concentrating close to their crossing point opposite the village of Nyaungu on the east bank of the Irrawaddy, with 17th Division and 255th Tank Brigade following behind. To maintain the deception and add to Japanese confusion, troops of IV Corps launched a feint towards Pakokku to the west to give the Japanese the impression that all of 14th Army's forces were converging on the Mandalay area. At IV Corps' request, the 5th Squadron P-47s bombed Japanese troop positions near Pakokku on 10 February 1945 in support of this feint. Meanwhile the main body of IV Corps advanced toward its crossing point 20 miles to the southwest. Under VCP control, and with the target area described over the radio and marked with mortar smoke, the Thunderbolts bombed and then swept in to make ten strafing passes on a small village where Japanese troops were entrenched. As the Air Commandos pulled off the target, they saw British tanks advancing to attack.

British officers and Indian troops watch as an Air Commando P-47 (center right) bombs a target in the bridgehead area , with the Irrawaddy River in the background. (Courtesy NASM)

The start of Operation Multivite. A IV Corps Sherman tank crosses the Irrawaddy River on February 14, 1945 under an umbrella of Air Commando protection. (Courtesy NASM)

The next day, twelve 6th Squadron Thunderbolts joined ten from the 5th to again attack troop concentrations near the town of Pakokku, dropping ten tons of bombs on the target.

Then, on 13 February as part of a second feint, the 6th Squadron sent 12 aircraft to bomb anti-aircraft positions at Chauk, further south down the Irrawaddy, while eight aircraft from the 5th Squadron escorted three B-25s from the 1st Air Commando Group's Bomber Section to hit targets around Pakokku.

As IV Corps concentrated at its crossing point, General Slim had XXXIII Corps escalate its attacks on Mandalay. The XXXIII Corps' 19th Division broke out of the bridgehead it had established some 30 miles north of Mandalay and drove south; meanwhile on the night of 12 February, the 20th Division made a loud and obvious crossing of the Irrawaddy at Myinmu, southwest of Mandalay, drawing an immediate and intense Japanese response.[53]

Slim's ruse worked. With the Japanese distracted by the British drive on Mandalay, IV Corps began its own crossing of the Irrawaddy. In the early hours of 14 February, troops of the 7th Division set off for the east bank of the river in motorized assault boats from a point four miles up river from Nyaungu. At this point the Irrawaddy was 2,000 yards wide, making this the longest opposed river crossing in World War II. At first the assault did not go well, leaving only a small British force clinging to the landing beaches. While the troops regrouped, the Visual Control Posts called in air strikes.[54]

The 6th Fighter Squadron had responsibility for cab rank patrols covering the crossing that day and the next. At 0645 hours, four P-47s took off from Hay field. They arrived over the bridgehead an hour later but initially had trouble establishing communications with any VCP post and had to orbit for over an hour. They were then directed to make strafing runs on a tree line in front of British troop positions.

The squadron dispatched flights of four aircraft at the hours of 0830, 0950, 1115, and 1300. Under VCP direction they dropped their bombs on several large buildings thought to be Japanese strong points and then, with the help of smoke markers, returned to make repeated strafing passes to silence Japanese machine guns. The air strikes helped stabilize the situation on the ground and, by early afternoon, a regular flow of troops were pushing across the river under cover of artillery and air support.[55]

The following day the crossing of the main body began. Tanks, more troops, and supplies poured across the river. The 6th Squadron again sent out five cab rank missions, covering the bridgehead area throughout the day, bombing and strafing under VCP control with excellent results.

On 16 February the 5th Fighter Squadron went back into action, taking over the cab rank duties while the 6th Squadron went off at full strength on an early morning sweep of Japanese airfields around Toungoo, Magwe, and Pyinmana in hopes of catching Japanese fighters that had strafed British troops near Myinmu the previous day. Pilots of the 6th found only a steamroller and some oxcarts to strafe.

Later that morning, eight 6th Squadron aircraft teamed up with two B-25s from the Bomber Section to hit enemy troop and gun positions at the request of IV Corps. After dropping their bombs the fighters returned to make four strafing passes over the target area.

The 5th Squadron sent up 40 aircraft on cab rank patrols, a record number. Beginning at 0645 hours, a flight of four aircraft departed every hour until late afternoon. The first few flights could not get in touch with the VCP controllers and had to jettison their bombs in enemy territory, but the remaining flights bombed Japanese positions, using tank fire to locate the target, and returned for strafing passes under VCP direction.

On the 17th, the 6th Squadron took over cab rank patrols, flying seven missions over the bridgehead area, and hitting Japanese troop positions. The VCP called the results excellent.

The 5th Squadron, meanwhile, sent 24 aircraft to join four Bomber Section B-25s attacking Japanese troop and anti-aircraft positions near the town of Chauk. A 6th Squadron aircraft acted as a forward air controller, pinpointing the AA positions for the 5th Squadron by dropping two bombs on the target area. The B-25s then made their bombing run, leaving a large section of the town on fire. All aircraft returned to strafe the area.[56]

These first few days set the pattern for operations of the 5th and 6th Squadrons over the next month. They alternated duties over the battle area, with one squadron flying cab rank sorties while the other covered assignments for IV Corps or carried out sweeps of roads, rail lines, and advance Japanese air strips in central Burma. During this period of combat the two units each flew 30 or more sorties a day, with the only semblance of a break being an occasional long-range escort mission with B-24s. This represented a tremendous achievement for the hard-working ground crews who labored around the clock to keep the maximum number of airplanes in commission.

The standard procedure for the cab rank patrols was a flight of four aircraft, each armed with two 500 lb. bombs and a 110-gallon drop tank under the belly. This gave them an hour and fifteen minutes over the target area. An unexpected benefit from these patrols was that the Japanese artillery, fearful of disclosing their location, tended to cease firing when fighters orbited nearby.

Air Commando P-47 pilots flew nearly every day. The missions followed the same pattern, day after day; taking off from Hay Field, climbing out over the Chin Hills, letting down across the Irrawaddy to the target area, bombing and strafing, then returning to Hay where there were few amenities to relieve the heat and monotony. The next day would be the same, and on it went, day after day. There was no glamour to it, no dog fights with Japanese fighters, just hot, hard work. The missions were, as one pilot put it, "the Air Force equivalent of infantry trench fighting."[57]

Fortunately, Japanese AA was generally light. As one pilot remembered, "Ground fire was not very bad, some occasional automatic AA and you might go days without any indication of resistance, when all of a sudden, coming out of a strafing run, you would say, 'My God, those were tracers coming after me!'"[58]

With repetition, the Air Commando fighters became very professional at this close support role. VCP officers consistently congratulated them for excellent results. As mutual confidence developed, the controllers brought the fighters in closer and closer to British positions. On one occasion, when the Japanese had pinned down a group of British troops, the VCP controller called in a strike to relieve the pressure. When advised that the Japanese positions were less than a hundred yards from the British, the flight leader told the controller that was too close. The reply was, "We're going to get it one way or the other, so come on in." The flight did its work, striking the Japanese without touching the British and breaking up a Japanese attack.[59]

The two squadrons suffered losses on the same day, 19 February. At 0650 hours two flights consisting of eight P-47s from the 5th Squadron set off to sweep the rail lines leading south from Meiktila, Thazi, Heho, and Pyinmana. One flight bombed the marshaling yards at Thazi and then went down to strafe three locomotives along the rail line. Instead of staying with his own "A" flight, Lieutenant Frank Byrne left to join "B" Flight which was heading south from Thazi. In company with the other pilots, Byrne strafed a number of boxcars along the rail line, setting off a dozen which appeared to be carrying fuel oil. Following this attack one of the B Flight aircraft had to return to base due to a lack of fuel. At the same time Byrne left to rejoin A Flight, which had been patrolling the rail line from Thazi to Heho. He never appeared, and no trace of his plane was ever found. He was listed as "Missing In Action."[60]

It's a poor candid shot but an interesting one of OLD IRONSIDES, a 5th Fighter Squadron P-47D at Hay Field. Two 500 lb. bombs were the standard load for so-called "cab rank" missions. (Courtesy William Burghardt)

That same day the 6th Squadron had been assigned to bomb several Japanese troop strongholds. The first flight of the day arrived over its target, a pagoda, at 1030 in the morning. The four aircraft dropped their bombs demolishing the pagoda and a building close by and starting a large fire. They then decided to sweep the rail line south to Mahlaing. Flying down the track, Second Lieutenant Keith Hughes turned suddenly to strafe what looked like camouflaged oil drums. The other pilots in the flight witnessed a huge explosion behind them and, when they circled over the area, saw large pieces of airplane scattered over a wide area. Hughes had apparently hit the ground in his strafing run.[61]

This eventful morning also saw a rare encounter with Japanese fighters. By now vastly outnumbered and without likely reinforcements, the 5th Hikoshidan could only mount night attacks and early morning sweeps over British bridgeheads along the Irrawaddy, usually involving less than a dozen Oscar fighters. On the morning of 19 February, the 64th Sentai sent 14 Oscars to escort two Lily bombers from the 8th Sentai in an attack on British armored units near Myinmu. While returning from this mission, a flight of five Oscars and one Lily ran into three P-47s from the 5th Fighter Squadron's B flight as the latter were patrolling the rail line south of Thazi.

Flying at 1,000 feet above the roadbed and searching below them for rolling stock, the three Thunderbolts failed to see the approaching enemy aircraft. One of the Oscars jumped the rear P-47 and managed to get three hits on the right wing. The flight leader, Lieutenant Marion Ball, immediately threw his aircraft into a very tight turn and came in behind one of the attacking Japanese. Closing to 100 yards he opened fire and saw strikes on the Oscar's cowl before it dived away smoking. Outnumbered and low on ammunition, the three P-47s hit the deck and at full throttle quickly pulled away. Ball received credit for one fighter damaged.[62]

General Messervy had ordered 17th Division's crossing of the Irrawaddy to begin on 17 February while 7th Division was still expanding its bridgehead on the east bank. By 20 February the Meiktila strike force was ready.[63]

The next day a column of over 3,000 vehicles set off for Meiktila, 82 miles away, as 6th Fighter Squadron provided aerial escort. Under directions from VCPs with the column, the flights bombed Japanese trenches and suspected troop positions in villages along the route of advance.

The 5th Fighter Squadron sent out several flights to join P-51s from the 2nd Air Commando Group and B-25s from the 1st Air Commando's Bomber Section in coordinated strikes on Japanese troop positions.

Later that day, 16 aircraft from the 5th Squadron went out on a sweep of the Japanese airfields at Toungoo, Pyinmana, and Lewe. While one flight flew top cover the other eight aircraft went down to strafe, but apart from a few boxcars and oxcarts, they saw nothing. After one run Lieutenant James Hutchinson radioed that his oil pressure had dropped to zero and he was heading back to base. He set off west, and was never seen again.[64]

17th Division's columns advanced rapidly along the road to Pyinbin through hot, dry, and very dusty country that was a far cry from the green jungle-clad hills to the north. The Japanese put up road blocks and fortified villages, but the surprise and speed of the advance gave no time for an organized defense. Senior Japanese commanders were still unaware that a major British force was advancing towards them and thought the reports of large numbers of tanks were exaggerated. The advance continued without letup. Artillery, tanks, and Thunderbolt air strikes took care of the roadblocks.

During the morning of 24 February, while the 6th Squadron flew cab rank patrols, the 5th Squadron sent 14 aircraft to join eight P-51s from the 2nd Air Commandos in a combined strike on Taungtha. Under VCP control the Mustangs went in first to drop napalm on the target area. The Thunderbolts were next, dropping 500 lb. bombs on Japanese positions and then returning to strafe, starting several large fires. That afternoon 48th Brigade captured Taungtha against light opposition.

The next day the 5th Squadron took over the cab rank duties and covered the advance of 63rd Brigade toward Mailing, bombing and strafing continuously as the tanks and troops advanced down the road.

The 6th Squadron dispatched twenty P-47s to escort thirty-six B-25s from the 12th Bomb Group to batter Japanese supply dumps at Meiktila. The fighters went in ahead of the Mitchells, attacking AA positions, so that when the bombers arrived over the target only one gun was left firing.[65]

While skeptical of the size of the allied force approaching Meiktila, the Japanese 15th Army was sufficiently concerned to request an air strike on the advancing columns of tanks and motorized infantry. The 5th Hikoshidan ordered the 64th Sentai to make the attack, and on the morning of 26 February 1945, they prepared for a strike at full strength: a mere 14 aircraft, all that were serviceable. That morning 14 Oscars took off from Mingaladon airfield armed with cluster bombs and headed north towards Mailing. There the Sentai would encounter Allied fighters and, in a series of running combats with British Spitfires and Thunderbolts from the 6th Fighter Squadron, lose one of their own. In return, they would claim the commander of the 1st Air Commando Group, Colonel Clinton Gaty.[66]

Gaty was an experienced pilot and a highly respected commander whose management of his disparate and far-flung units was both effective and appreciated. However, he was not a fighter pilot by training and he did not fly regular combat missions with the fighter squadrons.

On February 21, 1945, 17th Division began its dash for Meiktila. The column of tanks and trucks stretched for miles while the Air Commandos flew cover overhead. (Courtesy Imperial War Museum)

The 6th Fighter Squadron was scheduled to fly cab rank patrols that day. The day before, Gaty had contacted Captain Jack Klarr, who was scheduled to lead one of the early morning patrols, and arranged to meet him in his patrol area. Gaty took a Thunderbolt that had been undergoing maintenance at Asansol and flew down to Hay Field first thing in the morning on the 26th. While his plane was being refueled and armed he revealed his intentions to Major Roland Lynn, the 5th Squadron's commander. Lynn tried to dissuade him, but Gaty was adamant. So, respecting rank, Lynn helped Gaty into his aircraft, and watched his departure.

Once airborne, Gaty contacted Klarr, already on patrol, and told him that he was on his way. Arriving over the patrol area, Gaty joined with a flight that was waiting for the VCP controllers to give them a target. He then advised the orbiting P-47s that he was going further south to reconnoiter, and headed off alone.[67]

It was at about that time that Oscars of the 64th Sentai began making their appearance in the area. At 1050 hours a flight of Spitfires patrolling at 7,000 feet along the Mailing-Meiktila road ran into a formation of six Oscars who came in out of the sun, but didn't open fire. The Spitfires dived to the deck and then climbed rapidly back to altitude to attack, but lost the Japanese in the sun and haze.

At 1115 hours a flight of four Thunderbolts led by Lieutenant Charles M. Posten, Jr. was circling east of Mahlaing at 10,000 feet when they saw four Oscars at 3 o'clock 2,000 feet above them. When one of the enemy fighters cocked his wing up as if he was about to dive, the P-47s dropped their bombs and belly tanks, made a diving turn, and passed underneath the Japanese. The Oscar flight was led by Captain Takeo Miyabe, a veteran 64th Sentai flight leader. Miyabe was preparing to bomb the Allied columns around Mahlaing when he had encountered the P-47s. He and his wingman, Sergeant Yoshiharu Watanabe, dived down and started firing at Posten and his wingman, Lieutenant Glen Feickert, while the other two Oscars broke away. The two P-47s not under attack climbed above the enemy fighters to give cover for Poston and Feickert. Miyabe continued firing. He thought he had damaged one of the P-47s, but couldn't catch it. Seeing four P-51s below, Miyabe broke off the fight with the P-47s and dove down to engage the Mustangs. In the heat of combat he was unaware that his wingman had not kept up with him.[68]

Poston pulled back up and saw an "olive drab-colored Oscar with large blotches of silver" making a slow climbing turn ahead of him at 9,000 feet. This was in all likelihood Sergeant Watanbe, who may have been circling looking for his flight leader. Poston got into position behind the enemy fighter and gave it a one second burst. He saw his tracers go into the Oscar, which fell into a spin, and watched as the fighter headed down to crash into the trees.

Feickert approached what he thought was the second Oscar, also at 9,000 feet, which he described as having "blotchy silver paint." The Oscar entered a split-S as Feickert opened fire. Feickert made a 360-degree turn and came in again. The Oscar made this maneuver four times, and each time the Air Commando pilot give it a burst, although he was not certain that he scored hits. Finally the Oscar crashed when Feickert was down to 200 feet.

When Captain Miyabe returned to Mingaladon, he found that Watanabe was missing. While 64th Sentai records are not necessarily complete for this period, histories of the unit mention only one pilot being lost on this date. Poston and Feickert were both awarded confirmed victories, but it appears more likely that both fired on the airplane, flown by Sergeant Watanabe. From the description of the combat it seems that Poston disabled Watanabe's aircraft, or possibly killed the pilot.[69]

Which leaves the question of Colonel Gaty. Orbiting over his patrol area, Captain Klarr repeatedly tried to raise Gaty over the radio, but heard nothing. On his return to Hay, he found that Gaty was missing. Despite a search of the area the next day, no traces of the Colonel or his aircraft were ever found. News of his disappearance was kept quiet, and does not appear in the squadron or group records.

That day the 64th Sentai submitted claims for one Thunderbolt confirmed destroyed and one probably destroyed. A possible, and likely, scenario is that on approaching the target area, the Sentai split into two or more flights for the attack. One of these flights, under Captain Miyabe, ran into Poston's flight. The flight that encountered the Spitfires may have later encountered Colonel Gaty's Thunderbolt and shot it down. Describing his experiences after the war, Miyabe remembered that visibility that day was poor due to the haze. It could be that Colonel Gaty, searching below for a flight of Thunderbolts, simply failed to see his attackers coming in from above. In what proved to be their last encounter with Japanese fighters, the Air Commandos lost a respected commander.

The 5th Fighter Squadron flew only one mission on 26 February but lost a pilot. Shortly after noon eight P-47s were on patrol over the Mahlaing area when ground controllers instructed them to bomb a small village. The Thunderbolts went down, one by one, and dropped their bombs in the target area, starting a large fire and sending up a column of smoke over 8,000 feet. As they rejoined, Lieutenant William E. Davison was missing. Radio calls brought no response. A search for Colonel Gaty and Davison the next day turned up the burned out remains of a silver aircraft, but whether this was Gaty's or Davison's plane could never be determined. Davison may have been shot down by ground fire, or may have simply crashed, flying too low in his bomb run.[70]

That same day, the 26th, a combined tank and infantry force from 255th Tank Brigade swept around Mahlaing and captured the airfield at Thabutkon, 13 miles from Meiktila. Bulldozers and a team of aviation engineers who had accompanied the tanks made quick repairs to the field, and that evening sent a signal to IV Corps to start the airlift of 99th Brigade.

Both the 5th and 6th Squadrons put up cab rank patrols on 27 February, with the 6th patrolling the Mahlaing-Meiktila area during the morning and the 5th covering during the afternoon.

The 6th Squadron's first flight into the area ran into intense ground fire. The Japanese had set up a strong road block eight miles from Meiktila where they had blown a bridge on the Mahlaing-Meiktila road and placed large numbers of machine guns and artillery. British armored cars, probing south, ran headfirst into this strong point and came under heavy fire. The VCP controllers reported the ambush to the first arriving flight of Thunderbolts and instructed them to bomb machine gun nests around the bridge. As the P-47s started their bomb runs, they encountered heavy and accurate automatic weapon fire. Returning to strafe, one aircraft was hit hard and on return to base was found to be unserviceable. Two other aircraft in the flight were hit as well, but not as badly.

While the Thunderbolts were making their strafing runs, they saw an unidentified in-line engine fighter, painted in brown and green splotches, which they believed to be a Tony. The unidentified fighter came in on the tail of one of the Thunderbolts but then just as suddenly broke off and turned south.[71]

The VCP controllers directed the second 6th Squadron patrol on to the same road block. Three Thunderbolts bombed and then returned to strafe, again in the face of intense machine gun fire.

Lieutenant Glen Feickert's plane was hit, but he stayed over the target. On his third pass, he was hit again, this time fatally. His P-47 crashed and Feickert was killed. A second P-47 was hit and began losing oil pressure, but fortunately made it to the recently captured airfield at Thabutkon where the pilot landed without incident. While Thunderbolts were bombing the roadblock, one tank force flanked and attacked it from the south, while another force made a frontal assault from the north. The combined attack forced the Japanese to retreat.[72]

Later that morning, the airlift began. First, a glider landed carrying field lighting and traffic control equipment and then the 1st and 2nd Air Commando transport squadrons, with ten more C-47s from the 1st Combat Cargo Group, began unloading the 99th Brigade. The 5th Squadron patrolled along the approach corridor to Thabutkon, while RAF Spitfire and Thunderbolt squadrons flew patrols south and east of Meiktila to block any Japanese fighters. No Japanese aircraft attempted to intercept the steady stream of C-47s, and by evening the transports had off-loaded a complete battalion. Over the next day and a half the rest of the 99th was flown in. The transports encountered occasional Japanese mortar and sniper fire, but no airplanes or troops were lost.

Indian troops board a C-47 from the 1st Air Commando Group's 319th Troop Carrier Squadron for the flight into Meiktila, March 17, 1945. (Courtesy NASM)

An operation that was supposed to take seven days was completed in three-and-a-half, a remarkable achievement.[73]

With the entire force in place, British tanks and infantry began a three pronged attack on Meiktila on 1 March 1945. The Japanese garrison, a mixed force of some 4,000 troops, had managed to hurriedly build bunkers and fortify buildings, assuring a tough battle.[74]

That day the 5th Squadron had cab rank duties, while the 6th Squadron joined 2nd Air Commando Mustangs in two heavy strikes on Japanese positions at Yenangyaung to the southwest to prevent reinforcement of Meiktila.

The 5th Squadron flew eight close support missions. From overhead the pilots could see troops and tanks advancing on the town and observe the explosions of Allied artillery fire. The first three flights carried "Daisy Cutters," 500 lb. bombs armed with extended fuses set to explode on contact with the ground. The ever-present VCP controllers marked their targets with smoke and called in the Thunderbolts to bomb and strafe Japanese gun emplacements, road blocks, and troop positions. Despite repeated air strikes, the troops made slow progress against heavy artillery and machine gun fire from the many fortified positions.[75]

The next day, 2 March, the 6th Squadron took over and sent six flights to Meiktila. Over the target area the flights separated, with two aircraft covering the air strip at Thabutkon, and a pair flying close support. The first flight over Meiktila was directed to attack an area around the railroad station in the south of the town. The Thunderbolts made ten strafing passes, encountering heavy small arms and 20mm fire which damaged one airplane. The next flight struck the same area, and again small arms' fire hit one airplane, this time in the engine.

A P-47 from the third flight went so low it was hit by bomb fragments, forcing the pilot to land at Thabutkon with zero oil pressure. A second airplane was damaged making a low level strafing run over one of the airfields to the east of the town. As the pilot came over the center of the field at 100 feet, a huge explosion erupted, possibly from a Japanese mine set to trap strafers. The explosion rocked the Thunderbolt, but the sturdy aircraft suffered only minor damage. The advance into the town continued and, as the 63rd Brigade later recorded, "the indefatigable cab rank was always in support," attacking fortified buildings just ahead of the tanks.[76]

By March 3 the three attacking brigades had surrounded the town. 6th Squadron joined the 2nd Air Commandos in strikes on Japanese troop positions around Meiktila while the 5th Squadron took up the cab rank duties, flying eight missions. On one of the last flights of the day, two Thunderbolts struck a Japanese road block with 500 lb. bombs and then returned to make three strafing passes, forcing the Japanese to retreat. The VCP complemented the pilots on their accuracy, as the British troops had been less than 100 yards from the enemy. By the end of the day Meiktila was in Allied hands, with troops mopping up the last remaining snipers. The Japanese garrison fought to annihilation.[77]

General Slim called Meiktila's capture "a magnificent feat of arms" which "sealed the fate of the Japanese army in Burma."[78] It was also a superb example of air-ground cooperation. Major General Cowan's 17th Division drive to Meiktila had been supplied entirely by air and had moved forward under an Air Commando fighter umbrella. The practice of cab rank patrols under VCP control had proved itself countless times.

With the fall of Meiktila, IV Corps sent the following message to the 5th and 6th Fighter Squadrons: "There is nothing IV Corps wants more than your continued support, which has been absolutely terrific. From the highest to the lowest soldier there has been nothing but admiration for the quality and quantity of air support which we have received."[79]

The loss of Meiktila came as a shock to General Kimura, commander of the Burma Area Army. The British thrust had captured the main supply center for the 15th and 33rd Armies, cut off the flow of oil from the oil fields in central Burma, and sat astride the main communications links between central and southern Burma. British possession of Meiktila put the Japanese in an untenable position, as the main Japanese force, fighting to hold on to Mandalay, could not retreat. Should this force be defeated or prevented from retreating, then Kimura would have no means of holding central Burma and preventing the fall of Rangoon. When Kimura finally became aware of the full import of the British moves, he immediately ordered 15th Army, and then 33rd Army, to retake the town. For the rest of March, Japanese units hurled themselves at the British forces around Meiktila in fanatic, but uncoordinated attacks.[80]

Although technically surrounded, Major General Cowan decided that an aggressive defense would deny the Japanese the initiative. Cowan chose to send out columns of tanks and infantry on sweeps of the surrounding area to disrupt Japanese communications and strike at Japanese troops as they approached Meiktila.

Attaching a 100 lb. incendiary bomb to a drop tank created an effective fire bomb. (Courtesy William Burghardt)

Still entirely dependent on supply by air, 17th Division abandoned the airfield at Thabutkon and the air supply effort shifted to the newly captured airfield just east of Meiktila. Air Commando fighter squadrons continued to provide close air support to IV Corps and 17th Division in the first week following Meiktila's capture, since the RAF had not yet advanced its fighter squadrons closer to the area of battle. As Cowan's columns ranged out to the north and east of Meiktila, VCP teams accompanied them, with the 5th and 6th Fighter Squadron patrols overhead.

From 4-12 March the two squadrons alternated cab rank duties flying escort to B-24 bombers and bombing targets assigned by IV Corps when not providing close support. Only occasionally did the VCP teams fail to provide a target. On several missions IV Corps directed attacks on Japanese headquarters that had been located through radio intercepts.

On 10 March the 6th Squadron had an exceptionally good day. They flew six missions, supporting a raid by a column of troops from the Border Regiment and tanks of the 5th (Probyn's) Horse, from 63rd Brigade. The flights attacked Japanese troop positions and fortified villages, bombing with great accuracy and following up with repeated strafing passes that left their targets in flames. At the end of the day, the VCP team told the last flight that results for the day had been excellent and said that the troops were extremely pleased with the quality of air support provided.[81]

The next day the 5th Squadron took over, flying six cab rank missions. The last flight was directed on to Japanese troop positions. After bombing, they made six strafing runs over the target area, sending in 5,600 .50-caliber rounds. After the strike, Allied troops advanced to find more than one hundred dead Japanese soldiers.

The squadron continued its ground support on 12 March, sending out five missions. On the second-to-last flight the VCP team instructed the Thunderbolts to patrol a road looking for Japanese gun emplacements. Returning up the road toward Meiktila, 2nd Lieutenant Charles Hess' airplane was hit. The Thunderbolt began to stream smoke and Hess made a hurried crash landing, the airplane exploding in flames soon after it touched down. Squadronmates saw Hess leave the cockpit with his flight suit on fire. Hess beat out the flames, stripped off his flight suit, and proceeded to walk away from the Japanese lines.

Captain Paul Oram flew back and landed at Meiktila airfield, where he persuaded a British L-5 pilot to attempt a rescue. They located Hess, but the L-5 couldn't land due to the surrounding trees, so they dropped a first aid kit and went to seek help from British tanks nearby. While the rest of the flight strafed the Japanese positions, the L-5 landed and explained the situation to a nearby tank commander. A VCP team then organized a foray by a group of armored cars, but heavy

Indian troops approach a burning village. The Japanese fought for every house, every tree line, requiring the Air Commandos to bomb and strafe with a high degree of accuracy. (Courtesy Imperial War Museum)

mortar and machine gun fire forced them back. At dusk the armored cars went out again, but searched without success. Hess was listed as "missing in action."

The 6th Squadron also lost a pilot that week. Returning from a mission on 7 March, Lieutenant John Akston spun in during a landing at Hay Field and was killed.[82]

On 12 March, just as the battle around Meiktila was intensifying, the RAF took over primary responsibility for providing close air support to IV Corps from the Air Commando fighter squadrons. No. 224 Group in the Arakan transferred No. 905 Wing, consisting of four Thunderbolt squadrons, to the operational control of No.221 Group.[83]

With a reduced commitment to close air support, the 5th and 6th Air Commando Fighter Squadrons shifted their efforts to other targets. During their assignment to the direct support of IV Corps, the 5th Squadron had flown 98 missions and the 6th Squadron 108 missions. Apparently IV Corps had requested that the Air Commandos continue their close support role, but the RAF insisted on the shift back to its own units.

At this point in time the Americans informed Admiral Mountbatten that they intended to withdraw the Tenth Air Force and all their other air units in Burma and shift them to China where the Japanese threat was great. Alarmed at this prospect, particularly by the loss of vitally necessary transport planes, Mountbatten persuaded the Army Air Force to delay the withdrawal until the capture of Rangoon or 1 June, whichever came sooner.

IV Corps, and 17th Division in particular, were deeply grateful for the support they had received. At the end of the battle for Meiktila, Major General Cowan sent the following message to the Air Commandos: "The direct support so willingly given to us by our American Allies was of a very high order throughout and contributed in no small measure to our victory. Well done. Thank you."[84]

There was still much to be done in Burma, and both squadrons flew missions nearly every day. March proved to be the busiest month in the 6th Squadron's history, with 641 combat sorties and 86 missions.

Allied intelligence had detected signs that the Japanese were moving all possible reinforcements towards Meiktila in a desperate attempt to retake the town. As a result, No. 224 Group received instructions to make Japanese lines of communications a priority target. From 13 March, 5th and 6th Squadrons attacked road and rail bridges and their bypass bridges on the main route from Rangoon to Mandalay to interdict the movement of troops and supplies north to the battle area. The Air Commandos bombed these spans repeatedly. As soon as the Japanese made repairs, they were bombed again.[85]

The Japanese made a determined effort to seize the airfield east of Meiktila, 17th Division's sole lifeline. As the Japanese poured more troops into the attack, the British flew in reinforcements and the Air Commandos were called back to provide support. On 15 March, transports began flying in the 9th Indian Infantry Brigade under an umbrella of RAF and Air Commando fighters. The 5th Squadron spent two days flying patrols along the air route to Meiktila, but no Japanese fighters intervened. While the air lift was in progress, both squadrons flew close support missions under VCP control to ease the pressure on the airfield. Japanese and British troops were fighting so fiercely near the perimeter that all landings had to be canceled on the 18th. The 6th Squadron achieved particularly good results on 19 March against Japanese artillery positions that were harassing the airfield.[86]

As soon as the troop reinforcement was completed, the two Air Commando squadrons went back to attacking bridges with the additional task of hitting Japanese supply dumps. These missions involved at least one entire squadron, and sometimes both. On 18 March, the 6th Squadron sent out 28 aircraft to bomb stores in the town of Padaung on the Irrawaddy River. Three days later the two squadrons flew a combined mission, bombing dumps in the Prome area with 34 aircraft, while 11 aircraft hit the ferry station at Henzada on the Irrawaddy.

In the midst of this operation the 5th Squadron changed commanders. Major Roland Lynn, completing his combat tour, handed the reins to Captain Malcolm Wilkins, Squadron Operations Officer.

On 26 March, twenty-one aircraft from the 5th Squadron and 26 from the 6th returned to Henzada to attack a Japanese headquarters and warehouses, leaving 20 buildings destroyed. The next day the 5th sent nineteen aircraft to bomb supply dumps at Swa, while 24 aircraft from the 6th hit dumps at Kyungan.

The last day of the month showed the unpredictable nature of Japanese anti-aircraft defenses. Having bombed the Toungoo railroad bridge on March 28th without incident, the 5th Squadron sent out a flight to bomb the bridge again on the 31st. This time the Japanese defenders threw up a barrage of anti-aircraft fire, hitting 2nd Lieutenant Ed Auman's airplane after he had dropped his bombs, and damaging a second airplane. Auman crashed and was killed.

That same day the 6th Squadron dispatched 16 aircraft to bomb railroad bridges at Thawatti and Ela. After rendering both bridges unserviceable with direct hits, the flights dropped down to strafe rolling stock along the rail line. Near Myolila, Lieutenant Ralph Selkirk's plane was hit by ground fire as he completed a strafing pass. His plane crashed before Selkirk could parachute.[87]

By the end of March, the battle for Meiktila was over and with it any hope the Japanese had of holding central Burma through another monsoon season. General Kimura had thrown in his reserves, but to no avail. British superiority in artillery, air support, and tanks had overcome even the most determined Japanese attacks and had inflicted heavy casualties. The Japanese 49th Division, for example, which had advanced on Meiktila with 10,000 men, suffered 6,500 casualties and the loss of 45 out of its 48 artillery pieces. To the north, Mandalay had fallen on 20 March 1945. British forces had pushed east from their bridgeheads on the Irrawaddy to capture the main Mandalay-Rangoon rail line between Kyaukse and Wundwin, and south to link up with Cowan's forces around Meiktila.

Slim had sought a decisive battle with the Japanese Army in central Burma and he had won. The seizure and defense of Meiktila had, as Slim had planned, forced the Japanese to do battle on conditions favorable to the British. Having suffered over 12,000 casualties and the loss of almost all its artillery, tanks, and supplies, the Burma Area Army was a shattered force bent only on retreat. The race for Rangoon was on.[88]

14th Army's advance to Rangoon was a race against the weather and the unalterable dictates of logistics. The monsoon rains would come in early May. While rapidly building up Meiktila as a supply base, once beyond it, 14th Army's divisions would be entirely dependent on air supply. Once the rains came, the advanced landing grounds for transport aircraft would become quagmires and the troops would quickly run out of supplies. In the background, too, was the American intent to pull their transport units out of Burma by June 1 at the latest. Slim had to capture Rangoon and its port before the monsoon began if his army was to avoid a logistical nightmare. His plan was to have IV Corps' mechanized divisions advance with all speed down the road and rail line to Rangoon, bypassing Japanese strong points, while XXXIII Corps advanced down the valley of the Irrawaddy River. As an insurance against the failure of the overland advance, Operation Dracula,

Sampans like these, vital to the Japanese Irrawaddy supply system, were a frequent target for the 5th and 6th Fighter Squadrons. (Courtesy NASM)

Stinson L-5s were invaluable to the Air Commandos in a variety of roles: liaison, artillery spotting, transport of the wounded, and more than a few exciting rescues. (Lambert Collection)

the amphibious assault against Rangoon, was set for the first week of May.[89]

For the 5th and 6th Fighter Squadrons, April was "an anticlimax," as the 6th Squadron's Intelligence Officer put it. The Royal Air Force had taken over the close air support role and, on 12 April, three Wings of Hurricanes and Spitfires covered IV and XXXIII Corps in their drive on Rangoon providing air cover for the constant stream of transport aircraft flying into advance landing grounds with supplies.

The task of the longer range fighters, including squadrons in the First Provisional Fighter Group, was to attack enemy lines of communications, warehouses, and ammunition and supply dumps, and to generally prevent an orderly Japanese retreat. The 5th and 6th Squadrons were assigned responsibility for keeping a section of the Mandalay-Rangoon railway unserviceable. They often flew these missions at full squadron strength, and sometimes together, with as many as 36 Thunderbolts plastering targets. During the first two weeks of April the squadrons dropped over 185 tons of bombs, damaging or knocking out nine railroad bridges and destroying numerous warehouses and supply dumps.

A combined strike by 35 aircraft in the Pyu area destroyed 20 rail cars, a good day's work by this time when lucrative targets were few and far between. Japanese air opposition was minimal, involving only four air-to-air encounters during the month of April, all with the RAF. Even ground fire seemed to have lessened. The marauding Thunderbolts rarely encountered AA fire, but when they did Japanese gunners could still find the mark.[90]

Anti-aircraft fire brought down Captain William Hemphill, 6th Squadron commander, on April 17. This would be the only aircraft lost to either squadron during the month. Fortunately, Hemphill was rescued. The mission that morning had been to bomb a railway station located five miles south of Toungoo. The two squadrons sent out 35 aircraft, with Hemphill leading the 6th.

There was no sign of anti-aircraft fire over the target, but Hemphill's Thunderbolt was hit as he pulled out of his dive. With his plane streaming black smoke and the canopy covered in oil, Hemphill bellied in, grabbed his equipment, and ran to find a hiding place as the wreckage burned. Some three hours later he heard the sound of engines and looked up to see an L-5 with an escort of P-47s searching for him.

On landing, the L-5 ran into a ditch and stood on its nose, miraculously without breaking the propeller. With the help of some Burmese, Hemphill and Captain Frank Davis, the L-5 pilot, got the plane out of the ditch and pointed toward a row of paddy fields. Davis headed out and, after a series of bumps, staggered aloft and flew back to Meiktila.[91]

14th Army's divisions drove south at a relentless pace, giving the Japanese no time to regroup and establish a line of defense. Town after town fell or was bypassed on the way south. On 22 April Toungoo was taken. By the end of April, 17th Division was in Pegu, a mere 50 miles from Rangoon. Here the offensive ground to a halt as the monsoon burst over the land. Torrential rains began on 2 May, causing the Pegu River to flood and washing out the one available bridge.

For the last two weeks of the month, 5th and 6th Squadrons continued their attacks on bridges and supply dumps ahead of the advance, alternating these attacks with sweeps of the road, rail, and water transport networks leading to the battlefield. These sweeps brought back a good tally of rolling stock, motor transport, and rivercraft destroyed and damaged.[92]

The 5th and 6th Squadrons flew their last combat operations in support of the seaborne invasion of Rangoon. The British force arrived at the mouth of the Rangoon River on 1 May. That morning, two transport squadrons from the 1st and 2nd Air Commando Groups dropped a battalion from the 50th Parachute Brigade to attack Japanese gun positions at Elephant Point at the mouth of the river. While 12 aircraft from the 5th Squadron escorted 12th Bomb Group B-25s in an attack on Elephant Point, 22 aircraft from the 6th Squadron escorted thirty-eight 7th Bomb Group Liberators in an attack on the same target. The next day landing craft proceeded up the river to Rangoon and landed near the city unopposed. The Japanese were gone, the garrison having evacuated the city several days before. On 3 May British forces occupied Rangoon. For the next several days, despite poor weather, the 5th and 6th Squadrons joined other Allied fighter squadrons in patrols over the Rangoon area and in escorting Allied transports airlifting troops and supplies. These patrols were uneventful and not a shot was fired nor a single bomb dropped. The campaign ended not with a bang, but a whimper.[93]

From the American perspective, the capture of Rangoon signaled the end of the Burma campaign. Japanese forces in Burma were no longer a threat to China's supply lines, so as previously agreed, American air units in Burma began to pull back to India soon after the occupation of Rangoon in preparation for their movement to China.[94]

On 8 May the 5th and 6th Squadrons flew their last combat missions, then stood down to prepare for their move back to Asansol. Stores and personal items were packed and by the 13th both units were back at their home base.

The campaign in Burma had levied a cost on 5th and 6th Fighter Squadrons. Between November 1944 and the end of March 1945, thirteen pilots were lost on operations and of these, ten were killed. The air war in Burma did not have the intensity of the air war in Northern Europe, but it did have its own unique qualities that were more akin to the war in the Pacific. The heat and discomfort were constant and affected the hard-working ground crews the most. And amenities were few and far between. Burma was the "Forgotten Front;" there was no glamour and little recognition at home of what was achieved with minimal resources. If pilots in Burma did not have to face anywhere near the same amount of flak as their counterparts in Europe, they did have to cope with the knowledge that if downed they would be subject to brutal treatment as prisoners of war or, at best, a hazardous journey through dreadful country. It was only in the last few months of the campaign, when the battle shifted to the flat central plains, that rescue behind enemy lines became remotely possible.

General Stratemeyer's Headquarters, Army Air Forces India-Burma Theater, and the Army Air Force's Operational Plans Division in Washington had been wrestling with the question of how to deploy the Air Commandos in future combat operations. The headquarters staff in the theater had long believed that maintaining Air Commando groups as separate organizations was an extravagant use of resources in a theater of war with constant logistical problems, and recommended that the Air Commando groups be broken up and formed into standard units that could still be used in air commando-style operations when needed. Stratemeyer's headquarters recommended that the 1st, 2nd, 5th, and 6th Fighter Squadrons be combined into a single fighter group and sent to China to join an offensive planned for the fall.[95]

Toward the end of April the 5th and 6th Fighter Squadrons received a small batch of late model, bubble canopy, P-47Ds. This photo shows a 5th Fighter Squadron P-47D-30. (Courtesy USAF Museum)

Thunderbolt of Captain Everett Kelly, 6th Fighter Squadron, showing 59 bombing missions, 15 cover missions, and 12 fighter sweeps, and Kelly's one air claim, an Oscar shot down over Rangoon on 18 October 1944. (Courtesy Thomas Y'Blood, Office of Air Force History)

To this end, during the last half of May 1945, 5th and 6th Squadrons traded their battle weary P-47s for brand new North American P-51Ks and transferred temporarily to Kalaikunda for joint training with the 1st and 2nd Fighter Squadrons.

There were mixed feelings about the transition. Some pilots were delighted with the Mustang's power and maneuverability, but others were reluctant to lose their tried and trusted Thunderbolts. They spent the next two months first at Kalaikunda and then back at Asansol in operational training with new mounts.

Many of the longer serving pilots rotated back to the United States, and fresh replacement pilots brought the squadrons back up to strength. They were still awaiting the move to China when the war came to an end. With the British responsible for occupation duties in Southeast Asia, there was little reason to keep Army Air Force units in the India-Burma region. The fighter groups, including the Air Commandos, began packing a few weeks after the war ended. The 5th and 6th Squadrons flew their Mustangs to a supply depot during the middle of September and in early October boarded a boat in Karachi for the voyage home. They were formally inactivated on 3 November 1945.[96]

In preparation for their consolidation with the 1st and 2nd Fighter Squadrons into a new fighter group the 5th and 6th Squadrons received new P-51Ks in May and spent the next few months training in their new mounts. (Courtesy NASM)

4

THE 1ST AND 2ND FIGHTER SQUADRONS IN THE RECONQUEST OF BURMA

The 14th Army depended, perhaps to a greater extent than other Allied armies, on air superiority. The reconquest of Burma could not have been accomplished without air transport. Had the Allied air forces not maintained control of the air, the prodigious achievements of the transport squadrons would have been impossible. Air supremacy allowed a far more economical employment of air power. Transports could fly to and from the front without the need for fighter escort, which allowed RAF and USAAF fighter squadrons to concentrate on providing close air support and relentless attacks on Japanese lines of communications.

Yet even when attrition had reduced the Japanese Army Air Force in Burma to a relative handful of fighters, the danger to Allied transport aircraft remained. Japanese fighters posed a threat to air supply operations until the end of the campaign. When dropping supplies to Army forces along the front line, Allied transport aircraft were often flying well beyond Allied fighter bases and the radar warning net. Surprise attacks could be deadly. On 8 November 1944, Japanese fighters pounced on a group of C-47s dropping supplies and shot down five. Fighters struck again on 12 January 1945, and shot down four transports. Had the Japanese concentrated on Allied air transport instead of making random ground attacks, they would have achieved far greater results. The 14th Army had reduced requirements for food, fuel, and ammunition at the division level to the bare minimum. Any serious disruption of air supply would have had an immediate affect on the advance.[1]

In Burma the most efficient means of achieving air superiority was to destroy the Japanese Air Force on the ground. In 1945, as in 1944, this was a fighter battle. The Japanese had established a network of airfields in their rear area, where their fighters and bombers were dispersed, protected by aircraft shelters and camouflage. Small groups of fighters could launch from any one of these airfields, make a quick hit and run raid on Allied positions, and then return to their airfields before Allied fighters could intercept. To remove the threat of such attacks, Allied fighters had to destroy Japanese aircraft on their airfields. Faced with heavy machine gun and light anti-aircraft fire over many air bases, Allied fighters normally would make a single pass and hope to find an aircraft in their sights, thus requiring that the same airdromes and landing grounds be visited again and again. Allied air superiority over Burma was, in Air Chief Marshall Sir Keith Park's words, "the result of hard work with small dividends upon the part of our fighter organization."[2]

In the final months of the Burma campaign, the battle for air superiority would become the special task of the 1st and 2nd Fighter Squadrons of the 2nd Air Commando Group.

Activated on 22 April 1944, the 2nd Air Commando Group was the first of the new air commando groups to be formed for General Arnold's planned airborne invasion force of Burma. Based on Colonel John Alison's organizational recommendations, the component units at activation were:

Headquarters Squadron
1st Fighter Recon Squadron (P-51)
2nd Fighter Recon Squadron (P-51)
317th Troop Carrier Squadron (Commando) (C-47)
127th Liaison Squadron (Commando) (L-5/C-64)
155th Liaison Squadron (Commando) (L-5/C-64)
156th Liaison Squadron (Commando) (L-5/C-64)

To ensure maximum mobility the personnel strength of the air commando squadrons was kept to a minimum. The number of personnel was sufficient to maintain the squadrons in the field on a temporary basis, but was well below the authorized strength of the average equivalent squadron. To provide more sustained engineering, maintenance, and administrative support, the 327th, 328th, 340th, and 342nd Aerodrome Squadrons were assigned to the 2nd Air Commando Group. These units were to remain at the main rear base while the air commando squadrons were operating behind enemy lines. On activation the group was assigned to the Third Air Force, and men and planes began to gather at Lakeland Air Force Base in Florida, under the command of Lieutenant Colonel Arthur R. DeBolt, an experienced civil and military flyer. With Colonel Alison's assistance, DeBolt immediately began selecting his senior staff from men he had known from his service in the Caribbean and with the First Fighter Command.[3]

When requesting General George Marshall's approval to organize four air commando groups and four combat cargo groups, General Arnold had promised that the personnel for these new groups would be drawn from existing Air Force units and would not require an increase in the Air Force's authorized strength. Arnold stated that reductions in units assigned to the Sixth Air Force and the disbanding of several tactical reconnaissance units in the continental United States would provide the manpower for the new air commando and combat cargo groups. The Sixth Air Force would form the cadre of pilots and personnel for the 2nd Air Commando Group's new fighter units.[4]

In March 1944 the Sixth Air Force's XXVI Fighter Command, which had been responsible for the defense of the Panama Canal Zone, disbanded three of its fighter squadrons: the 29th, 31st, and 52nd. Pilots and ground personnel returned to the United States to become the nucleus for the 2nd Air Commando Group's 1st and 2nd Fighter Squadrons. The day after their arrival at Lakeland AFB, Florida, DeBolt held a meeting where he reviewed the operations of the 1st Air Commando Group and described the mission of the newly-formed 2nd Air Commandos. He was candid, because the air commando mission would be rugged and would likely involve operations behind enemy lines. 2nd Air Commando Group, like the 1st, would be an all-volunteer outfit. The prospect of being a member of a volunteer outfit, with what sounded like an exciting mission, proved attractive to the majority and an immediate boost to morale.[5]

The table of organization was set at 30 pilots, seven ground officers and 90 enlisted men. For squadron commanders and flight leaders, Colonel DeBolt drew on senior pilots from the Panama squadrons and combat veterans recommended by Colonel Alison, assuring that the 2nd Air Commandos went to war with a core of veterans.

Major Paul B. Ash, former squadron commander of the 29th Fighter Squadron, became commander of the 1st Fighter Reconnaissance Squadron. Colonel Alison brought in Captains Matthew Gordon, Donald Brookfield, and William Hawkins, who had all flown with the 23rd Fighter Group in China, and assigned them to the 1st Fighter Reconnaissance Squadron as flight leaders. To provide a leavening of combat experience for the 2nd Fighter Reconnaissance Squadron, Colonel Alison selected Major Roger Pryor, a China ace and former squadron executive officer in the 23rd Fighter Group, as squadron commander. Captain William Grosvenor, another China ace, joined the squadron as operations officer.[6]

The demands of administrating and coordinating the activities of five separate squadrons with three distinctly different roles brought out the need for a separate commander who would be responsible for controlling and directing the two fighter squadrons on all offensive operations. As Deputy Group Commander, Colonel Alison selected Lieutenant Colonel Levi Chase, who had fought with the 33rd Fighter Group in North Africa. Chase brought a wealth of experience in fighter operations under demanding conditions. In nine months of combat, Chase had become commanding officer of the 60th Fighter Squadron and had shot down ten German and Italian aircraft, emerging as the 33rd's top ace.

Colonel Arthur Debolt, lower center, with Major William Buxton, 1st Fighter Squadron commander on his right and Captain William Hawkins, Group Operations on his left. On the wing (L-R), Major Roger Pryor, 2nd Fighter Squadron commander, Major Kevin Mallen, Group Intelligence Officer, and Captain Charlie Gordon, Group Operations Officer(Courtesy World War II Air Commandos Association)

To their joy, the fighter pilots found that the 1st and 2nd Squadrons were to be equipped with P-51 Mustangs, C models. For pilots who had been flying P-39s and P-40s, the Mustang was a "hot ship," and the pilots were delighted with the new mount. P-51Cs began arriving on 8 May, and within a few days each squadron had 30 aircraft. After quick check rides in the Mustang, they began an intensive flying program designed to make them thoroughly familiar with the aircraft and the basic tasks they would need to perform in combat. In addition to their flying training, the pilots received training in basic engineering and maintenance so that they would be able to help maintain their own planes when operating from fields behind enemy lines.[7]

On 6 June the designation of the fighter squadrons was changed. The reconnaissance term was dropped, even as the 2nd Air Commando Group trained intensely, unaware that the question of their deployment was the subject of a debate among General Arnold, Admiral Lord Louis Mountbatten, and the Joint Chiefs of Staff. When his plan for the aerial reconquest of Burma failed to receive support from either Mountbatten or General Joseph Stilwell, Arnold canceled activation of what would have been the 4th and 5th Air Commando Groups, but the fate of the 2nd and 3rd Air Commando Groups remained undecided. As a result of this indecision, the 2nd Air Commando Group's alert for overseas movement was canceled on 24 June. The cancellation came as a bitter disappointment, since the group had been keyed up in expectation of quickly going overseas. However, it relieved the pressure on the training program and gave more time for the next phase of training, operating as a combined air commando group in an air commando operation.[8]

After each squadron had completed its own specialized training syllabus, Lieutenant Colonel DeBolt and his staff planned a series of maneuvers that would test the entire group in air commando operations. The five-day exercise involved seizing a forward air base, flying in troops and supplies, and conducting offensive operations from the forward base.[9]

During this period Major William Buxton, who had commanded the 31st Fighter Squadron in Panama, transferred over from Group Headquarters to assume command of the 1st Fighter Squadron. Over the next several weeks flights from the 1st and 2nd Squadrons took off regularly, returning several days later having flown nearly 5,000 miles over a good-sized section of America. These practice missions provided cross-country experience for what was to come.[10]

The Octagon Conference, where the Combined Chiefs of Staff settled on the fate of new air commando groups, ended on 16 September 1944. Nine days later the 2nd Air Commando Group received its Warning Order. The next few weeks passed in a blur of activity as the squadrons prepared for deployment. Finally, on 28 October, the majority of the group boarded trains for the West Coast, arriving in Los Angeles five days later. An advance party consisting of DeBolt and his key staff flew to India. The balance of the unit shipped out on the USS *General John Pope* and set sail for India on 10 November, arriving a month later after an uneventful voyage across the Pacific. Early the next morning they boarded old passenger cars for the trip across India to the Air Commando's assigned operational base at Kalaikunda, 70 miles west of Calcutta.

The sights, sounds, and above all the smells of India assailed them along the way. For all but the few China veterans this was their first encounter with Asia and a culture vastly different from their own.

Kalaikunda had been built as a B-29 base, yet quarters and facilities were rudimentary. The squadrons scoured the field for scraps of lumber and other materials to build and equip the offices and work areas. Kalaikunda served as the main rear supply depot and maintenance base for the entire group, supporting the individual squadrons who would be based closer to the front.[11]

The first Mustang arrived at Kalaikunda on 7 January 1945, to the delight of the pilots who had not flown in over two months. By the end of the month each squadron had a complement of 22 brand new aircraft, nineteen P-51Ds and a trio of F-6Ds for tactical reconnaissance. The engineering staff and the crew chiefs swarmed over the aircraft, checking to make sure that everything worked. Spray guns were brought out to paint on theater and squadron markings. Headquarters, Air Command Southeast Asia, issued instructions in January that all aircraft except four-engine bombers and night fighters carry theater recognition markings. For aircraft finished in natural metal, these markings consisted of broad chordwise bands across the wings, horizontal stabilizers, and vertical tail surfaces. The 1st and 2nd Fighter Squadrons painted these markings on their Mustangs in black. To distinguish the relatively unfamiliar profile of the Mustang for other Allied fighters and gunners, the two squadrons chose to paint dramatic lightning bolts on the top and bottom of the wings, and along the fuselage sides. The 1st Air Commando Group had painted some of its aircraft with a question mark on the tail as a group symbol; the 2nd Air Commandos chose an exclamation point. Finally, to distinguish between the two fighter squadrons, the 1st Fighter Squadron painted the propeller spinners of its Mustangs black, while the 2nd Squadron's Mustangs had the forward half of their propeller spinners left in natural metal and the rear half in black.[12]

Finally, after months of organization and training, the fighter squadrons were alerted for movement to the RAF base at Cox's Bazar, on the Bay of Bengal. On 4 February the entire 327th Aerodrome Squadron, with additional personnel from the 328th Aerodrome Squadron, flew to Cox's Bazar. The men of the 327th set about building hardstands for the fighters through the simple expedient of laying down bamboo matting on the sand, then covering this with runway matting of pierced steel planking (PSP). On 12 February 1945, the squadron engineering officers and the crew chiefs flew to Cox's, and the next day the 1st and 2nd Fighter Squadrons arrived.[13]

The 2nd Air Commando Group had arrived in India as General Slim and the staff of 14th Army were planning the assaults on Mandalay and Meiktila. They were assigned to the Combat Cargo Task Force, joining the 1st Air Commando Group to provide support to IV Corps in its dash to Meiktila. In early February the Combat Cargo Task Force set up the First Provisional Fighter Group, bringing together the 1st, 2nd, 5th, and 6th Fighter Squadrons and the 1st Air Commando Group's Night Intruder Section into one organization under the command of Lieutenant Colonel Levi Chase. To help coordinate air support for IV Corps, the 2nd Air Commando Group sent Major Bill Hawkins, Assistant Operations Officer, and Major Kevin Mallen, Group S-2 Officer, on temporary duty with the CCTF team at IV Corps.[14]

Right: The 1st and 2nd Fighter Squadrons added distinctive lightning stripes to the standard SEAC theater markings to identify their Mustangs.

Below: To distinguish between the two squadrons the 1st Fighter Squadron painted the propeller spinner on their Mustangs black, while the 2nd Fighter Squadron left the front half in natural metal. (Courtesy World War II Air Commandos Association)

Lacking HF radios, the 1st and 2nd Squadrons concentrated on targets assigned directly by IV Corps. In practice, IV Corps would identify Japanese troop positions or supply dumps through aerial reconnaissance or through intelligence passed up from advance units on the ground. This was then passed on to Major Mallen at IV Corps headquarters, who would relay it to Levi Chase. When the VCP controllers wanted a joint strike on a target, the 5th or 6th Squadron flight leaders, who were equipped with VHF radios, would act as forward air controllers, passing on instructions from the ground teams to the Mustangs. Later in the campaign a few of the VCP teams acquired VHF radios, providing them with direct communication.[15]

On 14 February 1945 1st and 2nd Fighter Squadrons flew their first combat mission supporting 7th Division's crossing of the Irrawaddy, bombing Japanese positions at Pakokku, east of 7th Division's crossing point at Nyaungu. The two strikes destroyed several buildings and started large fires.

The next day both squadrons attacked the same area with 500 lb. bombs and napalm and then went back in to strafe. After the mission 7th Division passed on its complements for the accuracy of the bombing.

Twelve aircraft went back to the bridgehead area the next day to bomb and strafe Japanese-occupied villages, followed on 17 February by a combined bombing and rocket strike on a reported concentration of Japanese light tanks at the town of Taungdwingyi.[16]

In preparation for 17th Division's advance on Meitkila, scheduled for 21 February, IV Corps requested the First Provisional Fighter Group to strike Meiktila and Pyinbin, an important road junction on the route to Meiktila and a key target for the first phase of the drive. A Japanese regiment was believed to have set up a roadblock at Pyinbin. Levi Chase organized a large combined strike by all squadrons.

1st and 2nd Squadrons dispatched 36 Mustangs to join 52 Thunderbolts from the 5th and 6th Fighter Squadrons and B-25s from the 1st Air Commando Group's Night Intruder Section. A combined force of Thunderbolts and Mustangs destroyed three villages in the Meiktila area, the Thunderbolts bombing with 500-pounders and the Mustangs following up with napalm, then strafing near Meiktila station. A second force accompanied B-25s to strafe Japanese troops in Pyinbin, around 15 miles from Nyaungu, with equal success. Later that day the 1st and 2nd Squadrons sent out 26 aircraft to bomb targets in the Nyaungu area.[17]

For daily ground support missions armorers reloaded the Mustang's six .50 cal. guns. (Courtesy World War II Air Commandos Association)

The advance began on the morning of 21 February 1945. For the next several days the 1st and 2nd Fighter Squadrons flew continuous missions in support of the advance on Meiktila. While the 5th and 6th Squadrons maintained cab rank patrols over the motorized columns, the 1st and 2nd Squadrons struck villages and Japanese assembly points along the route of the advance and to the flanks to limit the possibility of counter attacks. Using napalm, rockets, and then strafing attacks, they hit village after village, where British recon patrols found hundreds of dead Japanese soldiers.

The missions had an air of unreality about them, as the pilots could rarely see the troops they were attacking or the small arms and machine gun fire the Japanese threw back at them. As one pilot wrote in his diary, "The amazing thing about combat is that we know we must be killing lots of Japanese, but you can't see them and it's very easy to believe that you aren't in any danger until you see the holes in the plane."[18]

The British crossing of the Irrawaddy at Nyaungu prompted a response from the 5th Hikoshidan, which ordered the 64th Sentai to strike troops in the bridgehead area. They sent out several flights of Oscars on early morning and evening sweeps along the Irrawaddy from Myinmu to Nyaungu.

On 17 February a flight of eight Oscars strafed vehicles and troops at Nyaungu and shot down an L-5. On the 19th, several Oscar flights made sweeps over the area, one flight jumping four Thunderbolts from the 5th Fighter Squadron. Patrolling Spitfires bounced some of these sweeps, claiming several kills.

In response to the Oscars' attack on the 17th, the 1st and 2nd Squadrons sent 19 Mustangs to strike the Japanese airfields at Toungoo and Magwe, and seven aircraft to strafe the Pyinmana group of airfields, which Allied intelligence suspected the Japanese were using as advanced bases. The Mustangs strafed hangars and dropped napalm, but found no Japanese aircraft. On the 23rd the 1st Squadron made a low-level attack on the Meiktila airfield, dropping napalm on hangars and revetments; again, no Japanese aircraft could be seen.[19]

To provide additional air cover over the bridgehead area during the early morning hours, IV Corps asked the 2nd Air Commando Group to station a flight of Mustangs at Sinthe, about 25 miles northwest of Nyaungu and a few miles from Corps headquarters at Pauk. On 22 February, the 1st Fighter Squadron sent six aircraft, pilots, and crew chiefs to operate out of Sinthe, and the 2nd Fighter Squadron sent four. For the next several days the Mustangs flew patrols over the bridgehead area and around Meiktila, beginning early in the morning and continuing throughout the day. These patrols proved to be uneventful until the 25th, when the 2nd Fighter Squadron lost two airplanes over enemy territory within the space of a few hours. The first of these incidents led to the 2nd Air Commando's first rescue of a pilot behind enemy lines.

Late in the morning on the 25th the team at Sinthe received a report that 12 Oscars were flying north towards Meiktila. Captain Ed Atha and Lieutenant Robert Beck, from the 2nd Fighter Squadron, scrambled to patrol the Meiktila area and hopefully intercept the Japanese. Atha planned to fly low, then cross the Irrawaddy River where it bends south of Mandalay and fly southwest to pick up the Irrawaddy farther downstream, passing Meiktila on the way. The two Mustangs completed the first part of their patrol without incident, seeing nothing. On reaching the Irrawaddy again, southwest of Meiktila, they turned and headed back along their patrol route. About halfway, near Meiktila, Lieutenant Beck experienced an explosion in the nose of his plane and saw a large piece of the left cowling fly off. His P-51 had been tracked and hit by some very accurate Japanese anti-aircraft gunners. He immediately turned northwest, back towards Sinthe, but in a few minutes his engine started to lose RPMs as it began to freeze. Beck had no alternative but to parachute.

Atha rushed back to Sinthe, where a rescue was immediately organized. In central Burma the first few months of the year before the monsoons arrive are hot and dry. The fields and rice paddies become hard as rock, making it possible to land a light aircraft. Major Charlie Gordon commandeered an L-5 and took off to look for Beck, with Ed Atha leading an escort of P-51s. Beck was hiding in a pile of brush when he heard the unmistakable drone of Mustang engines and then saw an L-5 landing about a half-mile away. Beck ran to the plane, Gordon starting his take-off as soon as Beck boarded. It was a small field, and with full power Gordon just made it off, hitting the top of a tree as he did so. Within a short while Beck was back on the ground at Sinthe, where Lieutenant Ed Reilly, the 1st Squadron's intelligence officer, offered him a slug of whisky. Beck drank half of the bottle. He had been in Japanese territory for a little more than two hours.[20]

Later that day Captain Atha went out on another sortie near 17th Division's advancing columns. His Mustang had an oil leak and the engine seized, forcing him to bail out behind Japanese lines a few miles from British troops. Even though it was late in the day, Charlie Gordon left again in the L-5 to attempt his second rescue. This time he came to grief. While trying to land near British troops, in the gathering darkness Gordon overshot the field and crashed into trees, wrecking the Stinson and breaking his jaw and one leg. Friendly troops quickly appeared on the scene to rescue him, but his injuries kept him out of combat for the rest of the campaign. Atha spent a lonely night hidden in the bush wrapped in his parachute for warmth, and was rescued the next morning. For his two gallant rescue attempts, Major Gordon was awarded the Silver Star.[21]

Ground fire was not always noticeable until the mission was over. This 2nd Squadron Mustang picked up a machine gun bullet in the spinner. (Courtesy World War II Air Commandos Association)

While the Air Commando transport squadrons airlifted the 99th Brigade to Thabutkon on 27-28 February, the 1st and 2nd Fighter Squadrons pounded targets in the area of Meiktila. On the 28th, a P-47 from the 1st Air Commando Group accompanied the 1st and 2nd Squadrons to serve as a forward air controller. The P-47 pilot contacted the VCP team and then relayed instructions to the circling Mustangs, directing them onto targets with pinpoint accuracy.

With the 5th and 6th Fighter Squadrons providing close support to troops fighting in Meiktila, the 1st and 2nd Squadrons shifted to attacking villages along the route of the British advance to prevent the Japanese from bringing up reinforcements. Using bombs, napalm, rockets, and strafing attacks, the two squadrons hit Japanese supply dumps and enemy-held villages. Flights of four aircraft went out daily to sweep the roads leading to Meiktila, strafing any type of transport that could be found. Neither squadron suffered any losses, despite hits by small arms or machine guns.[22]

By 4 March 1945 Meiktila had been captured and Operation Multivite completed. The battle would continue to the end of March, but the 1st and 2nd Fighter Squadrons turned to long-range operations, leaving responsibility for providing close air support to the RAF. On 1 March 1945, General Stratemeyer ordered that operational control of the First Provisional Fighter Group would shift from the Combat Cargo Task Force's representative with IV Corps to a newly-appointed CCTF representative at the headquarters of No. 224 Group on March 5. While the 5th and 6th Fighter Squadrons continued to concentrate on supporting the ground battle, the longer-legged Mustangs of 1st and 2nd Fighter Squadrons received a new mission: "responsibility for counter air force activity within the range of their aircraft."[23]

The air battles during 1944 had broken the back of the Japanese Army Air Force in Burma and inflicted a blow from which they never recovered. In early November 1944, at the end of the monsoon season, the Japanese 3rd Kokugun had just 478 aircraft deployed in Southeast Asia, with approximately 111 in Burma under the 5th Hikoshidan. The 5th Hikoshidan's two air brigades, the 4th Hikodan and the 25th Hikodan, had responsibility for the defense of Burma, Thailand, and French Indochina. The Burma front was still the responsibility of the 4th Hikodan, which controlled the following Hikosentai:

50th Sentai	20+ Ki-84 (Frank)
64th Sentai	30+ Ki-43 (Oscar) and 10 Ki-44 (Tojo)
204th Sentai	20+ Ki-43 (Oscar)
81st Sentai	15+ Ki-46 recon (Dinah)
8th Sentai	20+ Ki-48 bombers (Lily)

Also available were the 13th Sentai (20+ Oscars) and the 58th Sentai with 15 Type 97 Heavy Bombers (Sally) of the 25th Hikodan in French Indochina. Replacement aircraft could only be drawn from other combat or operational training units in Malaya and Sumatra. None of the air units in Burma were ever up to full strength, and all suffered constantly from problems of serviceability.[24]

By January 1945, combat attrition had reduced the operational air strength of the 3rd Kokugun in Southeast Asia to around 300 aircraft, with less than 100 deployed in Burma. From this time on, Japanese air strength in Burma steadily declined. The demands of other combat zones obliged the Japanese Army Air Force to begin stripping its Burma squadrons.

The 204th Sentai went to the Philippines in November 1944 and did not return. After US Navy carrier strikes on French Indochina during January 1945, the 5th Hikoshidan transferred the 50th Sentai to Saigon for convoy protection, leaving the veteran 64th Sentai as the sole fighter unit in Burma. In early February the 3rd Kokugun transferred the 7th Rensei Hikotai (Operational Training Unit) to Burma with ten Ki-61 fighters (Tony) to assist the 5th Hikoshidan with the defense of Rangoon.[25]

More critically for the Japanese Army, the Allied advance into central Burma and the constant depredations of Allied fighters and bombers forced the 4th Hikodan to withdraw from airfields in central Burma. The Hikodan's units retreated to airfields around Rangoon and then withdrew further to airfields in Thailand. In mid-January the 64th Sentai, the 8th Sentai, and the 81st Sentai moved from their bases around Meiktila to the airfields around Pyinmana. In early February, the 64th moved again back to Mingaladon, followed shortly thereafter by the 8th and 81st Sentais. The 8th Sentai's Lily bombers began using the fields in upper Burma to stage their nocturnal raids, returning to Rangoon before daybreak.

Following the loss of Meiktila in early March, the main airfields around Rangoon — Mingaladon, Hmawbi, Hlegu, and Zayatkwin – became the forward bases and the 8th Sentai withdrew its bombers to Thailand. At the beginning of March, Rangoon bases held the 64th Sentai with approximately 20 Oscars, the 7th Rensei Hikotai with eight to ten Tonys, and the 81st Sentai with approximately eight recon Dinahs. The aircraft stayed in protected revetments away from the main fields under heavy camouflage.[26]

During late 1944 and early 1945, the Japanese had developed a string of airfields in Thailand in the event that their hold on Burma became untenable. The main Japanese base in Thailand was Don Muang, just north of Bangkok, the Thai capital, and roughly 400 miles from Rangoon. Don Muang had been a major supply and maintenance center for the 4th Hikodan since the beginning of the war. By 1945 Don Muang had two all-weather runways, extensive hangars and maintenance facilities, and shelters for 85 aircraft. It was also the headquarters of the Royal Thai Air Force, still ostensibly allied with the Japanese. The Japanese had built or expanded a number of airfields and landing grounds running north from Don Muang to Chiengmai, creating a defensive line. These fields could support bomber or fighter aircraft, and each field had 40 or more aircraft shelters.[27]

Captain William Hawkins, assigned to Group Headquarters, flew this 1st Fighter Squadron F-6D on combat missions. This was a photo recon version of the P-51D-15NA. Note camera ports in fuselage just aft of national insignia. (Courtesy USAF Museum)

The Nakajima Ki-43 Hayabusa (Oscar) was the Japanese Army fighter most frequently encountered in S.E. Asia. An Oscar from the *64th Sentai* lies derelict at Mingaladon air field after the capture of Rangoon. In two and a half months of combat the 1st and 2nd Fighter Squadrons claimed 60 Japanese aircraft destroyed in the air and on the ground, and a further 40 probably destroyed or damaged. (Imperial War Museum)

By early 1945, the depleted Japanese Army Air Force in Burma had no ability to influence the outcome of the ground battle. Allied air power was overwhelming. However, advancing Allied ground forces presented the Japanese with a host of lucrative targets. Transport and liaison aircraft shuttled back and forth to the front lines throughout the day. During one week in mid-February, Allied transport and liaison squadrons flew over 14,000 sorties in and around Burma.

As soon as practical, the RAF moved squadrons of Spitfires and Hurricanes closer to the front. These forward strips often had little capacity for dispersal. Ground targets were even more numerous. 14th Army's dependence on air supply meant that every forward strip was piled high with supplies of fuel, food, and ammunition. The trucks used to transfer supplies to the fighting units at the front were in the open and vulnerable to strafing attacks along the few roads and tracks available. In the open plains artillery and troop positions were easily identifiable from the air. While the sheer quantity of supplies available to 14th Army was vastly superior to the Japanese, every pound of supply, every gallon of gasoline, and every piece of equipment had to come over an aerial supply line that was stretched to its limit. General Slim and his staff had cut the average division's allocation to about 1/3 of what a British division fighting in Europe would have received. Even so, the transport squadrons were under an enormous strain. 14th Army's air supply plan made no allowance for interference from the Japanese, and General Slim admitted after the war that "we were never without acute anxiety on the supply and transport side."[28]

However, the Japanese never took advantage of the situation. For unexplained reasons they never seemed to have deliberately sought out Allied transport aircraft. The few occasions when the Oscars wrecked havoc among the transports were random encounters. There were, apparently, numerous differences of opinion on targets between the 5th Hikoshidan and Burma Area Army, which constantly demanded that priority be given to ground support rather than attacks on Allied lines of communication. Interdicting the Allies tenuous supply line would have been far more productive.[29]

As a result, the 64th Sentai's Oscars flew repeated ground attack sorties, causing comparatively minor damage, while Allied transport planes flew over Burma almost entirely unmolested. But the risk to Allied transports, and to the increasingly long columns of motor vehicles, was seen as a constant threat that increased as the Allies moved steadily south toward the Japanese airfields in lower Burma.

In the Mustangs of the 2nd Air Commando Group, the Allies had a fighter with the range and the performance to crush the Japanese wherever they could be found. 1st and 2nd Fighter Squadrons began that job on 7 March 1945 with an escort mission, accompanying seventy-five B-24s from the RAF and the AAF 7th Bomb Group to the dock area at Martaban near Moulmein. This six-hour mission proved uneventful, and the squadrons saw no Japanese aircraft.

The next day Levi Chase scheduled an afternoon sweep over two Rangoon area airfields. He lead 14 Mustangs from the 1st Squadron to Mingaladon while 16 aircraft from the 2nd Squadron struck Hmawbi. As the 1st Squadron approached Mingaladon, the flights spread out and dropped down to the deck. Coming in over the field they fired at whatever was in their path, though few aircraft were visible. Chase lined up an Oscar and fired at it, seeing strikes and then flames. A second Oscar attracted his attention and he banked slightly and fired again, seeing more strikes. Chase claimed one aircraft destroyed and one damaged, but intelligence reduced his claims to one probably destroyed. Captain Bob Eason found two Oscar fighters parked outside a hangar and fired at both, damaging one of them.

The raiders surprised the airfield's defenders, who failed to respond until the P-51s had flown past the revetment area. The pilots were flying so low that some of the anti-aircraft fire went over them. A burst of machine gun fire completely shattered the canopy on 2nd Lieutenant Ben Lundberg's Mustang, but he was unscathed. Ground fire hit one other aircraft and then the Mustangs were gone. The 2nd Squadron found no aircraft at Hmawbi, but gave the hangars a good strafing.[30]

On 9 March, the Mustangs joined 1st Air Commando Thunderbolts to escort RAF and 7th Bomb Group B-24s to attack a major Japanese supply dump at Victoria Park north of Rangoon. This mission to the Rangoon was an exciting prospect, as the month before a dozen Japanese fighters had intercepted a bombing mission to the same target. 1st and 2nd Squadron members looked forward to what they assumed would be an opportunity to engage in air combat, but the enemy failed to offer any resistance. Two days later the squadrons escorted RAF Liberators back to the same target, and again, the Japanese failed to make an appearance. Unknown to Allied intelligence, the 5th Hikoshidan had imposed a ban on aerial combat to conserve 64th Sentai's fighters.[31]

The results of these first few missions were a disappointment. However, Levi Chase had been working on a plan for a more effective strike against the Japanese Army Air Force. Photo intelligence revealed that the Japanese were steadily pulling aircraft out of Burma and transferring them to Thailand. In mid-February the 4th Hikodan had approximately 82 aircraft in Burma, comprised of 59 fighters, 13 Lily bombers, and ten Dinah reconnaissance aircraft. The count of airplanes in Burma as of 9 March was just 41, while the number in Thailand underwent a corresponding increase. Air activity had declined as well. While the 8th Sentai's Lily bombers made several night raids during the first 12 days of March, the 64th Sentai refrained from flying any daylight sweeps and simply sent out one or two planes on reconnaissance. To Chase, the conclusion emerging from this analysis was straightforward. If the Japanese could not be brought to combat in the air, and if they could not be found in sufficient numbers on the airfields in Burma, then the key to their destruction was to strike the airfields in Thailand where the Japanese were concentrating in seemingly safe havens.[32]

Chase flew to Eastern Air Command headquarters in Calcutta to present his idea for a raid on the Japanese airfield at Don Muang. General Stratemeyer was skeptical. The distance from Cox's Bazar to Don Muang was 750 miles, the equivalent of flying from London to Vienna. The mission would involve a round-trip of over 1500 miles, and a fighter mission of that length had never been attempted before in the Burma theater. Allied intelligence was unsure what type of radar the Japanese were operating in Thailand that might alert them to the approaching fighters. If the pilots had to engage in air combat over Don Muang, and there was every prospect that they would, they might not have enough fuel to return. Losses could be very high.

Levi Chase was a great organizer and a careful planner. He delivered a convincing argument that the Don Muang mission had a good chance of success. Based on the fuel consumption data the 1st and 2nd Squadrons had acquired during their training, Chase showed that, with long-range tanks, the Mustangs had the ability to fly to Don Muang, attack the field, and fly return to Cox's Bazar. The margin of error would be tight, but the risk was acceptable. Anyone running short of fuel on the return flight could divert to alternate advance fields at Akyab and Ramree Island. Chase pointed to the experience level in the 1st and 2nd Squadrons and the reputation they had established in their first weeks in combat. The majority of pilots had hundreds of hours in fighters and had demonstrated impressive flying discipline. Chase was convinced that the two squadrons could succeed, and Stratemeyer finally approved the mission, albeit reluctantly.[33]

Photographic coverage of Don Muang on 12 March revealed over 50 aircraft, including eight large twin-engine aircraft identified as Ki-21 (Sally) and Ki-49 bombers (Helen), and Ki-57 transports (Topsy), nine medium twin-engine aircraft thought to be mostly Lily bombers; 31 fighters; and several that were unidentified. By this stage the Allies had developed contacts with the Thai underground, who were receiving clandestine support from the Royal Thai Air Force. They confirmed the number of Japanese aircraft to the Thai underground, who quickly radioed the information to Eastern Air Command at Calcutta.[34]

In preparation for the mission, Chase called in the squadron operations officers and told them that they were to prepare 20 aircraft from each squadron for a mission the following day and that the mission would require full 110-gallon drop tanks under each wing. He did not disclose the destination. Captain Donald Branyan and Captain Alvin Williams, Engineering Officers for the 1st and 2nd Squadrons, notified their maintenance crews and those of the 327th Aerodrome Squadron that 40 Mustangs had to be in perfect condition for mission the next day. The individual crew chiefs and everyone else who could lend a hand, spent the rest of the day preparing the aircraft and checking every system. No crew chief wanted his plane to abort, or worse, to suffer mechanical problems during the mission.

That evening, Chase held a preliminary pilot briefing. When he told them where they were going and when the pilots saw the long stretch of ribbon on the wall-mounted map starting at Cox's Bazar and going deep into Thailand, there were some expressions of surprise tinged with disbelief. Could they actually fly that far? But when Major Kevin Mallen, Group S-2, started handing out reconnaissance photos of Don Muang showing the host of Japanese aircraft on the field, the pilots immediately became enthusiastic. Mallen gave a detailed description of the field while everyone studied the photos. Element leaders received maps marked with indicated courses and target photos.[35]

ploded in flames. Flying to
Chase counted 15 to 20 indi
remembered most was, "the
field, with everyone firing a
ing to avoid hitting each oth

Lieutenants Haro
Morrison found several scar
nese reconnaissance effort.
north end of the field and st
ued on and found another
strafed as well. This target
stroyed. Morrison also foun
of the field, which he straf
south he sighted another w
centrated burst of the P-51'

Despite the dictum t
the field, the absence of a
fire encouraged Chase to o
served the last of the Musta
for one more strafing run fr
pilot heard him, but those
and came in again.

Chase saw a Lily b
fired at it, getting many stri
nothing in his path but th
sprayed. (Dixon later attem
chief to paint a wind sock o

Nearly every pilot in
a claim for aircraft destroy
Captain Warren Modine, le
lost. His Mustang was last
cockpit.[40]

High scorer for the
Spann, who was leading th
William Buxton's flight. Wh
sance photos of Don Muan
sion, Spann had noticed tha
the airfield that passed ove
aircraft. From that particula
almost in a line. He boastin
the path he would follow,
chances of being so perfec
his amazement, when he le
the next morning, he found
tion he had seen on the pho
was a row of twin-engine a
ers. He banked down and fi
side a revetment, which bu

In order not to over
he chopped his throttle, pul
then straightened out and d
burst and this airplane beg
same maneuver to fire at a
over the tail and hitting ano
fifth twin-engine plane in a r
this aircraft explode. There
aircraft in his line of sight

JAPANESE AIRFIELDS IN THAILAND

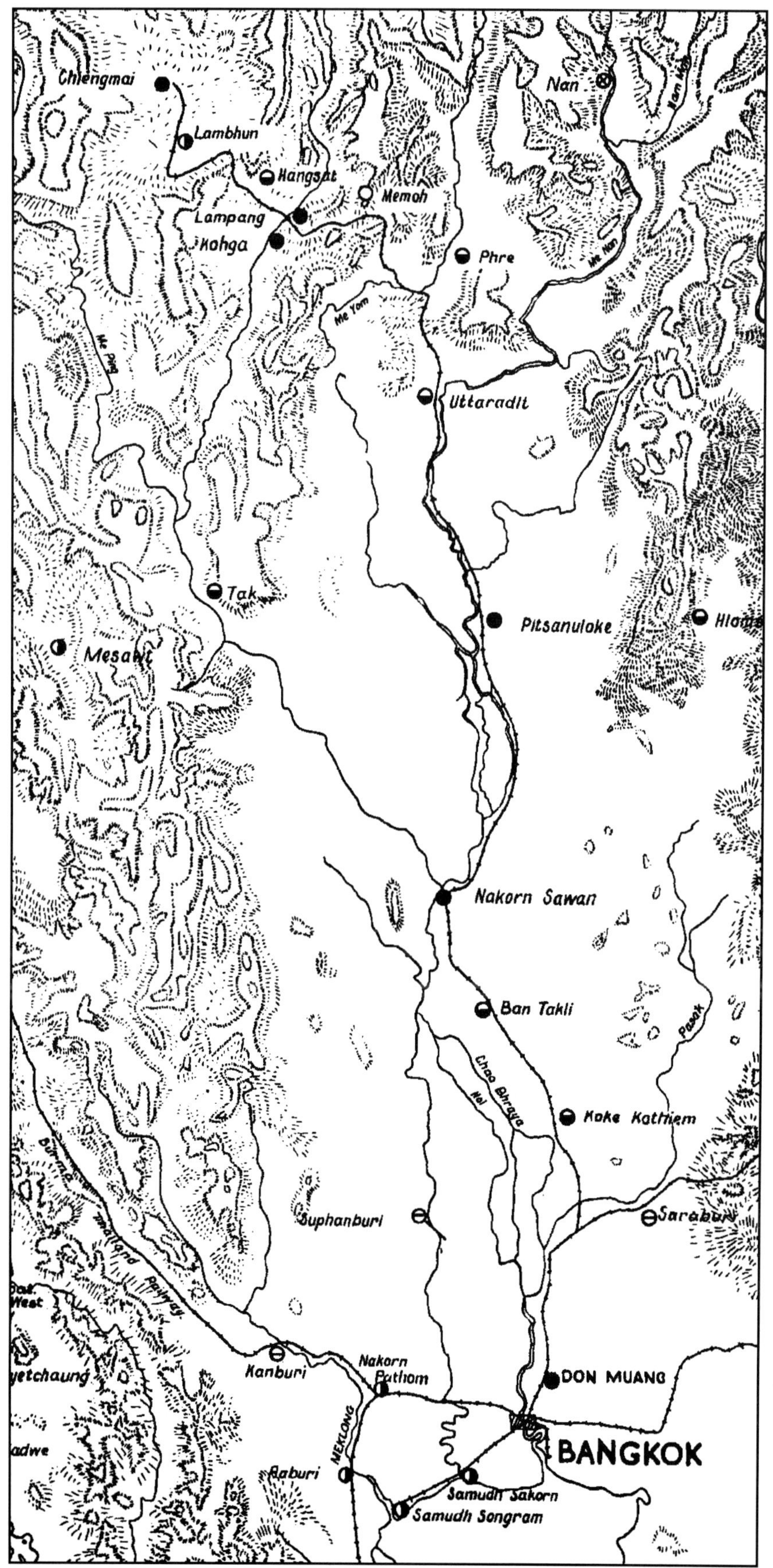

Source: *Public Records Office*

At 0800 hours c
the operational briefing
20 aircraft organized int
to the Initial Point (IP),
Chao Phraya River, abo
Here they would split.
Fighter Squadron almo
Muang from the north.
Fighter Squadron and fl
Don Muang from the w
Squadron had complete
tack run, the flights wou
formation to provide m
structions were clear: c
briefing on anti-aircraf
escape and evasion (t
shot down, to surrend
would provide far bette
the pilots went out to th
of water and some a s
would be a long trek.[36]

At 1019 hours
airplane #85, named '
Hadley Dixon as his wi
the field as the other
squadrons had joined,
feet and set course for
fuel mixtures and redu
droned on over cent
Salween River and th
Burma-Thailand borde
Thailand's central plai
down to low altitude wit
ron close behind. Chas
featureless jungle wa
exactly on schedule, th

About ten mile
wing tanks, and Pryo

1st Lieutenant Bob Spann
morning of March 15, 194
Association)

Another low quality gun camera clip shows that Spann's last ground target was a Sally bomber in a revetment. Note the staff car in front of the bomber. (Courtesy W.R. Eason)

> to jerk away, leaving me my twin to shoot at again. By this time I was very close, probably 100 yards, and overtaking it. As I went over the Sally there was an explosion and it began to tumble as I passed over it."[42]

The two "poachers" were Buxton and his wingman, 2nd Lieutenant William Holman. They had also seen the Sally heading away from the field and joined the hunt. Buxton approached from astern and opened fire, not seeing Spann's Mustang in pursuit. Holman saw the bomber approaching from his left with two P-51s right behind. Holman joined in and it appears from the gun camera films that the three pilots fired more or less at the same time, Holman closing in to almost point blank range. All three saw the Sally crash. As they completed their final runs across the field, each joined up with whoever they could find and headed home. The 1st Squadron's strike had lasted only a few minutes.[43]

A tired Bob Spann, right, talks with Captain William Marshall, left, who led the second flight across Don Muang, and 1st Lieutenant George Dent, 1st Fighter Squadron adjutant, after the return to Cox's Bazar. Spann submitted claims for 7 aircraft destroyed or damaged.

The 2nd Squadron came in right on the heels of the 1st. Long columns of black smoke rising into the air identified the target from several miles away. As they neared the target, Major Pryor gave his squadron the order to drop tanks and spread out. At full throttle the pilots pulled up to gain a little altitude and roared onto the field. Coming in from the west the 2nd Squadron's approach crossed over the main runways, which ran north-south, and led directly to the many hangars that lay on the eastern side of the field. Although the 1st Squadron had left a trail of destruction, there were still many undamaged aircraft remaining. Protective revetments around the field faced in different directions, making it difficult to hit many aircraft on a single pass. It had been for that very reason that Chase directed the two squadrons take different approaches. 2nd Squadron pilots fired into revetments and hangars that faced west, adding to the havoc, but in going across the field rather than along its length they had fewer opportunities.

Pryor found a large revetment in front of him that held two Tony fighters, most likely from the 7th Rensei Hikotai. Opening fire, he saw one fighter burst into flames and strikes cover the other before he had to pull up. Major Grosvenor, Squadron Operations Officer, also scored twice, setting one single-engine fighter in a revetment on fire and then taking out a twin-engine aircraft in another revetment across the field.

After strafing aircraft in revetments, several pilots fired into the large hangars, filling them with bright flashes as their bullets struck the aircraft inside. Seeing a Lily bomber within one hangar, 2nd Lieutenant Charles LeFan dropped down on the deck below the hangar line and fired through the open doors setting the aircraft afire.

Some pilots had time for a quick turn and another pass, and then they were on the other side. Circling to the west, Chase watched the 2nd Squadron make its attack. By this time the Japanese had started to react, and he saw AA fire coming from the south end of the airfield. When the last of the Mustangs had pulled away from the target, he called for everyone to break off and head for home.[44]

The first planes arrived back at Cox's Bazar around 1700 hours, the pilots having flown on average six-and-a-half hours. They were tired but jubilant at their success. Surprise had been complete, only one pilot (Modine) had been lost, and they had left a mass of burning aircraft behind.

Coming in from their planes, the pilots took a few minutes to describe the attack to their crew chiefs and to other ground staff who were relieved to see them

Major Roger Pryor, 2nd Fighter Squadron commander, with the members of his flight on the first Don Muang raid. (L-R) 1st Lieutenant B.J.Mayer, 1st Lieutenant William Wilson, Major Pryor, 1st Lieutenant Charles LeFan. Pryor destroyed two airplanes on the first raid while Wilson and LeFan destroyed one each. (Courtesy World War II Air Commandos Association)

back and eager to learn what had happened. Word quickly spread that Bob Spann had strafed seven aircraft.

At the debriefing, the intelligence officers tried to make sense of who had shot up what. Preliminary claims were for three aircraft destroyed in the air, 28 destroyed on the ground, five probably destroyed, and eight damaged. Thirty twin-engine and 11 single-engine aircraft were claimed as destroyed or damaged. After debriefing, group intelligence radioed Eastern Air Command headquarters that the raid had been a complete success. Stratemeyer was standing by waiting for the results and later admitted his fear that half the long-range raiding force might be lost.[45]

A reconnaissance photo of Don Muang taken the day after the raid showed just 19 operable aircraft, remains of a dozen burned-out hulks in revetments, and a pile of aircraft wreckage in a corner of the field. Further analysis reduced the total number of ground claims to 17 destroyed, four probables, and 18 damaged. Counting the three air kills, the total of destroyed and damaged aircraft was one quarter of the estimated number of Japanese aircraft in Burma, Thailand, and French Indochina.

Japanese Army Air Force records of the period did not survive the war, but it appears that the 8th Sentai suffered most in the attack. Allied intelligence had estimated that in the days before the Don Muang raid the Japanese had 30 light bombers in Burma, Thailand, and French Indochina, with an additional ten in Malaya. The following week this estimate dropped to 25 total.

The fighter estimate saw a decline of ten aircraft. By pulling fighters from training schools and operational units in Malaya and Sumatra, the Japanese rebuilt their fighter strength, but the losses in medium bombers and reconnaissance aircraft were never made good.[46]

In the days following the raid, congratulations came in from Admiral Mountbatten, Air Marshal Sir Keith Park, Allied Air Commander-in-Chief, Southeast Asia Command, and Major General Stratemeyer. Admiral Mountbatten's message read as follows:

> "Please convey my heartiest congratulations to Nos. 1 and 2 US Squadrons of 2nd Air Commando Group on their magnificent attack on Don Muang airfield Bangkok....This remarkable achievement carried out by single-seat aircraft reflects most favorably on 2nd Air

Staff Sergeant Charles Pearce, crew chief, left, 1st Lieutenant Edwin Harkins, pilot, smile for the camera while Harkins' armorer points to the newly painted flag representing the aircraft Harkins destroyed on the first Don Muang mission. (Courtesy World War II Air Commando Association)

> Commandos as a whole and in particular on high standards of training and determination of pilots concerned."[47]

The Don Muang raid was the longest fighter mission, in terms of distance, ever attempted in the Burma theater and one of the longest fighter missions of World War II.

During the second half of March, the 2nd Air Commandos revisited Japanese airfields around Rangoon and Moulmein. On 18 March, twelve P-51s from the 1st Squadron went on a sweep of Mingaladon and Zayatkwin, while 16 aircraft from the 2nd Squadron covered Hmawbi and nearby Hlegu airfields. Both squadrons departed in predawn darkness in order to reach their targets at first light. A night takeoff from Cox's dusty runway, by the light of a few flare pots, was a hair-raising experience, but there were no accidents.

Captain Bob Eason led the 1st Squadron to Mingaladon, beginning the attack run at 0635 hours from the southwest. Before hitting the field, Eason called for the other two flights to go in trail, echeloned to the right. They surprised several Oscars parked in revetments. Eason found a pair of Oscars sitting in a revetment at the edge of the field. He opened fire and sent several long bursts into the two fighters before he swept past. 2nd Lieutenants Dean Wimer and Richard Fishburn each strafed an Oscar, Wimer claiming a destroyed and Fishburn a probable. All four claims were subsequently downgraded to damaged.[48]

The 2nd Squadron found no aircraft at Hmawbi on their strafing runs, so went on to Hlegu. As they approached the field, Captain Edward Atha, leading one of the flights, observed a twin-engine aircraft approaching from the south. His combat report described the short and swift fight that ensued:

> "I called it in over the radio and thought it was probably a Mosquito or Beaufighter on a rhubarb. I flew a collision course with it at about a 90 degree angle. When about a thousand yards away it made a turn towards my flight. I saw the Red Ball markings of the Japanese Air Force on the wing and fuselage and thought that it was a 'Dinah'. At 400 yards range I opened up with a burst which hit his left engine. The engine and wing burst into flames with smoke trailing. I did a sharp chandelle and then dove, shooting a burst into his right engine. By this time, my second element leader had positioned himself and was firing into the ship from the left. The 'Dinah' exploded in mid-air and crashed to earth in a mass of flames."[49]

Two days later the squadrons flew to northern Thailand to strafe the airfields at Chiangmai and Phrae, Thai bases that the Japanese were using as staging areas. Nearing Chiangmai, Captain William Marshall came across a small single-engine airplane which he promptly shot down. This turned out to be a civilian Fairchild 24 of the Aerial Transport Company of Thailand, which was unfortunate enough to be in the wrong place at the wrong time. The two squadrons swept over the fields strafing hangars and other buildings, but found no aircraft.[50]

On March 21 the targets were airfields deep in southern Burma. The 1st Squadron carried out an uneventful sweep around Tavoy. The 2nd Squadron had better luck at Moulmein where Lieutenant Julian Gilliam destroyed one twin-engine bomber, most likely a Lily from the 8th Sentai , while 2nd Lieutenant Paul Kent probably destroyed an Oscar.

On the return to base, the 2nd Squadron made a quick sweep over Zayatkwin but found it empty. Antiaircraft fire hit Lieutenant Gilliam's Mustang in the tail and elevators. Gilliam struggled back to Cox's Bazar, where he was forced to belly-land his aircraft.

Three days later, while the 1st Squadron flew escort to RAF B-24s, Lieutenant Colonel Chase took three flights from the 2nd Squadron on a sweep of Mingaladon and Moulmein airfields. He damaged one heavily camouflaged airplane at Mingaladon while the rest of the pilots strafed hangars and other buildings, leaving them in flames.[51]

On the night of 25 March, the 4th Hikodan organized a raid on British ships in Akyab harbor and airfield with three Sally bombers from the 58th Sentai, four Lily bombers from the 8th Sentai, and seven Oscars from the 64th Sentai. British intelligence detected that the Oscars had all returned to Hmawbi following the night raid and flashed the news to the First Provisional Fighter Group.

Chase reasoned that the Oscars would likely fly back to airfields in Thailand after they refueled at Hmawbi, and he was determined to catch them before they did so. He quickly organized a sweep of Hwambi, Mingaladon, and the airfield at Moulmein, all possible staging bases.

At 0440 hours Chase led off the 1st Squadron, with Lieutenant Harold Hettema flying as his wingman and Lieutenant Bobby Spann leading the second element. Major Pryor and the 2nd Squadron took off immediately after the 1st on what would prove to be a long and costly day.[52]

Chase was about three miles north of Hmawbi field at around 0625 hours, flying at 1,000 feet, when he observed three Oscars coming toward him. Captain Yoshio Nakano, from the 64th Sentai, had just taken off with Warrant Officer Kokichii Kitajima and Lieutenant Shinitchiro Kato, most likely to return to bases in Thailand. Captain Nakano saw the Mustangs approaching head-on and immediately led his flight in a steep climbing chandelle toward the south in a desperate but futile attempt to escape.

1st Lieutenant Hal Hettema, left, with his crew chief Staff Sergeant Ray Lunde, and his armorer, Charles Augustoni, on the wing of Hettema's Mustang, No.35, PASADENA KID, named after the town where Hettema grew up. (Courtesy World War II Air Commandos Association)

The Mustangs were approaching at high speed and quickly overtook the fleeing Oscars. Chase pulled up behind Nakano, Hettema off his left wing and Spann off his right. Hettema and Spann fell in astern Nakano's wingmen. The three Americans opened fire at the same time, and all three Oscars were well hit. They went straight in, striking the ground in a V formation and exploding. None of the pilots survived. The fight was over in less than a minute.[53]

As Chase pulled away from Hmawbi, Captain Bob Eason, who was leading the trailing flight, called Chase to warn him that his aircraft was leaking coolant. As the P-51s passed over the airfield, the Japanese had sent up volleys of small arms and machine gun fire. A lucky shot had hit Chase's Mustang in the coolant system. Soon the engine began to run rough, coolant temperatures started rising, and the oil pressure dropped to zero. Chase knew he had to leave the plane, but when he looked at his altimeter he found he was already down to little more than 300 feet. He bellied into a field about 20 miles west of Hmawbi airfield. When his flight saw that Chase was safely away from his plane, Bobby Spann went down and strafed, setting the Mustang on fire to prevent it falling into the hands of the Japanese.[54]

Around the time that Chase and the 1st Squadron hit Hmawbi, Pryor was leading the 2nd Squadron over Mingaladon. They swept across the field but found no airplanes. As they pulled away from the field, the other pilots in Pryor's flight saw that his aircraft was streaming coolant, "like a fire hose," as one pilot remembered. Like Chase, Pryor had been hit by ground fire that no one had seen. Realizing that he could not return to base, Pryor called his wingman to stay with him and calmly ordered the rest of the squadron to complete the mission. Pryor flew away from Mingaladon and bailed out about 25 miles northeast of Chase's position.[55]

Lieutenants Edwin Pearle and Charles LeFan each found and damaged a twin-engine bomber Moulmein airdrome. Seeing a machine gun firing at his element leader, LeFan sprayed the position but took a hit to his own airplane. His canopy was instantly covered with oil which also flooded into the cockpit. Unable to see, he climbed away from the field as fast as he could and then cracked his canopy open a few inches so he could make out the horizon.

Captain Al Abraham, LeFan's flight leader, escorted him back to the RAF base at Akyab. Coming in to land, Abraham radioed LeFan and said, "Charlie, move to your left a little." LeFan did so, narrowly missing a squadron of Spitfires lined up along the runway which he could not see through his canopy. He found out years later that Abraham had turned off his radio after the attack and only remembered to turn it on just before LeFan landed.[56]

When Bob Eason saw that Chase had managed to land safely, he immediately began to think about organizing a rescue attempt. The nearest Allied airfield was on Ramree Island, 200 miles away. Eason headed there with his wingman, Lieutenant Fishburn. On the way he learned that Major Pryor had also been downed. Shortly after Eason and Fishburn arrived at Ramree, Spann and Hettema joined them. Eason and Spann looked for a rescue aircraft and saw two L-5s belonging to one of the 2nd Air Commando Group's Liaison squadrons. Pulling rank, Eason arranged to "borrow" the L-5s to fly back for Chase and Pryor. Despite the obvious risks, Eason and Spann loaded the L-5s with five-gallon cans of gas and tied the cans to the rear seats. They

Lt. Col. Levi Chase with the two men who rescued him from behind enemy lines on 26 March 1945. Captain Bob Spann, left, and Captain W.R. Eason, right. (Courtesy W.R. Eason)

took off from Ramree and returned to Chase's crash site, with Hettema and Fishburn flying escort.[57]

Once on the ground Chase had headed away from his aircraft and soon encountered several Burmese who escorted him back to their village. The elder, who spoke broken English, welcomed Chase and fed him while he decided what to do with the foreign airman who had dropped into their midst. Greatly in fear of Japanese reprisals if they helped him, the elder and the village headman had decided to hand Chase over to the local Burmese police when Chase heard the sound of a P-51 engine overhead. He told the village elder that his friends had come to get him. They smiled and wished him luck. Chase began walking back to the crash site and was soon amazed to see an L-5 overhead and another making a distant landing approach.[58]

Eason had landed in a rice paddy but ran into a patch of moist ground and his plane became mired in the mud. He immediately got out and started refueling the L-5 as Spann landed on a patch of harder ground nearby. Soon Chase ran up and the three men tried as hard as they could to free Eason's L-5, but failed. By then a number of villagers had gathered, including one who spoke some English. By giving them silver rupees from his money belt, Eason persuaded the Burmese to help. Eason and Chase leapt into the L-5 while Spann and the villagers pushed it clear of the mud. Eason then made a bone-jarring run across several paddy fields, slamming into the dikes between each field until the tail skid had been forced up into the fuselage of the plane. This worked to free the plane and Eason managed to get off the ground and set course for Ramree with the two escorting Mustangs.

Spann refueled his L-5 and took off without incident to search for Pryor. With only a rough idea of where to look, and despite searching for as long as he dared, Spann failed to find any sign of the CO.

The Japanese had captured Pryor soon after he had landed and taken him first to Mingaladon and then to a prisoner of war camp in Rangoon. For their courage in attempting a rescue 200 miles behind enemy lines in unarmed liaison planes, both Eason and Spann were awarded the Silver Star.[59]

The remainder of the 1st and 2nd Squadrons had diverted to Akyab, also in the hope of arranging a rescue. As the planes landed they raised a cloud of dust on the airfield, and this led to a tragic accident. Captain Sherard Sorrenson, a highly experienced flight leader in the 2nd Squadron, had just completed his landing role when his engine quit on the runway. Another pilot landed right behind him, but unable to see clearly through the dust, he collided, killing Sorrenson instantly. The day ended with four Mustangs destroyed, one pilot killed, and an experienced squadron commander captured. Suffering no more than a few bruises, Levi Chase flew back to Cox's Bazar that afternoon. Major William Grosvenor took over command of the 2nd Squadron.

The next day Chase led a combined force on an escort mission to Bangkok. B-24s bombed supply dumps near the city while the Mustangs cruised overhead hoping the Japanese fighters would attempt to intercept, but all was quiet. On the return flight Major William Hawkins, from Group Headquarters, spotted a Lily bomber sitting on the airfield at Pegu. Hawkins left the formation with his wingman, did a quick 180 degree turn, and dove down to strafe it, passing over the field at 350 mph.

More bad luck hit the 2nd Squadron that day. 2nd Lieutenant Robert Morris was seen to drop away from his flight with his cockpit on fire. Frantic calls from his flight leader to "jump" brought no response. His Mustang dove straight into the ground.[60]

During March 1945 the 1st and 2nd Fighter Squadrons had made six strikes against Japanese airfields in Burma and Thailand and claimed seven Japanese aircraft destroyed in the air, 18 on the ground, and a further 34 probably destroyed or damaged. This amounted to 82 percent of all Japanese aircraft claims by Allied units during the month. The effect on Japanese Army Air Force offensive operations was demonstrable. While the 4th Hikodan managed to increase the number of bomber sorties flown during the month, the combination of a policy of avoiding aerial combat in favor of selected airfield strikes had reduced the number of offensive fighter sorties flown during the month to less than half the February total. The 4th Hikodan's fighter force had flown 100 offensive sorties in January, 54 in

"Daisy cutters" were fragmentation bombs employed in some ground attack missions against personnel. (Courtesy World War II Air Commandos Association)

February, and a mere 22 in March, all night missions. The Allies, in contrast, were averaging more than 600 fighter sorties every day. Such was the magnitude of Allied air superiority. During the climactic battle for Meiktila, the battle that broke the back of the Japanese Burma Area Army as a fighting force, the Japanese Army Air Force in Burma was reduced to impotence and had no alternative but to abandon the army to its fate.[61]

During April the primary mission of the 2nd Air Commando fighter squadrons remained air supremacy. No. 221 Group assigned the 2nd Air Commandos sole responsibility for counter air strikes so that all other fighters could devote their effort to ground support of 14th Army and interdiction of Japanese strong points and retreat routes.

The loss of airfields in central Burma and the continued pressure on airfields in the Rangoon area throughout the month of March forced the 4th Hikodan and its component units to withdraw further into Thailand and French Indochina. After the first Don Muang raid, the 8th and 81st Sentais pulled some of their aircraft back into Cambodia to avoid the marauding long-

Loaded and ready. The 1st Fighter Squadron was nicknamed "The High Pockets." (Courtesy World War II Air Commandos Association)

On the first Don Muang raid Major Pryor's claim for one twin-engine aircraft turned out to be two Tony fighters in the same revetment. Captain Ed Atha, a big fan of Al Capp's "Lil' Abner" comic strip nicknamed Pryor "Weak-eyes Yokum" after a character in the strip. Pryor then had Atha give all the pilots names from "Lil'Abner." Robert Heisick (above) became Cyclone McGoon. (W W II Air Commandos Association)

range Mustangs. Toward the end of March, the 7th Rensei Hikotai appeared to have moved to Thailand, and the 64th Sentai began basing some of its fighters at airfields in Thailand's central plain, using its former main bases around Rangoon as staging fields. The only Japanese aircraft left in Burma at the beginning of April were a dozen 64th Sentai Oscars at Hmawbi. During April the 1st and 2nd Fighter Squadrons concentrated their attacks on the airfields in Thailand.[62]

On 1 April 1945, the Air Commandos launched a raid on Mingaladon and Hmawbi airdromes. This time, instead of looking for aircraft, the squadrons targeted the aviation installations, particularly machine shops, to damage each airfield's capacity to service aircraft. Forty P-51s participated, 24 carrying 500 lb. bombs and 16 carrying 110 gallon napalm tanks. All bombs and napalm went into the designated target areas.

High scorer was the 1st Squadron's Hal Hettema, seen here in his Mustang after scoring his first and only air victory. Hettema finished combat with one air victory and four ground kills. The 1st and 2nd Squadrons used red hinomaru on a white field to indicate air victories and a rising sun flag to indicate ground kills. (World War II Air Commandos Association)

The next day the squadrons went back to Thailand to strike Japanese airfields in the central plain. The 1st Squadron hit the airfield at Nakhon Sawan, some 120 miles north of Don Muang, while a combined force from the 1st and 2nd Squadrons covered Ban Takhli and Koke Kathiem, south of Nakhon Sawan. Lieutenant Herman "Doc" Lyons found a twin-engine bomber at Nakhon Sawan, which he left enveloped in flames after three strafing passes. Intelligence identified this as a Nakajima Ki-49 Helen, but it was more likely to have been one of 58th Sentai's Sally bombers. The other pilots found no airplanes at Ban Takhli or Koke Kathiem, but heavily strafed buildings around the fields.[63]

Photo reconnaissance of Don Muang during the first week of April revealed a slight build up in Japanese fighter strength. The 5th Hikoshidan was transferring fighters from Sumatra north to Thailand and French Indochina. Based on this intelligence, Levi Chase decided to launch another strike on Don Muang on 9 April. This time he would lead 32 aircraft from the 1st and 2nd Squadrons to Don Muang while two flights from the 2nd Squadron attacked the Japanese airfield at Nakhon Pathom, 20 miles to the west. Suspecting that the Japanese defenses would be better prepared the second time around, Chase decided not to repeat the approach from two directions as done on the first raid, but to have the entire formation approach from the north, with the flights spread out as before.[64]

Once again Chase's navigation was precise and the formation hit IP on the Chao Phraya River right on schedule. Here two flights from the 2nd Squadron broke away for an attack on Nakhon Pathom, while the rest of the formation continued on south to Don Muang. As they approached the field Chase called for the pilots to drop their external tanks, go to full throttle, and to spread out line-abreast. It was akin to a cavalry charge.

Chase fired at one fighter and destroyed it, then continued down the length of the field. His wingman, Lieutenant Malcolm MacKenzie, saw two single-engine fighters and a twin-engine bomber straight ahead of him and fired at all three. He then pulled up to gain some altitude for another pass farther down the field. As he nosed over he heard and felt an explosion, and his cockpit filled with white smoke. He cracked open the canopy to clear the smoke and headed west.

Lieutenant Ben Lundberg from MacKenzie's flight, who destroyed two bombers on his pass, pulled up alongside as escort. MacKenzie made it across the Chao Phraya River but, with a failing engine, belly-landed in a rice paddy a few miles away. Grabbing his carbine and escape kit, MacKenzie headed off while Lundberg came in to strafe the Mustang. This time the Japanese were quick to react. Almost as soon as the Mustangs hit the field, anti-aircraft fire started seeking them. As the flights swept across the field, more Mustangs began to take hits.[65]

Don Muang was rich in fighters that day, though there were fewer targets than on the first mission. Captain William Marshall, leading the second flight from the 1st Squadron, destroyed two fighters but took hits near his engine and after-coolant area. Captain Bob Eason destroyed two fighters sitting in a revetment on his pass. Lieutenants Harold Hettema and James Mason each destroyed one bomber and one fighter, while five other pilots claimed single kills against fighters.

Newly-promoted Lieutenant Colonel William Buxton, 1st Squadron commander, had his Mustang shot up and his hydraulic system damaged but managed to limp away. Lieutenant Dean Wimer, in the fourth flight, took a direct hit to his coolant system as he sped across the field at 50 feet. He had just enough time to climb to about 500 feet and bail out before his Mustang exploded.

Major William Grosvenor, leading three flights from the 2nd Squadron, found nothing in his path, but Lieutenant Charles LeFan destroyed two twin-engine bombers and Lieutenant Roy Long claimed a fighter and a bomber. Other pilots claimed six more aircraft. Leading the last flight across the field, Captain Al Abraham pulled up as he approached the field to look for a target. A 40mm shell found him immediately, taking out his coolant system. Abraham flew past the airfield and bailed out.[66]

Captains Glen Charpie and Jullian Gilliam led the two flights attacking Nakhon Pathom. To confuse any anti-aircraft fire they separated and attacked from different directions. They found several fighters parked around the field. Charpie and Lieutenants Beckner, Garibaldi, and Pike each destroyed one. There was no anti-aircraft fire, so they made repeated passes, strafing several motor vehicles and setting fire to many of the buildings.

Total claims for the two airfields were nine twin-engine aircraft and 21 fighters destroyed, and one twin-engine aircraft damaged.[67]

Abraham, MacKenzie, and Wimer were quickly captured. They had been briefed to surrender if possible to the Thai police instead of the Japanese. The Thais had an agreement with the Japanese forces in Thailand that if they captured an Allied pilot, the pilot would be their responsibility, and vice-versa. Fortunately, Thai police located each of them within a few hours, and all were taken to an internment camp in Bangkok for Allied civilians and military prisoners of war.

A few days later they were warned that they were to be taken to the Japanese for interrogation in the presence of Thai officers. The three had time to concoct a story that contained some elements of truth and a large amount of exaggeration. They were interrogated one at a time, and though clearly not satisfied with the answers, the Japanese bowed to Thai jurisdiction. The Mustang pilots spent the next four months fighting boredom and learning to play cricket.[68]

Major William Grosvenor, a five-kill China ace, took over command of the 2nd Fighter Squadron after Pryor was shot down. (Courtesy World War II Air Commandos Association)

General Stratemeyer paid a visit to the Air Commando fighter squadrons at Cox's Bazar and awarded the Silver Star to Chase for organizing the two long distance raids on Don Muang. The general commended both fighter squadrons for their excellent work inflicting significant damage on the Japanese Army Air Force.

That evening Chase called a general meeting for all personnel where he stressed that the award of the Silver Star was not a personal award, but for the unit as a whole. In his view the medal was an expression of appreciation from the higher command for the effort and contribution that every member had made.[69]

Lt. Charles LeFan led the 2nd Fighter Squadron in total aircraft destroyed with four ground victories. (Courtesy World War II Air Commandos Association)

In April the 1st and 2nd Fighter Squadrons joined the attack on Japanese supply dumps in southern Burma. Captain William Gadow's "Mary Jane" on the flight line armed with 4.5 inch rockets. Gadow's tally at the time of sixty bombing missions is painted underneath the cockpit. (World War II Air Commando Association)

Over the next ten days the Air Commandos were called on to support IV Corps' advance toward Rangoon. No. 224 Group assigned the 1st and 2nd Fighter Squadrons the task of destroying Japanese supply dumps around Pegu, a major town on the road to Rangoon that lay ahead of IV Corps' advancing columns. The two squadrons sent out several flights a day to bomb and strafe suspected supply dumps at Pegu and in villages in the surrounding area.

In preparation for Operation Dracula, the seaborne invasion of Rangoon scheduled for early May, the fighter squadrons were briefed on a special assignment. Invasion planners needed low level photographs of the Rangoon River's banks, and the Air Commando were detailed to attack nearby AA positions and provide diversionary cover for the photo recon planes. As one pilot observed, "It was a good way to get one's ass busted."[70]

The briefing was detailed and thorough. Timing was critical as the Mustangs had to hit the anti-aircraft batteries from different directions and at just the right time for the photo planes to make their inflexible runs.

Armed with 500-pounders and rockets, 16 aircraft from the 1st Squadron and 20 from the 2nd proceeded down the Rangoon River to its delta on 20 April 1945. The mission was a success, but anti-aircraft fire hit Lieutenant "Doc" Lyons' Mustang hard. Lyons, from the 1st Squadron, managed to get as far as Bassein where he parachuted successfully.

Captain Bob Eason, Lyons' flight leader, immediately flew to Ramree Island and contacted the 2nd Air Commando Group's 127th Liaison squadron. An L-5 was dispatched but failed to find any sign of the downed pilot. Eason went back to the Bassein area the next day and in two missions spent nine hours searching for his squadron mate, but to no avail. After the war was over the 2nd Air Commando Group learned that the Japanese had captured Lyons. When the Japanese Army retreated they beheaded him.[71]

During the last week of April, with advance columns of IV Corps nearing Rangoon, No. 221 Group intensified the campaign against enemy lines of communications in southern Burma. To cover the road and rail lines that were beyond the range of the group's Hurricane squadrons, they asked for assistance from the First Provisional Fighter Group's Mustangs. Starting on April 25th the 1st and 2nd Squadrons sent out several flights a day on regular sweeps. The toll of trucks, bullock carts, locomotives, and rolling stock mounted quickly.

The prize went to Lieutenant Colonel William Buxton who had the good fortune to find a complete

Captain Bob Eason named his F-6D ANNA BELLE after his wife. Eason commanded B flight, and all members of the flight named their airplanes accordingly. Eason's was QUEEN BEE (painted on the right side), Lt. Robert Fishburn was DRONE BEE, Lt. Robert Cason was LAZY BEE, Lt. Benjamin Lundberg was BUZZING BEE, and 2nd Lt. Herman 'Doc' Lyons was SON OF A B.

train in daylight. No. 224 Group's intelligence officer had alerted Major Kevin Mallen on 23 April that a train would be leaving Rangoon and heading east to Thailand heavily loaded with supplies and badly needed gasoline. The Air Commandos searched for two days without success. On the morning of the 25th Buxton and his flight found the train at a small station en route to Pegu. The Mustangs pounced on it and with no anti-aircraft fire to bother them, destroyed it completely. At one point Buxton came in low and fired at a box car which instantly exploded, sending flaming 55-gallon drums of gasoline high into the air and over his Mustang.[72]

On one these rhubarbs Captain Glen Charpie was leading a flight from the 2nd Squadron when, having failed to find any suitable targets, they passed across a field filled with stacks of rice straw. Out of boredom one member of his flight dropped down and fired at a stack. To his amazement the straw pile exploded. The Japanese had hidden drums of gasoline under every stack, and there were over 50 around the field. Charpie led his flight back and forth across the field until they had blown up every one.[73]

On 28 April, while on a mission to southern Burma, Captain William Marshall strafed a staff car but failed to note a line of trees in his flight path. He clipped a tree and his engine began shedding parts. Marshall pulled up and gained enough altitude to parachute.

Lieutenant McGinnis Clark, Marshall's wingman, carefully marked the location and then raced back to Cox's Bazar to initiate a rescue. Clark flew to Akyab where he and Master Sergeant Stanley Morris, from the 127th Liaison Squadron, took two L-5s loaded with 5-gallon cans of gas to search for Marshall. They found the site where Marshall had bailed out but saw no sign of him. Marshall had been helped by friendly Burmese and moved to their nearby village.

Morris called Clark and told him he needed to land and refuel. Morris landed while Clark circled overhead but the tail of the L-5 aircraft got stuck. Clark landed alongside and together they worked the Stinson loose and quickly refueled both aircraft. Clark said it felt eerie to be standing there refueling an L-5 more than 100 miles behind enemy lines.

Arriving back at Akyab after dark, Clark found that he couldn't locate the L-5's landing light. He called Morris who told him to pull in tight alongside. Morris then led both planes using only the landing lights on his aircraft.[74]

Clark and Morris tried again early the next morning, going back to the scene of the crash. Meanwhile, Marshall was distancing himself from the crash site, heading north in a bullock cart, when he spotted two flights of P-51s, which turned out to be from the 2nd Squadron. He got out his signal mirror. Lieutenant Joe Hagemann noticed the flashing light and dropped down to investigate. When he saw Marshall on the road, Hagemann contacted Clark and Morris and led the L-5s

Lieutenant William Nash with his crew chief, Staff Sergeant William Minarick, left, and his armorer, Sergeant Kimmey, left, standing by Nash's WINNIE THE POO. Note Nash's claims for two sampans and one basha destroyed. (Courtesy World War II Air Commandos Association)

to Marshall's location. Morris landed on the road and retrieved the Mustang pilot for the trip back to Akyab.[75]

On 29 April the 1st and 2nd Fighter Squadrons flew their last sweep of airfields in central Thailand. Operation Dracula was scheduled to begin on May 1st, and as a precaution against enemy air attack, Chase wanted one more strike against Japanese air bases in Thailand.

A mixed force of 16 aircraft from both squadrons attacked Koke Kathiem while eight Mustangs from the 1st Squadron hit Nakhon Sawan. At the same time the 459th Fighter Squadron sent 23 Lightnings to strafe Ban Takhli. Nakhon Sawan was empty, but at Koke Kathiem they found a 7th Rensei Hikotai Tony, what appeared to be a Tojo fighter from the 64th Sentai, and one other unidentified single-engine fighter. These aircraft had most likely participated in a raid into Burma earlier that morning. Twelve 64th Sentai Oscars had strafed a convoy near Toungoo before returning to their bases in Thailand. This turned out to be the 4th Hikodan's last attack of the war. Lieutenant Edwin Harkins from the 1st Squadron destroyed one of the fighters while Lieutenants John Harris and Charles LeFan claimed two others. The 459th were lucky as well, destroying one Tony and one twin-engine bomber at Ban Takhli.[76]

The 2nd Squadron flew another mission that day in preparation for Dracula, which resulted in the last combat loss for either squadron. For some time the RAF had searched without success for ten motor torpedo boats that the Japanese had captured from the Dutch in the Netherlands East Indies and had since used to patrol the Gulf of Martaban. The MTBs posed a threat to the invasion force's transports and landing craft which were gathering in the Gulf for the amphibious assault on Rangoon.

The 2nd Squadron dispatched eight aircraft on a shipping sweep along the east coast of the Gulf around the Moulmein area. Two flights stumbled on the elusive MTBs off the town of Amherst, south of Moulmein. The Mustang pilots immediately attacked, firing rockets, and then closing to strafe. The rockets and concentrated machine gun fire left two sinking and damaged six others. But return fire from the MTBs hit Lieutenant Roy Long's airplane. He crashed into the sea nearby and was killed.[77]

On the last day of April, Eastern Air Command informed the 2nd Air Commando Group that the 1st and 2nd Fighter Squadrons and the 327th Aerodrome Squadron had been awarded the Distinguished Unit Citation for the initial raid on Don Muang on 15 March. They would be the only Air Commando units so honored during the war. Late that night the 2nd Squadron received even better news. Roger Pryor, who had been listed as "missing in action," was known to be alive and a prisoner of war in Rangoon.

Lieutenant Roy Long, 2nd Fighter Squadron, who was killed on 29 April 1945, while strafing Japanese motor torpedo boats. Long is wearing a money belt around his waist filled with silver rupees which the pilots wore in case they had to bail out and seek help from local villagers. (Courtesy World War II Air Commandos Association)

The two air commando groups played a key role in the invasion of Rangoon. Its C-47 squadrons, the 319th Troop Carrier from the 1st Air Commando Group, and the 317th Squadron from the 2nd Air Commando Group had spent the last two weeks of April training with the 50th Parachute Brigade, which was to be dropped at Elephant Point on D-Day minus 1.

The 1st and 2nd Fighter Squadrons were to escort the transports to Elephant point, but on the appointed day the weather was absolutely foul, the monsoon having arrived in full force. The transports made it to the drop zone by flying right down on the deck, but of the 40 Mustangs which started out on the mission, only six managed to break through the thunderstorms and provide an escort. In any event, it wasn't needed. The Japanese Burma Area Army had abandoned Rangoon and so had the Japanese Army Air Force.

On 2 May 1945, a dozen P-51s from the 1st Fighter Squadron flew the last counter air mission, a sweep of the airfield at Moulmein. One unidentified aircraft, by this time most likely a derelict, was strafed without any satisfying results.[78]

Late on the afternoon of 1 May 1945, RAF planes flying over Rangoon had seen the words "Japs gone" and "Extract Digit" (RAF slang for "get moving") on the roof of the Rangoon jail that held Allied prisoners of war. The next morning, the British invasion force started landing at the mouth of the Rangoon River without encountering any opposition. An RAF officer landed his Mosquito fighter at Mingaladon airfield that afternoon and made his way to the jail where he found 1,400 prisoners of war. Japanese troops had withdrawn from the city three days before. Commandeering a launch, the RAF officer went downstream to bring the news to the invasion force and effect a recovery of the POWs. British and Indian troops occupied Rangoon on 3 May.[79]

The day the city fell, Colonel Art DeBolt and Lieutenant Colonel Jack Ball, Deputy Group Commander, flew to Rangoon in a B-25 to retrieve Roger Pryor, who would return to the 2nd Air Commando Group a lieutenant colonel, having been promoted along with William Buxton in early April. DeBolt and Ball landed at an airfield north of Rangoon and commandeered a British jeep to take them into the city. Arriving at Rangoon jail, they persuaded the senior allied officer in command to allow them to fly Pryor back to India. After a brief reunion with the personnel of the 2nd Squadron Pryor took time to shave off the beard he had grown in captivity then proceeded back to Combat Cargo Task Force Headquarters for debriefing before going into the hospital for medical attention. During his time in the Rangoon jail, Pryor had been beaten several times and had lost a considerable amount of weight, but was otherwise relatively healthy.

The 1st and 2nd Fighter Squadrons, together with the 5th and 6th Fighter Squadrons, were committed to the defense of Rangoon until D-Day plus 7. They alternated patrols over the Rangoon area, usually flying at full strength. Apart from the weather, which was often poor, the patrols were uneventful.

Under the agreement worked out between the American and British Chiefs of Staff earlier in the year, all American units in Burma were to withdraw after the capture of Rangoon or after 1 June, which ever came earlier. With Rangoon in British hands, the 1st and 2nd Fighter Squadrons left Cox's Bazar and returned to Kalaikunda on 11 May.

DeBolt and Levi Chase left soon after to return to the United States. Lieutenant Colonel Jack Ball took over command of the group, and a number of pilots went on leave to Kashmir.

In their last month of combat, the 1st and 2nd Fighter Squadrons had claimed 34 Japanese aircraft destroyed and one damaged. Their total claims were:

8 aerial victories.

52 destroyed on the ground.

6 probables and 32 damaged on the ground.[80]

This made the two 2nd Air Commando Group fighter outfits the highest scoring squadrons in the last phase of the Burma campaign. These numbers amounted to approximately 1/3 of the total number of aircraft the Japanese Army Air Force had available in Southeast Asia. To maintain its front line units in Burma and French Indochina, the 3rd Kokugun had drawn down virtually all its reserves, even taking fighters and crews from operational training units and denuding its strength in other parts of Southeast Asia. Had it been more effectively employed, the 4th Hikodan could have exerted a far greater impact on the campaign than it did. Unlike their Japanese counterparts, RAF and USAAF commanders in Burma employed their aircraft in a manner that first won air superiority and then supported the ground offensive.

The two fighter squadrons remained at Kalaikunda through the monsoon rains periodically flying training missions, dog-fighting with P-38s from the nearby 459th Fighter Squadron, and awaiting orders. The end of the war on 15 August 1945 canceled all plans for transferring units to China. In mid-September the 1st and 2nd Squadrons flew their Mustangs to a collection airfield and on 21 October they boarded a boat in Karachi for the long voyage home. They arrived at Camp Kilmer, New Jersey, on 11 November 1945. The following day the 2nd Air Commando Group was inactivated, passing into history.[81]

Lt. Col. Roger Pryor at Cox's Bazar after his release from Rangoon prison. (WW II Air Commandos Association)

Bob Spann with his BIG GAS BIRD near the end of the Burma Campaign. (Bob Spann)

5

LEYTE TO JAPAN THE 3RD AND 4TH FIGHTER SQUADRONS

The 3rd and 4th Fighter Reconnaissance Squadrons, the last air commando fighter units formed during World War II, were activated at Lakeland AFB in Florida on 1 May 1944 as part of the 3rd Air Commando Group. The organizational structure of the 3rd Air Commandos mirrored that of the 2nd Air Commandos with two fighter, one transport, three liaison, and four aerodrome squadrons:

3rd Fighter Reconnaissance Squadron
4th Fighter Reconnaissance Squadron
318th Troop Carrier Squadron (Commando)
157th Liaison Squadron (Commando)
159th Liaison Squadron (Commando)
160th Liaison Squadron (Commando)

The 334th, 335th, 341st, and 343rd Aerodrome Squadrons provided maintenance, engineering, and administrative support to the air units. Like the 2nd Air Commando Group, the 3rd Air Commandos drew pilots and maintenance personnel from units that were surplus to Army Air Force requirements. Personnel for the 3rd and 4th Fighter Squadrons came from the 23rd and 97th Tactical Reconnaissance Squadrons of the 76th Tactical Reconnaissance Group, which had been disbanded on 15 April 1944. The pilots from the 23rd and 97th Squadrons had been trained in tactical reconnaissance and close air support. Flying Bell P-39s, the two squadrons had spent their time providing air support for Stateside infantry divisions in training.[1]

Like the pilots from Panama who had comprised 1st and 2nd Fighter Squadrons, the pilots and squadron officers from the 23rd and 97th Tactical Reconnaissance Squadrons had hundreds of flying hours in fighters, but little combat experience. As he had done with the 2nd Air Commando Group, Colonel John Alison assembled combat veterans to form the cadre. The new CO of the 3rd Air Commando Group, Lieutenant Colonel Arvid Olson, had fought in Burma and China with the American Volunteer Group and served as Operations Officer of the 1st Air Commando Group. Lieutenant Colonel Elmer Richardson, former commander of the 75th Fighter Squadron in China and an ace with seven victories, became Group Operations Officer. Major Walker Mahurin, a 20-victory ace with the 56th Fighter Group in England, took command of the 3rd Fighter Squadron.

In addition, a number of pilots with combat experience in the North African and Italian campaigns joined the two fighter squadrons. Captain Steve Wilkerson, who had commanded the 97th Squadron, became commander of the 4th Fighter Squadron. Mediterannean vet, Captain Charles Adams (six victory P-38 ace), from the 23rd Squadron, became Operations Officer for the 3rd Fighter Squadron, while Captain Raymond Lahmeyer, from the 97th, was appointed Operations Officer for the 4th Fighter Squadron.[2]

The two squadrons began a period of intensive training in June with a mix of P-40s and P-51Bs and Cs. The first priority was to complete transition to the Mustang and to practice basic fighter skills. The pilots spent hours on ground and aerial gunnery, formation flying, bombing, practice strafing missions against local airfields, and dogfights with obliging Navy fighter planes. Major Mahurin lectured both squadrons on fighter tactics while Lieutenant Colonel Richardson shared his experiences fighting the Japanese in China. In the 3rd Fighter Squadron, Mahurin introduced a technique he had learned in England for making rapid takeoffs. He trained his pilots to take off and land in pairs, to speed assembly over the airfield and to minimize the time aircraft spent waiting on the runway. This would pay considerable dividends when the fighter squadrons operated in the Philippines.[3]

Both squadrons completed their Phase III air and ground training in August and moved on to their Phase IV training, which involved more complicated tactical problems as well as continued emphasis on gunnery and bombing. Intercepts under ground control, scrambles, escort missions, and photo reconnaissance all entered the training curriculum. The culmination of the Phase IV training was an air commando-type operation that involved all units of the group seizing and holding an airfield behind enemy lines. At the end of September, the 3rd Air Commando Group was pronounced ready to move overseas. Its destination would be the Philippines.[4]

At the Octagon Conference the Combined Chiefs of Staff had agreed to allocate the 3rd Air Commando Group to General George Kenny's Far East Air Force to support the Philippine invasion. The initial strat-

Pilots for the 3rd and 4th Fighter Squadrons were drawn from the 23rd and 97th Tactical Reconnaissance Squadrons who had trained in tactical reconnaissance and close air support. Captain Ray Lahmeyer, who became operations officer in the 4th Fighter Squadron, stands at left with several other pilots from the 97th Squadron. They flew the Bell P-39Q. (Courtesy World War II Air Commandos Association)

North American P-51Cs of the 3rd Air Commando Group flying over Lackland in a tight formation. (Courtesy World War II Air Commandos Association)

The 4th Fighter Squadron's A Flight with one of the Squadron's P-51Cs, "BUGZELEEZER II." Counterclockwise from bottom: Lt. John Tillou, Lt. Fergus Mead, Lt. John Weidman, Captain Bleecker. Lt. Casey Bower on wing. (Courtesy Rex Pealer)

egy included plans for an air task force to establish airfields behind Japanese lines in territory held by Philippine guerrilla forces, a mission ideally suited to the Air Commandos.

In early October, the 3rd Air Commando Group moved to Drew AFB, near Tampa, Florida, to prepare for overseas deployment. It would turn into quite an odyssey. The 3rd and 4th Fighter Squadrons received instructions to form a ground echelon, which would travel by sea, and an air echelon consisting of the pilots, selected engineering staff, and senior crew chiefs, which would fly out to the Pacific. No one knew that it would be two months before the two groups were reunited. Shortly after the move to Drew, Lieutenant Colonel Olson and an advance party of the group staff left the United States by air for the Pacific. On 24 October, four days after the invasion of Leyte, the entire group entrained for California. After a week of preparation, the 3rd Fighter Squadron's ground echelon joined with the rest of the group and boarded the USS *Hersey* on 7 November for the long trip to Leyte. The 4th Fighter Squadron's ground echelon left on a troop ship a week later bound for Biak, off the coast of New Guinea. After several days of riotous parties in San Francisco and a nonstop poker game at the Officers Club at Hamilton Field, the pilots and ground staff of the fighter squadrons' air echelon boarded a C-54 and flew to Nadzab, in New Guinea.[5]

The 3rd Fighter Squadron's ground echelon arrived off Leyte on 30 November 1944 and disembarked the next day to find complete confusion. As one participant put it, the 3rd Air Commando Group arrived, "unknown, uninvited, and unwanted." No one seemed to know where they were supposed to be located, or even why they were there. To make matters worse, their equipment had been put on another cargo ship and offloaded in New Guinea. Arvid Olson was not even advised that his group had arrived on Leyte. Driving to a meeting at V Fighter Command Headquarters on December 15, two weeks after the group had landed, he was astonished to pass a tented camp with a "3rd Air Commando Group" sign in front. The fighter pilots arriving at Nadzab were delighted to find brand new P-51Ds waiting for them, but puzzled to be told to sit in Nadzab and wait.[6]

Airfield construction on Leyte had fallen well behind schedule. Much of the ground had proved unsuitable for building airfields, and to compound the problem, torrential rains in the month following the invasion turned the entire beachhead into a sea of mud. Only one field, Tacloban, was operational, and this quickly became heavily congested as the Fifth Air Force's V Fighter Command put in more and more fighter squadrons to cope with an unexpectedly strong Japanese response, including the first Kamikaze attacks.

Fifth Air Force decided to continue landing ground echelons of various air units but left many of their air echelons behind. In these circumstances V Fighter Command gave priority to its veteran units, the 49th, 475th, and 348th Fighter Groups, which flew up to Tacloban as soon as space could be found for them. The 3rd Air Commando Group had to wait.[7]

To their great frustration, the pilots of the 3rd and 4th Fighter Squadrons sat in Nadzab reading about the intense aerial battles going on over the Philippines. Meanwhile pilots and crew chiefs prepared the P-51Ds for combat. They also checked out a group of replacement pilots on the Mustang and flew completely uneventful patrol missions to Rabaul and bypassed portions of New Guinea, and waited.[8]

The capture of Leyte took longer than expected. This forced General MacArthur to delay the invasion of his next target, Luzon, destined to involve more U.S. Army troops than were employed in Italy. The Sixth Army, which was responsible for the initial invasion of Luzon, had an assault force of 191,000 men in the I and XIV Corps. The Sixth Army's two corps would land at Lingayen Gulf. The XIV Corps would then drive south to seize the central plain, with its all-important airfield complex around Clark Field, and the area around Manila. The I Corps would guard XIV Corps' left flank and prevent any Japanese counterattack. Once the airfields and Manila and its harbor had been taken, MacArthur's troops would turn to the annihilation of remaining Japanese armed forces on Luzon.[9]

General Tomoyuki Yamashita, commander of the 14th Area Army on Luzon, knew that he had no hope of repelling an American invasion. Whatever chance there might have been had been lost in the cauldron of the battle for Leyte. Yamashita planned to fight a static, defensive battle of attrition to delay the conquest of Luzon, and the subsequent advance to Japan, for as long as possible. To defend Luzon, Yamashita had approximately 275,000 men but the sheer number was not a measure of their capability. His infantry units lacked strength and critical equipment. He had no hope of getting additional supplies or reinforcements, and knew that no more air support would be forthcoming. His logistical problems on Luzon were severe. Allied air attacks would soon compound these difficulties.[10]

Yamashita divided his forces into three groups. He knew he could not defend the central plain against MacArthur's legions, so he decided to concentrate his own troops in three mountain strongholds. The Kembu Group, with 30,000 men, would hold the mountains west of Clark Field. The Shimbu Group, with 80,000 men, would defend southern Luzon. The largest group, the Shobu Group, would have 152,000 men under General Yamashita's direct command and would defend the most important sector, the approaches to the Cagayan Valley, Luzon's second most important food-producing area. Nature had prepared powerful defensive positions that would take months to clear.[11]

The Fifth Air Force had responsibility for providing air support to the Sixth Army for the invasion of Luzon, but until airfields could be taken or built, U.S. Navy escort carriers provided close air support. In the week prior to the invasion and for two weeks thereafter, V Fighter Command was responsible for neutralizing Japanese air power on Luzon and in the central and southern Philippines and for isolating the battlefield by disrupting lines of communication on Luzon to delay the movement of Japanese supplies and reinforcements. Once Sixth Army engineers had completed airfields at Lingayen Gulf, V Fighter Command would begin moving fighter and attack bomber units to Luzon and assume responsibility for close air support from the Navy.[12]

Conditions on Leyte were basic. Staff Sergeant Ray Van Order, a 4th Squadron crew chief, stands in front of his tent at Tanauan. (Courtesy Ray Van Order)

Amidst this grand plan however, 3rd Air Commando Group was without a mission. The strategy for the recapture of the Philippines no longer called for an air task force to support a major operation behind enemy lines, nor did the plans for the invasion of Luzon offer any opportunity for air commando-type operations. Colonel Olson, Lieutenant Colonel Richardson, and the squadron commanders realized that the only alternative was to employ the Group's component squadrons in their regular roles, taking on whatever tasks or assignments came their way.

In December 1944, the 3rd Air Commando Group was assigned to the 86th Fighter Wing, V Fighter Command. Toward the end of the month the 3rd and 4th Fighter Squadrons received word that they would finally be moving up to Leyte. Army engineers had built a second airfield at Tanuan, south of Tacloban, and by early January had completed a 6,000 foot steel mat and asphalt strip. This would be home, temporarily, for the Air Commando fighter squadrons. Since the 3rd Fighter Squadron's ground echelon was already on Leyte, the 3rd Squadron moved first. The 4th Fighter Squadron's ground echelon set off from New Guinea on 30 December, arriving at Tacloban on 5 January and moving to Tanuan to prepare for the Squadron's air echelon.[13]

The 3rd Squadron flew to Leyte via Biak and Morotai with a B-25 doing the navigation, arriving on 7 January 1945, two weeks after Leyte had been secured and two days before the invasion of Luzon. They cre-

On arrival in the Philippines the 3rd and 4th Fighter Squadrons applied standard theater markings, wide black and white bands around the wings and rear fuselage. The tail was painted blue with the aircraft letter in yellow. The 3rd Fighter Squadron's aircraft carried a blue propeller spinner while the 4th Squadron used red. When the squadrons had more than 26 aircraft assigned, they would use Greek letters for their additional aircraft, as shown here on Lt. Jacques Young's Mustang with the Greek letter "omega." (Courtesy Jacques Young)

ated quite a stir on landing. Sixteen P-51s arrived over Tanuan in tight formation, then broke into flights and landed in pairs as Major Mahurin had trained them, much to the consternation of the staff in the control tower, who had never seen aircraft landing in pairs. The entire squadron was on the ground in less than three minutes.

When the 3rd and 4th Squadrons began flying combat missions from Tanuan, they took off in pairs. Later they would depart in flights of four. The savings in time on heavily congested airfields was considerable and meant fewer delays in rendezvous and specified "Time Over Target." These Air Commando tactical approach and departure initiatives soon became standard operating procedure for other AAF units.[14]

The combat debut of the Air Commandos, ended in tragedy. On the day after their arrival at Tanuan, two eight-plane flights went to Mindanao in the morning, one to bomb and strafe the airfield at Surigao and one to do the same at the airfield at Del Monte. The morning mission was uneventful, and two flights returned to the same targets again in the afternoon. They found an unserviceable Oscar fighter which was strafed and set on fire. Off the coast of Surigao, 1st Lieutenant Earl Thibideaux and 2nd Lieutenant William Tudor saw several barges and went down to strafe. Coming off their runs they collided and were killed instantly.[15]

Three days later, the Squadron caught two Zeke 32s on the ground at Bulan airfield on the south eastern tip of Luzon and set them on fire. Four Mustangs on a sweep of the southern Luzon peninsula on 13 January discovered a choice target of opportunity, a Japanese truck convoy stopped at a ferry crossing. They made several passes, destroying seven trucks, including three filled with ammunition. These blew up with such force that they destroyed the ferry pier and a ferry barge alongside. The Mustangs then continued on down the road leading out of the town and found thirteen more trucks camouflaged to resemble thatched huts. These were destroyed as well. The flight made a quick sweep of Bulan airfield on the way back to Leyte, finding a Zeke in a revetment which was left in flames.[16]

As the Japanese Army Air Force and the Imperial Navy Air Force had effectively abandoned the defense of Luzon, the opportunities for air combat were few, but on 14 January the 3rd Squadron got lucky. That morning Bud Mahurin led ten Mustangs to cover a B-25 strike on the town of Appari on the northern coast of Luzon. After Mitchells had hit, the P-51s strafed the nearby airfield, destroying a Tony, a Nick, a Sally, and one other unidentified airplane.

Returning south down the Cagayan Valley at around 10,000 feet in two flights of four with one element as top cover, the 3rd Squadron spotted a Sally bomber passing north at 5,000 feet at their three o'clock position. Flying nearby was a reconnaissance Dinah. Captain Charles Adams, Squadron Operations Officer, dropped down with his wingman and came up directly behind the Sally. Closing to short range, Adams opened fire and the bomber crashed into the mountains.

When the pilot of the Dinah saw the attack on the Sally, he did a 180-degree turn and set off at full throttle. Major Mahurin dropped his wing tanks and gave chase. After ten minutes he caught up with the speedy recon aircraft and gave it several short bursts, causing it to roll on its back and crash.[17]

The most successful of these airfield missions occurred on 16 January when four Mustangs went out on a sweep of the Clark Field complex. At Angeles airfield, they found four Tojos sitting on the runway with engines running, waiting to take off. 1st Lieutenant Glenn Larimore dropped a 500 lb. bomb, which exploded on one of the airplanes and set fire to the other three.

The P-51s went on to Clark, where they found more Japanese fighters on the ground. In their attacks they claimed another five aircraft destroyed and three damaged. The next day four Mustangs caught two Oscars on the ground at Legazpi airfield in southern Luzon and spotted another on take-off. They strafed the two on the ground, setting one on fire and damaging the other, then set off after the Oscar that had gotten airborne. They were closing in when the lucky Japanese pilot lost himself in a rain shower.[18]

Regular sweeps of the road and rail network on Southern Luzon and on other islands brought back a growing tally of trucks, cars, and trains destroyed or damaged. In the course of one day's missions over Luzon, the 3rd Squadron destroyed two locomotives and damaged another; shot up 22 boxcars, destroyed eleven trucks, damaging seven more; and shot up a pair of tractors, three staff cars, assorted warehouses, and a saw mill. These missions were not without cost.

On 16 January, Captain Charles Adams was hit by anti-aircraft fire while strafing targets on Negros Island. Fortunately, he made it out to sea where he parachuted. Friendly Filipinos rescued him, and the next morning a Catalina returned him to Leyte. On the 20th, while strafing a truck on Mindanao, 2nd Lieutenant William Isgrigg crashed into a tree and was killed.[19]

The 4th Fighter Squadron arrived at Tanauan on 16 January 1945, "several weeks after the WACS had been well-established on the island," as one squadron member put it. The next day they put up seven flights on sweeps over Cebu and southern Luzon.

Late in the afternoon on the 18th, Captain Ray Lahmeyer led a flight of four Mustangs on a sweep of Del Monte airfield on Mindanao. V Fighter Command intelligence suspected that the Japanese were using Del Monte to stage night raids on Leyte and ordered the 4th Squadron to reconnoiter before dusk.

As Lahmeyer approached Del Monte, he saw a flickering light on the field. At first he thought it was an airplane, but then discerned large puddles and assumed the light was simply a reflection of the sun on the water. As he got closer he suddenly realized that the flickering light was spinning propellers on a twin-engine aircraft.

Lahmeyer quickly turned and dove toward the airstrip. As he opened fire he noticed a group of Japanese running away from the bomber. His long burst tore into the Mitsubishi G4M Betty and it exploded. The rest of the flight came down with him and strafed the operations building and barracks around the field.[20]

The 3rd and 4th Fighter Squadrons did not tarry long on Leyte, as they were needed on Luzon. Two days after the initial landing at Lingayen Gulf, Army engineers began improving a Japanese landing ground near the invasion beaches. The Fifth Air Force assigned responsibility for all air power based in the Lingayen area, which

On January 14, 1945, Major Walker Mahurin destroyed a Dinah over Luzon to add a Japanese aircraft to his 21 victories scored in Europe. The photo is of marginal quality but the subject is rare. (Via the author)

The 4th Fighter Squadron chose a rearing Mustang as its squadron insignia and painted it beneath the cockpit on the Squadron's Mustangs in yellow and black. Here Lt. John Weidman stands next to his aircraft on Luzon. (Courtesy Rex Pealer)

included Army Air Force fighter and attack groups and two Marine air groups, to the 308th Bombardment Wing. The 308th had the task of providing air support to the Sixth Army, maintaining air superiority over Luzon, and coordinating attacks on Japanese forces on Formosa.

The close air support role began on 17 January, the day after its first fighter group arrived at the Lingayen strip, and engineers immediately began building a second airstrip at Mangaldan, a small village about eight miles east of Lingayen, to hold additional fighter, attack, and medium bomber squadrons. Within little more than a month, 308th Bombardment Wing's component units, the 110th Tactical Reconnaissance Squadron, the 547th Night Fighter Squadron, the 35th, 49th, and 475th Fighter Groups, the 38th and 312th Bomb Groups, the 24th and 32nd Marine Air Groups, and the 3rd Air Commandos, were based at Lingayen and Mangaldan airfields. At Mangaldan the engineers leveled a large area of rice paddies creating a landing strip that was several thousand feet long and several hundred feet wide. The hot sun soon baked the dirt as hard as concrete.

On 20 January, C-47s from the 318th Troop Carrier squadron flew an advance team of engineering and maintenance crews from the 334th and 335th Aerodrome Squadrons to Mangaldan to prepare for the arrival of the Air Commando Mustangs.[21]

The 3rd and 4th Fighter Squadrons flew their last mission from Leyte on 23 January, sending 32 aircraft to bomb General Yamashita's headquarters around Baguio in Luzon. Each P-51, carrying the hefty load of a 1,000 lb. bomb under each wing, hit barracks and administration buildings at Baguio, leaving a column of smoke that rose to 8,000 feet.

The 3rd Fighter Squadron's pilots flew back to Tanauan, refueled, and then flew up to their new base at Mangaldan where they watched in fascination as the local Filipinos constructed their new quarters out of bamboo, using the simplest of tools. It took the Filipino workers only a few hours to build a bamboo platform to support the standard four-man tent, with a raised floor and sidewalls of bamboo and even bamboo furniture. An operations office, armament, and engineering offices for each squadron were built the same way, using the same material. The 4th Fighter Squadron arrived at Mangaldan three days later.[22]

By this time Sixth Army troops had been advancing across the plain of Luzon for two weeks against little opposition. While I Corps progressed on the left flank, XIV Corps pushed rapidly south toward Clark Field and Manila. By 23 January, its advance units were nearing the Clark Field area but had begun to encounter stiff resistance from elements of the Kimbu Group holding the Zambales Mountains to the west. XIV Corps had to eliminate the Kimbu Group's positions to secure the Corps' right flank for the advance to Manila. After three weeks of hard fighting, advance units entered the outskirts of Manila on 3 February, but Manila would not be completely retaken until 3 March, after a horrendous house-to-house battle that destroyed much of the old city.[23]

Both I Corps and XIV Corps were dependent on air support to soften up Japanese resistance ahead of the advance. As it was advancing at a faster pace than I Corps, XIV Corps was particularly dependent on air support to guard its left flank against surprise attack.[24]

On 29 January, while the 3rd Squadron attacked enemy gun emplacements at Plaridel south of Clark Field, 16 Mustangs from the 4th Fighter Squadron bombed suspected Japanese positions in three small towns in Bulacan Province northeast of Manila, along the route of XIV Corps' advance. Philippine guerrillas reported that the strikes killed over 500 Japanese troops and destroyed several ammunition dumps. So effective were these attacks that General Krueger sent the 4th Squadron a personal letter of commendation.[25]

Luzon, Philippine Islands

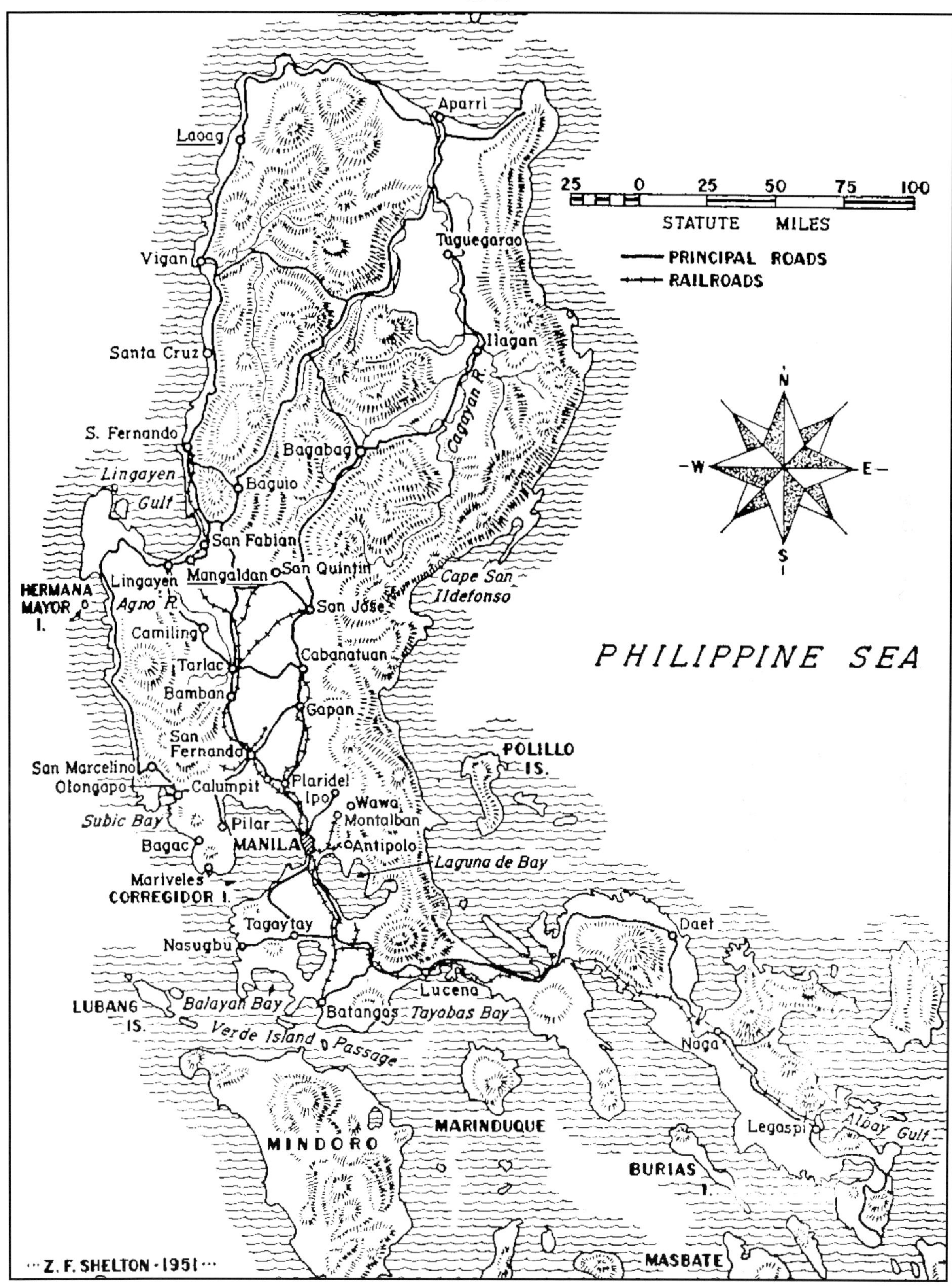

Source: *The Army Air Forces in World War II, Volume V*

Going native in relative luxury. (Above) Officer's quarters at Mangaldan, Luzon. Using only bamboo, Filipino laborers built these huts in just a few hours. (Courtesy Rex Pealer)

(Below) A few decorative touches and some bamboo furniture made the quarters quite livable. (L-R) Lt. Robert Ankrom, Lt. Robert Chappel, Lt. Mosher, Lt.William Belton. (Courtesy Rex Pealer)

The real work began as American troops began probing into the hills and valleys of the Caraballo Mountains toward the Shobu Group's positions. General Yamashita's plan of defense was to hold the approaches to Cagayan Valley. He withdrew his forces into a defensive triangle, with one base at Baguio and the other at Bambang 35 miles due east. The apex of the triangle was the town of Bontoc, 50 miles to the north.[26]

The mountains were ideal for defense. Rising to heights of between 6,000 and 8,000 feet, both the Cordillera Central and the Caraballos presented a rugged series of densely covered ridge lines, one after the other. The few narrow roads and trails snaked through the mountains, providing no avenues for an attack on a broad front and giving even a small defending force innumerable opportunities to slow an advance. General Yamashita's troops had been building mutual support defensive positions in the mountains since December, bringing in large numbers of artillery pieces and placing them in positions to cover all possible approaches and building a network of caves to protect supplies and men. The battle against the Shobu Group became, in the words of the U.S. Army's official history of the Luzon campaign, "an arduous, time-consuming, and costly process of clearing the adjacent terrain inch by inch."[27]

This turned the fighting along the Villa Verde Trail and up through the Balete Pass into "a knock-down, drag-out slugfest that combined mountain and jungle warfare at its worst."[28]

The only advantages American forces had over the Japanese were more artillery and a prodigious amount of close air support. In the confined terrain, American troops were reduced to making a continual series of frontal assaults against Japanese positions. Patrols would probe forward to locate Japanese strongholds, then air strikes and artillery would be called in to soften up the enemy and support the attack.[29]

When one position was taken, there was another beyond. This went on, day after day, for three-and-a-half months. As an example of how difficult and time-consuming the fighting was, it took the 25th Infantry Division from the third week of February to the middle of May to battle its way through the Balete Pass, a distance of 25 miles. Every bomb or strafing pass that eliminated a machine gun position or destroyed a gun emplacement, eased the path of the infantry as they struggled forward over the rugged hills.[30]

Fifth Air Force had achieved complete air superiority over Luzon, which meant that the fighters could devote the major part of their effort to close air support. Neither the fighters nor the bombers ever had to worry about enemy interception.

Practice made perfect, and within a few months the fighter squadrons were routinely getting 80% to 90% of their bombs directly on the target. The techniques of forward air control improved as well. Most of the fighter and bomber groups had a ground liaison officer from Sixth Army who would provide a daily briefing on the ground situation and the day's target. At the front, an Air Force or Marine forward air observer team, usually a few men in a jeep in radio contact with the fighters overhead, controlled all air strikes. The forward-most troops would use colored panels to mark their own positions for the planes above. The air observer team would talk the fighters down on to the target, which mortars or artillery would mark with phosphorus or other colored smoke, and then direct the fighters on repeated strafing passes until ammunition was expended. After the Air Commando liaison squadrons arrived at Mangaldan air strip, L-5s began to carry forward air controllers who would direct air strikes from the rear seat, with the L-5 often swooping low to drop flares or smoke grenades on targets.[31]

The 3rd and 4th Squadrons developed their own procedures for bombing in the close support role. Close support missions usually involved two or four flights of Mustangs. A typical day would see two missions in the morning and two in the afternoon. The usual load was a pair of 500 lb. General Purpose bombs, but often half the flights would carry 500-pounders while the other half carried napalm tanks. Fragmentation and incendiary bombs would also be utilized if better suited to situation.

The front lines were a short flight from Mangaldan strip, rarely more than 30 minutes away. Once near the target area, P-51s would orbit awaiting target assignment. Jacques Young, a pilot with the 4th Squadron remembered the frequently heavy traffic.

> "Sometimes there were airplanes all over the place and we had to wait our turn. We might have been scheduled [for a set time], but still there were so many airplanes in there ahead of us, squadron after squadron, so we would just get in line and wait our turn. Of course, we could watch what was going on, and you could see the target. They'd call us in, and it was real quick. All we did was drop our stuff and get out of there. And then we were real close. From the Lingayen Gulf air strip [Mangaldan] right up to the Villa Verde Trail wasn't too long. We had lots of short missions."[32]

Close support for I Corps became a primary mission for the 3rd and 4th Fighter Squadrons. Here pilots get a briefing from the ground liaison officer prior to a mission. (Courtesy Rex Pealer)

Low-level bombing with precision in the highlands of Northern Luzon required great skill, where deep river valleys were surrounded by mountains up to 8,000 feet. In this picture, typical of the terrain where the 3rd Air Commandos sortied, a pair of Japanese positions are under attack by Fifth AF P-38 Lightnings (unit unknown). The forested hilltop in the lower left is burning from a napalm hit. Smoke rises from a strike on another target, center, with a perfect smoke ring as a cap. Note the absence of any roads. The step-like features are native rice terraces that provided no cover for the Japanese. (AAF via National Archives)

When the forward air controller summoned the air commando squadrons, they would go in by flights. The flight leader would identify the target and signal the flight to go into a close echelon to the right. The flight leader would then approach the target at about 5,000 feet altitude, slow his plane down until he was just past the target, then do a "Split-S" and pull down onto the target. When the aiming point was just about to disappear under the nose he would release ordnance at around 3,000 feet and pull away, other members of his flight following the same procedure.

> As Jacques Young recalled, "We'd fly over the target, level, and the target would go under the wing. We'd be slowing down, and slowing down, pull up, and just do a wing over. Slightly beyond the target, pull over, and then come straight down. Line the target up on the seam. We had a gun sight, but just line up on the seam of the cowling was the best we did. We'd drop on straight down and pull out, and either hit the deck or pop up again and come back and strafe, depending on the opposition. Sometimes, if there was any gunfire, which I didn't see much of, I'd stamp the rudder a little bit, left, right. You'd skid. Don't keep the ball in the center was my tactic. They'd shoot to the right, and I'm going to the left."[33]

During February the two squadrons flew 523 bombing and strafing sorties, mostly in support of I Corps, and dropped 226 tons of bombs and napalm. March proved to be an even busier month.[34]

Progress along Route 5 and the Villa Verde Trail against the well-entrenched Japanese proved to be painfully slow. The 3rd and 4th Fighter Squadrons were repeatedly called on to add their weight to the attack, often flying four full squadron missions a day on close air support missions or on strikes against Japanese supply points behind the lines. The close air support missions were often frustrating for the pilots, as only rarely could they see any results of their attacks. One hill looked more or less like every other one, and one column of smoke pretty much looked like another. Satisfaction came from congratulatory messages from forward air controllers attesting to excellent results.

A description of just a few of the missions flown during March gives a flavor of this operation. The month began with a strike on the Villa Verde Trail. The air observer team directed 16 Mustangs from the 3rd Squadron onto Japanese troop concentrations on a hill along the trail. The bombing started two large fires in the area, probably an indication of a supply dump. Subsequent strafing passes started a grass fire that covered the entire area. The smoke was visible from Mangaldan strip.

A few days later, the 3rd Squadron went after gun emplacements and targets of opportunity around the town of Santa Fe. They bombed two ammunition dumps and then strafed a motor convoy hidden under some trees, destroying 15 trucks. On 10 March, sixteen 3rd Squadron Mustangs attacked a small Japanese-held village with 500 lb. bombs, setting off numerous explosions and sending up a huge column of heavy black smoke. The pilots came back to strafe the town, setting off more fires and explosions as more supplies and ammo went up in flames.

Major Steve Wilkerson, 4th Fighter Squadron commander, with his crew chief, Staff Sergeant Golini with their P-51D-20, THE BISCUIT HEAD, at Mangaldan, February 1945. (Courtesy Rex Pealer)

Colonel Arvid Olson's Mustang, THE POKER PLAYER'S FRIEND. (Courtesy World War II Air Commandos Association)

Ten days later the 4th Squadron attacked a bridge and enemy gun emplacements nearby. Near misses damaged but did not destroy the bridge, but strafing passes destroyed three gun emplacements. One day toward the end of the month the two squadrons flew a combined total of 50 sorties, during which they dropped 21 tons of bombs and expended 20,900 rounds of .50-caliber ammunition on Japanese troop concentrations, buildings, and gun emplacements.[35]

During the course of these March missions the Air Commandos added a new innovation to the practice of close air support. The 32nd Division was having a particularly difficult time seizing one ridge line along the Villa Verde Trail. The Japanese had dug in artillery along the steep slope of the reverse side of the ridge, preventing an effective counter-barrage that in turn frustrated an infantry assault. Major General William Gill, the division commander, called Colonel Arvid Olson to see if the Air Commandos could find a way to hit the Japanese battery. Olson had Major Walker Mahurin and several flight commanders from the two fighter squadrons go to the front lines to observe the topography themselves. After studying the situation they convinced the infantry commander that the Japanese positions could be bombed without undue risk to his troops.

Returning to Mangaldan, Mahurin and the other flight commanders carefully briefed their squadron mates and then led a successful attack on the Japanese artillery. American infantry took the ridge with minimal casualties.

Major General Gill sent a personal letter of thanks to Colonel Olson in which he praised the work of the 3rd and 4th Fighter Squadrons, saying:

> "The bombings have been precise and accurate; their strafing runs have been to my mind perfection itself. It is my belief that your unit is the first one in this theater from which pilots of the supporting air force have voluntarily visited the forward ground units to view the terrain and study the tactical situation prior to their employment. Subsequent close support missions have conclusively demonstrated the value of such visits. I believe that you are the pioneers in the development of a closer understanding between the air arm and the ground infantry and that your example will soon be followed by other Air Corps commands."

The results of this approach were so successful that the two fighter squadrons adopted it as standard practice. During the rest of the campaign on Luzon, selected pilots frequently visited the front lines to get a better appreciation of their targets.[36]

The 3rd and 4th Squadrons flew 1,238 bombing and strafing sorties during March and dropped 540 tons of bombs, almost double the results achieved in February. Accuracy improved too, with nearly 80% of all bombs on target.[37]

Remarkably, given the number of missions flown on close air support during the month, only two planes were lost. While well-supplied with artillery, the Japanese did not have much in the way of anti-aircraft cannons. Few missions over Luzon encountered visible ground fire, but that did not mean it was not present as Japanese infantry did not use tracers. On 22 February, 2nd Lieutenant Thomas Thibodeaux crashed while making a strafing pass, possibly the victim of ground fire, which caught Captain Ray Lahmeyer, 4th Fighter Squadron Operations Officer, the following month.

On 17 March, Lahmeyer was leading a flight of Mustangs to bomb Japanese artillery positions near Balete Pass. The weather that day was cloudy, and the flights had to begin their bombing run at a lower altitude, which meant that they would pull out at a lower level as well. Lahmeyer ran into trouble after his bomb run.

> "As I pulled off the target I felt a bump, just like you were running through some prop wash, along with that a little popping noise. I thought there was something wrong with my engine, but it worked perfectly, and I still heard the popping noise. Pretty soon I looked out at my left wing, and every time I'd get a pop, a puff of smoke would come over the leading edge of the wing. So I kept watching and gaining altitude, and heading back to where I thought our friendly lines were.
>
> "When I got to 7,000 feet I looked out, and the wing just sort of opened up and flames started coming out. So I decided this was where we part company. I unhooked everything and released the canopy. I grabbed the rip cord and just rolled her upside down, and let go. As I saw the tail section go by I pulled that ripcord. You get quite a jolt at 150 miles an hour. But that felt good. The airplane just went over like that and blew up. Then it gets very quiet.
>
> "You're hanging up there and you think you're never going to get down. I was looking around, and here was a truck coming up my way, and I didn't know whose it was. So I hit in an open field, and you're supposed to be able to change your direction by managing those cords so you can land forward. Well, that didn't work. I landed going backwards. I hit pretty hard. I did a somersault, got back on my feet, spilled the air out of the chute, got out of my harness, and got my trusty .45. I ran to the top of a hill and took a look and there was a personnel carrier from the American troops. They picked me up. They had a cold beer down there and that tasted very good."

A light plane returned Lahmeyer to Mangaldan strip an hour after he had been shot down.[38]

During the first half of April, I Corps' divisions continued to make slow forward progress, hampered by heavy rains and tenacious Japanese resistance. Advances were measured in hundreds of yards. The 3rd and 4th Squadrons spent a good deal of time over the Villa Verde Trail area, sending two or more flights of Mustangs out in relays throughout the day to bomb and strafe Japanese troops and gun emplacements. Most often the flights carried combinations of 500 lb. bombs and 75-gallon tanks of napalm, but the squadrons tried other methods as well in an effort to make their strikes more effective. The ground troops found napalm to be effective against the many caves the Japanese had dug. Napalm had the added benefit of burning away the brush that hid Japanese positions.

Occasionally the Air Commandos would come in low and drop their underwing tanks, then return and strafe to start gasoline fires. The 4th Squadron's armament officer, Lieutenant Fredrick Mulligan, was particularly inventive. Mulligan designed special fittings and attachments for the Mustangs to carry clusters of five 100 lb. incendiary bombs or three 265 lb. fragmentation bombs under each wing. The variety of weapons employed, and the sheer volume of air strikes had a cumulative impact. Japanese forces defending the Baguio-Balete Pass area found it increasingly difficult to sustain their troops. The constant attrition from relentless ground attacks, artillery, and air strikes, and attacks on a shrinking transportation network was slowly wearing down General Yamashita's forces, but there was another month of hard fight ahead.

Captain Ray Lahmeyer, left, and Major Steve Wilkerson, right, improve the walk outside their quarters wearing casual apparel. Lahmeyer was forced to parachute over Luzon. (Courtesy Ray Lahmeyer)

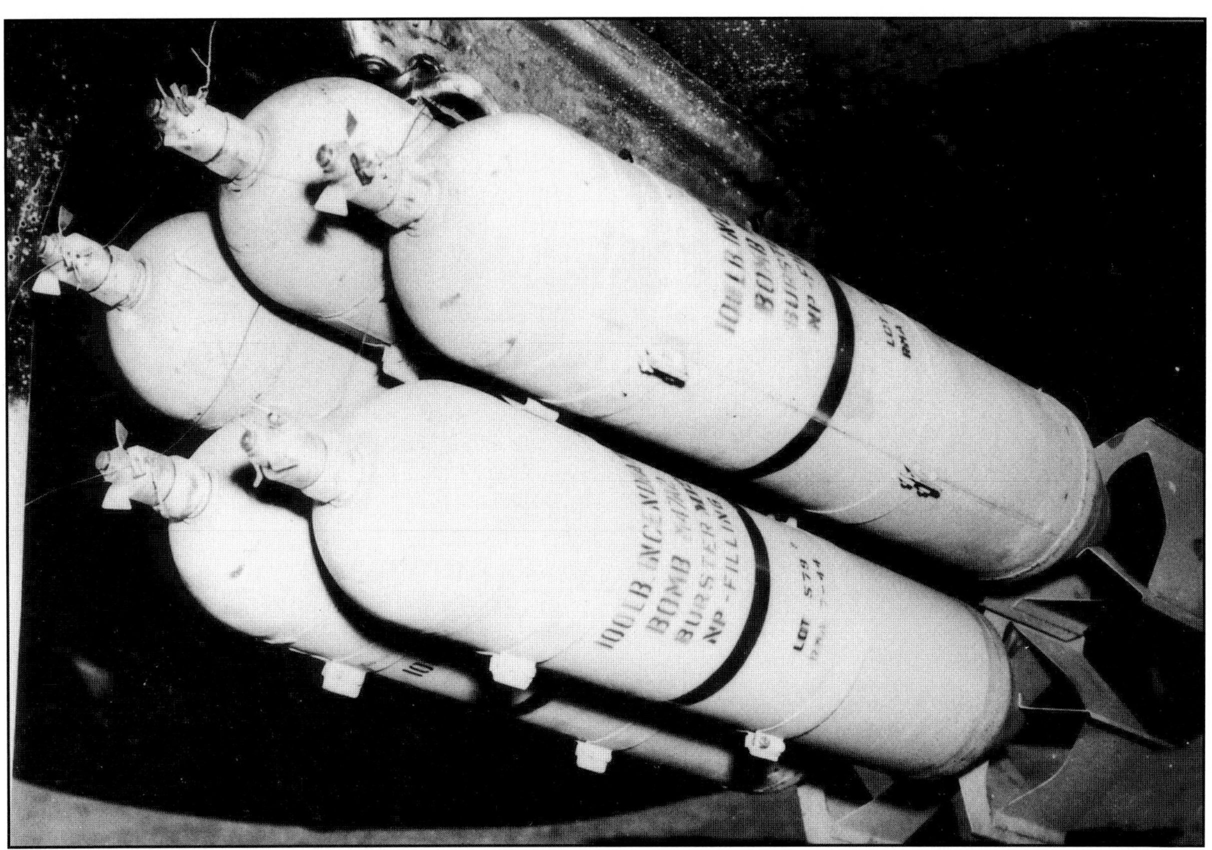

The Air Commando fighter squadrons employed a variety of weapons in addition to the standard 500 lb. bombs, including 100 lb. incendiary bombs in clusters shown above.

A 75-gal. napalm fire bomb, used to clear the jungle covering Japanese positions is shown below. (Courtesy Ray Lahmeyer)

While supporting the ground campaign on Luzon demanded a greater proportion of the Air Commando effort, Formosa claimed a far greater number of casualties. The air campaign against the Japanese bastion of Formosa would last five months, from the end of January until the middle of June. During that operation Fifth Air Force employed heavy and medium bombers, attack aircraft, and fighters to establish and maintain air superiority, attacking airfields, port facilities, factories, and transportation. Bomber escorts and fighter sweeps to Formosa alternated with close support for Luzon to become part of the regular pattern of missions for pilots of the 3rd and 4th Fighter Squadrons.

The island of Formosa (now Taiwan) had been a Japanese colony since 1895. By the outbreak of World War II, it was a key link in Japan's military program. It supported and guarded the lines of communication between Japan and South East Asia, protecting the sea lanes and providing port facilities for the ships and tankers carrying raw materials to Japan. As a manufacturing base, Formosa was a source of alcohol for aviation gasoline and produced 10% of Japan's aluminum as well as supplying iron, copper, and other needed raw materials. The island also served as an unsinkable aircraft carrier. The Imperial Japanese Navy Air Force and the Japanese Army Air Force maintained six major air depots on Formosa, 17 airfields, and a further 28 landing grounds. In January 1945, following withdrawal from the Philippines, army and navy air units on Formosa had over 600 aircraft available.[39]

Formosa had long been a candidate for invasion among American military planners, who saw it as a stepping stone to the China coast, but it was generally acknowledged that conquering the island would be a costly venture. When the US Chiefs of Staff abandoned the idea of seizing territory on the coast of China, the objective of taking Formosa immediately became mute. The Philippines were more logical as a stepping stone for the advance and fulfilled an American obligation to the Filipinos. Nevertheless, Formosa had to be isolated and neutralized both to protect American forces fighting on Luzon and soon on Okinawa, and as part of the campaign to blockade Japan and cut off the supply of raw materials. This became the primary assignment of the Fifth Air Force.[40]

Missions to Formosa had a completely different character than those flown over the Philippines. Formosa lay some 250 miles northeast of Luzon, so any mission to the island involved an over-water flight of some 500 miles. The U.S. Navy stationed submarines and PBYs off the Formosan coast for aviators who were forced to bail out. If a pilot could make it to these air/sea rescue units, well and good, but to get shot down over the island meant certain capture and likely harsh

The 4th Fighter Squadron's GYPSY was a popular background for photos. L-R: **Lt. Robert Milliken, Lt. Herbert (Hap) Arnold, Lt. Moosenick, Lt. Fergus Mead, Captain John Bleecker (KIA), and Lt. John Tillou (KIA), with Lt. John Weidman on the wing. (Courtesy Rex Pealer)**

treatment from a hostile population, unlike the Philippines where the locals invariably aided downed pilots to reach safety. And the flak over Formosa was, as the pilots put it, "the Real McCoy." Its anti-aircraft defenses were far more developed and more lethal than anything in the Philippines, and worse than anything the Fifth Air Force had previously encountered. Major Mahurin thought the flak over Formosa was more intense and accurate than what he had encountered over Germany. The island seemed littered with high caliber rapid-firing 25mm and 40mm cannons. Air Commando pilots soon began referring to Formosa as the "Isle of Hate."[41]

The 3rd and 4th Fighter Squadrons began these operations in early February and, despite poor weather, flew 11 missions to the island during the month. Anti-aircraft fire became more intense and more accurate with each succeeding mission.

The first was on 7 February 1945, when the 3rd and 4th Squadrons escorted B-25s from the 38th Bomb Group on a shipping strike to Takao on Formosa's southwest coast (present day Kao-hsiung). The fighters went down to strafe and destroyed two trucks and a few staff cars. On the return, 1st Lieutenant Louis Curdes, a flight leader in the 4th Squadron, found a Dinah flying off the southern tip of Formosa and downed the reconnaissance aircraft. (This was another success for Curdes, an eight-victory ace in a previous combat tour with the 82nd Fighter Group in the Mediterranean.)

However, Formosan flak claimed its first victims. While attacking the airfield at Takao, two pilots from the 3rd Squadron, 2nd Lieutenants Marvin Mentor and Clifton Huntington, took hits. A 40mm shell burst directly underneath Huntington's airplane, blowing gaping holes in the fuselage and knocking out the landing gear. Mentor's P-51 was hit in the wing and the engine. Both pilots headed out to the coast, where Mentor bailed out. He was last seen getting into his dingy but was never found. Huntington managed to get his damaged plane back to Mangaldan.[42]

The next day, it was the 3rd Squadron's turn to intercept a Japanese aircraft. The mission was again an escort for B-25s, but bad weather over Formosa forced the bombers to turn back. On the return flight, Lieutenant Glenn Larimore spotted a Sally bomber headed toward Luzon and promptly shot it down.

10 February proved to be an unusual day in the annals of AAF history. That morning Curdes was scheduled to lead a flight up to Formosa to search for three missing air crews from a mission the previous day. They flew at low level to the west coast of Formosa and searched without success, but found a Dinah flying off Takao. 2nd Lieutenant Robert Scalley, leading the second element, was in the best position to attack and went after the Dinah, setting the right engine on fire on his first pass. On his second pass Scalley set the left engine ablaze, and by the third pass the Dinah, engulfed in fire, crashed into the sea.

Following this combat, Curdes decided to split his flight to cover a greater area. He ordered Scalley and his wingman, 2nd Lieutenant Robert LaCroix, to search in a different direction and then check the Japanese airfield on Bataan Island, which lay between Luzon and Formosa. By incredible good fortune, the two encountered another Dinah en route to Bataan Island. LaCroix closed to silence the rear gunner, then put a long burst into an engine and wing, causing a fire and subsequent crash into the ocean. Coming over Bataan Island the two pilots saw three or four Japanese airplanes on the small air strip on the island. Despite the presence of several anti-aircraft guns they went down to strafe, destroying two Tony fighters in three passes.[43]

> Coming off his third pass, LaCroix was hit. "When climbing out from the field I suddenly heard a series of riveting gun noises under the plane, my leg was knocked off the rudder pedal, and the cockpit was filled with hot coolant and smoke. In view of the annoyance we had been to the Japs, it didn't seem likely they would greet me with love, so I stuck with the plane long enough to get offshore, though not far enough as I soon discovered. Pulling up to about a thousand feet I jettisoned the canopy and rolled the plane over to drop out. Unfortunately, I had not put enough trim-tab in and the plane fell with me, locking me on the armor plate, half in and half out. Reaching up with my foot I kicked the stick, tore loose, and fell. Sudden silence. I pulled the ripcord. No reaction, so I threw it away figuring I was done and a telegram was going to my family. The parachute suddenly opened, but I was upside down, my shoulder harness having caught in the parachute shroud. I tore it loose, swung up-right, and hit the water."[44]

LaCroix shed his chute, inflated his dingy, climbed aboard, and soon found that the Japanese on the island were shooting at him. Scalley had called Curdes as soon as he saw LaCroix get hit, and Curdes and his wingman joined Scalley, who was circling over LaCroix's dingy.

Leaving Scalley to orbit LaCroix, Curdes and his wingman turned toward Bataan attempting to silence the Japanese guns. They made repeated strafing passes over the island, and it was apparently this activity that attracted an AAF Douglas C-47 transport.

The pilot of the C-47, who was lost, had seen the Mustangs making low passes near an air strip and simply assumed they were buzzing an American field. As the C-47 began a landing approach to the Japanese

Lt. Louis Curdes in his Mustang showing one Japanese flag for his Dinah shot down on 7 February, and the C-47 shot down on the 10th, along with his seven German and one Italian victories from combat in the Mediterranean. (AAF via National Archives)

held island, Curdes carefully shot out one engine, forcing the transport to ditch. By this time it was well into the afternoon, and there could be no rescue that day.

Curdes and Scalley returned to Mangaldan. LaCroix spent an anxious night as a storm came up and brought high waves which he feared would drive him back to the island. The next day he got another fright when he thought he saw Japanese boats approaching his dingy, but it turned out to be the dinghies from the C-47. That afternoon a Navy PBY landed in the still rough seas, rescuing LaCroix and the C-47 occupants, 13 people in all. Curdes was decorated for his nimble thinking and superb marksmanship.

Scalley's and LaCroix's Dinahs would be the last Japanese aircraft the two fighter squadrons would encounter in the air for nearly two months. Ironically, that same day, the 35th Fighter Group shot down ten Japanese aircraft in a running battle over Formosa.[45]

While the bombers went after the major airfields and ports on Formosa, Fifth Air Force sent the fighters after everything, particularly Formosa's road and rail network. The 4th Squadron went on a sweep of southern Formosa on 12 February and came back with a bag of ten trucks and three locomotives destroyed. One pilot, 2nd Lieutenant Robert Ankrom, developed a coolant leak, probably from ground fire, and had to bail out ten miles from Mangaldan.

On the 16th the 3rd Squadron flew to Formosa, destroying three trucks, three locomotives, and a bus. Again one aircraft was hit by anti-aircraft fire.

Two days later, while the 3rd Squadron bombed marshaling yards at Takao, the 4th Squadron flew up the east coast of Formosa and then followed the east coast rail line down to Taito (present day T'ai-tung). Along the rail line they destroyed a railroad station, nine locomotives, four trucks, a railroad crane, and a water tower, and badly damaged 11 locomotives and 42 boxcars without loss.[46]

On the return flight 2nd Lieutenant Elder Bower spotted a cave in a cliff on the Luzon coast and conducted a strafing run. Misjudging his pass, he ended up plowing through a line of trees just above the cliff. With his Mustang leaking coolant he headed west toward the coast to get away from the Japanese, but his engine soon seized and he bellied into a paddy field, narrowly missing two water buffalo. He made contact with Filipinos who told him that the Japanese had pulled out of the area a month before. The villagers prepared a feast for him, a welcome change from the constant diet of Spam at Mangaldan, and then took him to an Army Signal Corps unit which was operating an early warning station behind enemy lines protected by Philippine guerrillas. Bower stayed with the Signal Corps team for two weeks until their resupply boat came and took him back to Mangaldan.[47]

The 4th Squadron had another banner day on 19 February strafing an airfield at Kerenko on the east coast of Formosa, destroying three unidentified aircraft and damaging ten more. They then headed south down the rail line, leaving a trail of destruction in their wake. The pilots found and destroyed seven boxcars, five locomotives, three trucks and a staff car, and two small power stations. They damaged a further seven locomotives, two trucks, and a staff car. Locomotives were always a favorite target. If a locomotive was under steam, and the pilot could get a good solid burst into the boiler, steam would erupt in every direction.[48]

Misfortune found the 3rd Squadron on 25 February during a planned fighter sweep along the east coast of Formosa. Weather had closed in over most of the island, forcing a return to Luzon. They discovered three oil trucks and a dump truck on the coast road, which were strafed and destroyed.

FORMOSA

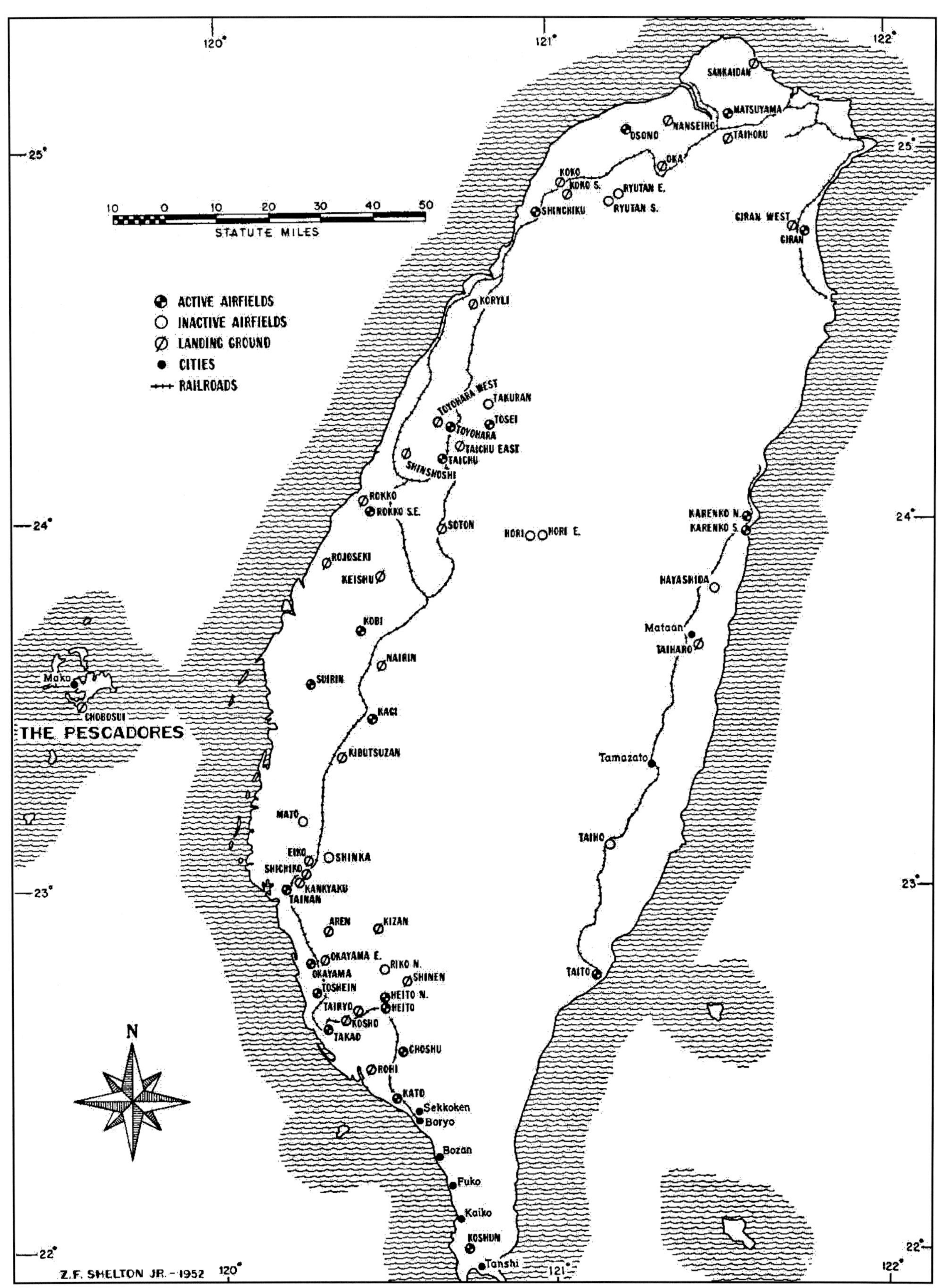

Source: *The Army Air Forces in World War II, Volume V*

At the flight line. Lt. Johnson, left, sits behind Captain Rex Pealer. (Courtesy Rex Pealer)

At the southernmost tip of the island the squadron saw a carefully camouflaged radar station protected by many nearby gun emplacements. They peeled off to strafe this lucrative target, but as they approached, the hillsides erupted in accurate, intense AA fire. Five Mustangs were immediately hit, two severely. F/O Sylvester Everhart had to bail out a half mile off shore. His flight saw him struggling to get into his dingy, but lost sight of him. A PBY landed to try to pick him up but found nothing more than a leather glove and a fragment of the dingy.

Lieutenant Scott Alexander's P-51 was also badly hit, and he was forced to parachute 30 miles from the coast, breaking his leg when he struck the tail. Alexander's dingy failed to inflate, but despite the intense pain he managed to inflate his Mae West and hang on until a PBY landed nearby and rescued him. A third Mustang crash-landed back at Mangaldan.[49]

The 4th Squadron flew the last Formosa mission of the month on 27 February. A fighter sweep resulted in one aircraft destroyed and one severely damaged on the ground, and one truck destroyed and one damaged. It had been a productive, but costly month. Between them, the two squadrons had shot down four aircraft, destroyed six on the ground, and damaged another ten, in addition to destroying 21 locomotives and 25 motor vehicles of various types as well as a number of buildings. Two pilots had been killed over Formosa and two others forced to bail out.

Despite poor March weather and constant calls for ground support on Luzon, 3rd and 4th Squadrons continued to send missions to Formosa. With the invasion of Okinawa planned for 1 April 1945, neutralizing the Japanese airfields on Formosa became a priority. For the month prior to the invasion and the month after, Fifth Air Force sent out heavy and medium bomber squadrons to attack the airfields whenever weather permitted. As there was always the risk of interception, fighter escort accompanied the bombers. However, Japanese fighters never rose to defend their bases, preferring to husband their strength against the threat of invasion.

When it became apparent that the Japanese would not strike at the bombers, the fighters began to carry bombs on escort missions and, once the bombers had completed their runs and were back out over the sea, the fighters would return for low-level attacks. On these missions the Air Commando Mustangs typically carried one drop tank and one 500 lb. bomb.

March 1945 began with a strike by 16 Mustangs from the 3rd Squadron on a sugar refinery. They attacked with 500 lb. bombs and napalm, covering the target and an adjacent railroad yard.

The next day, the 3rd Squadron escorted B-24s bombing shipping in Takao Harbor while the 4th escorted Libs to Matsuyama at the northern tip of Formosa (near present day Taipei). When the bombers turned for home, the Mustangs went down to strafe along the east coast of the island, destroying a railroad station and a power transformer and damaging several boxcars.

These slim pickings proved to be the norm much of the time, for the constant fighter sweeps had brought daytime movement on Formosa to a grinding halt.

Once again the 4th Squadron seemed to have the better luck. On a sweep down the east coast on 5 March they destroyed two locomotives and a truck, and damaged five boxcars. Ten days later on a sweep along the west coast, the 4th found and destroyed five trucks, a locomotive, and a switch engine, and damaged a number of boxcars and trucks.

During the morning of 1 April, the 4th Squadron sent eight P-51s to sweep the west coast of Formosa where they destroyed 13 trucks, three boxcars, two buses, and two locomotives, and damaged another locomotive, the best bag for some time.

An indication of how cautious the Japanese were with their aircraft came that afternoon when two flights from the 4th Squadron went up the east coast of Formosa to investigate Giran Airfield. Flying at high altitude, they observed what looked to be 14 parked twin-engine bombers and two bombers taxiing near the runway. The Mustangs flew past the airfield, turned, let down, and began an attack run. In those few minutes the Japanese had cleared the field. Not one airplane was left as a target.[50]

In the middle of March Lieutenant Colonel Elmer Richardson, the 3rd Air Commando Group's Operations Officer, was transferred to the 308th Bombardment Wing as Operations Officer. Major Walker Mahurin replaced him, and Captain Charles Adams replaced Mahurin as commander of the 3rd Squadron. Captain Thomas Williams replaced Adams as Operations Officer.[51]

During March the squadrons had begun flying missions to the China coast, escorting bombers or fighter sweeps. These were long missions. The coast of China was more than 500 miles from Mangaldan, involving flights of six hours or more, all of it over water. Many of the pilots noticed that their Merlin engines, which purred like kittens over Luzon, developed a variety of odd sounds once out over the ocean. Using cruise control techniques that had now become standard, the pilots would depart from Mangaldan, lean out their mixture and reduce the RPM, and settle back for a boring few hours flying over the South China Sea. Major Mahurin took to bringing a mystery novel along and reading during the flight to and from the coast, keeping an eye out from time to time on the formation leader. Apart from one mission to Hong Kong, which resulted in the Air Commandos' first and only encounter with Japanese fighters, the escorts and sweeps to the China coast proved uneventful.[52]

On 2 April 1945, the 3rd and 4th Squadrons joined the 49th Fighter Group to escort a group of B-24s attacking port facilities in Hong Kong. The Mustangs were scheduled to rendezvous with the Liberators over Hong Kong harbor at around 1230 hours, but the bombers were late. The pilots spent some 30 minutes circling over Hong Kong, looking down at the city below. Finally the bombers showed up and began their run.

Two flights from the 3rd Squadron were escorting the bombers just east of Hong Kong harbor, flying at around 15,000 feet when a call went out that bogies were coming in at twelve o'clock high. The pilots looked up to see two Zekes, flying about 500 feet above the Mustangs. The Zekes apparently intended to bounce the leading Mustangs, but then changed their minds and started a side pass on the second flight, led by Lieutenant Glenn Larimore. Larimore turned his flight into the attack and pulled up to get a head-on shot. Both Zekes came straight at them, firing.

Second Lieutenant Joe Singletary, number four man in the flight, couldn't fire without hitting his element leader but remembers the tracer fire from the Japanese fighters whipping by him. As the enemy swept past the Mustang flight one of the Zekes broke down and away, but the second executed a tight Immelman and came in right on Singletary's tail. Larimore ordered the flight to dive away to regain a more favorable position, as they had been trained not to try to turn with the Zeke. The P-51s pushed over into a dive, dropping their external tanks, all except Singletary who had trouble jettisoning his. Since his speed had slowed when he pulled up into the head-on attack, it took a few seconds for Singletary's laden P-51 to get going, even though he had the throttle fire-walled. With the Zeke coming down on him, Singletary screamed out, "Get this son of bitch off my ass!" He dove past his element leader with the Zeke still hot on his tail.

Second Lieutenant Barret Wagner, a replacement who had just 19 hours of combat flying, had dived to the left as the Zekes passed and then pulled around to the right, positioning himself on the tail of Singletary's pursuer. Seeing Wagner behind him, the Japanese pilot broke off the attack and then unaccountably dived away. Wagner stayed with him and started firing as they approached 3,000 feet, getting strikes on the Zeke's fuselage and wing roots. The enemy pilot dived down close to the water and, apparently failing to pull up soon enough, caught a wing tip and spun into the water.

Meanwhile, Larimore had pulled his flight back up to 12,000 feet where he observed two more Zekes at his level going away from him. The Japanese aviators also saw the Mustangs and turned back for a head-on pass. Larimore opened fire when the Zekes were around 600 yards away and kept it up as they closed, seeing some hits around the engine and pieces of cowling flying off one aircraft. The Japanese fighters broke right and went spiralling down toward the water.

Larimore broke away and was looking for his wingman when he saw another Zeke below him flying above a flight of P-51s, apparently attempting to make a pass on them. He dove toward this new menace and opened fire from 800 yards away, getting strikes on the fuselage and wings as he closed to 25 yards. Passing under the Zeke and pulling up to the right, Larimore saw the enemy fighter roll over on its back and dive down, seemingly out of control, but lost sight in mist and haze below him.

Wagner received credit for one Zeke destroyed, and Larimore was credited with two probables. The pilots all commented that the Japanese seemed to be experienced and fought aggressively.[53]

By March 1945, guerrillas of the U.S. Army Forces in the Philippines (Northern Luzon) (USAFIP(NL)) had forced the Japanese to withdraw from northwestern Luzon, backing them into the Cordillera Central and freeing several towns along the coast, including the town of Laoag, 160 miles north of Lingayen. Here the Japanese had built a small, rough airstrip at

B Flight, 3rd Fighter Squadron, March 1945 in an interesting but low-quality photo. On the wing (L-R) Lt. Maiga, Lt. Burrel Dykes, Lt. Bramble, 2nd Lt. Barret Wagner, Lt. Glenn Larimore, 2nd Lt. Joe Singletary, Lt. Planta; Standing (L-R) Lt. Hayes, Lt. Edward Lyons, Captain Donald Songer, flight leader. On April 2, over Hong Kong, Barret Wagner chased a Zeke off Joe Singletary's tail and shot it down. (Courtesy World War II Air Commando Association)

the village of Gabu a few miles away. Fifth Air Force C-47 Dakotas began using the strip to land supplies for guerrillas and reported that it could be used as an emergency field. Since Laoag was 160 miles closer to Formosa than Lingayen, the 308th Bombardment Wing began talking with the USAFIP(NL) about building a more permanent airfield that could serve both as an emergency strip for damaged airplanes returning from strikes on Formosa and as a base for fighters. The USAFIP(NL)'s American commander agreed to provide troops to guard the airfield which, although free of Japanese troops, still remained well behind enemy lines.[54]

The Gabu strip was little more than a dirt field, with no facilities for maintaining aircraft. Since the Air Commandos had trained and were equipped for just these conditions, the 308th Bombardment Wing decided to transfer the 3rd Air Commando Group, less its Liaison squadrons, from Mangaldan to Laoag. Headquarters for the Air Commandos was established in a school six miles from Laoag, while the two fighter squadrons were based three miles from Gabu strip. The 318th Troop Carrier Squadron began flying in teams from the 334th, 335th, and the 343rd Aerodrome Squadrons to prepare for the fighters, and then flew constant shuttle missions to bring in fuel, ammunition, and supplies.[55]

On 19 April the 3rd Squadron set out from Mangaldan on a close support mission near Baguio, hit their target, and then flew up north to their new home near Laoag. The next day the squadron escorted B-24s to Formosa. The 4th Squadron flew up a few days later, again without any disruption to combat operations. Once again, local Philippine labor set to work building bamboo offices and quarters for the officers and enlisted men. The pilots had to suffer several weeks of bone-jarring take-offs and landings, due to prior bomb damage, until an all-weather strip could be put down.

For the first few weeks of operations from Gabu strip, the 318th airlifted all supplies as the west coast road was still closed. Truck convoys began coming up the coast in early May, and the Army built a small dock on the coast so that bombs and fuel could be supplied more easily. This several weeks of isolated operations was the closest the 3rd Air Commandos ever came to functioning as they had trained. Fortunately, the Japa-

A 4th Fighter Squadron Mustang comes to grief at Gabu. (Courtesy Rex Pealer)

nese never chose to contest the American occupation of their former airfield, though the guerrillas continued to patrol the mountains east of the field for several months after the move.[56]

Missions continued without let up. Fortunately the supply of replacement pilots and planes had increased to the point where the 3rd and 4th Squadrons could each add two extra flights, giving each squadron more than 40 pilots and around 25 aircraft. This was a relief for the original pilots who had been flying two missions a day for weeks on end.

With the chance of encountering Japanese fighters over Formosa practically nil, only single flights of four aircraft escorted bombers as the pounding of airfields and port facilities continued. Often, instead of escorting the bombers to the target, the Mustangs were assigned to patrol over the rescue submarines or PBY flying boats orbiting off Formosa. These "cover" missions became a regular, but boring, feature of operations in the months following the move to Laoag.

Being that much closer to Formosa made little difference to the pilots, apart from shaving off some time getting to and from the island. Leaving the enemy bastion behind was always an exhilarating feeling. As the 3rd Fighter Squadron's intelligence officer put it, "A pilot had only to ride over the island of Formosa to know that the Isle of Hate is one big virtual flak gun." While targets were fewer and farther between, the flak never let up in its intensity. Invariably a run of good fortune would end with a pilot shot down or wounded.[57]

During the last week of April, the 4th Fighter Squadron joined the attack on Formosan airfields bombing several with 500-pounders and fragmentation clusters. These missions did a great deal of damage to airfield facilities but failed to destroy a single aircraft. By this time the Japanese had moved most of their planes away from the main airdromes and, in a careful plan of dispersal, had hidden them in farms and villages, sometimes miles away. At the end of April, Far East Air Force intelligence estimated that the Japanese had no more than 89 aircraft on Formosa, but in actual fact they had over 700.[58]

Ironically the only planes the 4th Squadron destroyed that month were on Luzon. A 28 April mission to bomb Okayama airfield on Formosa had to be canceled due to bad weather over the target. The Squadron turned back to Luzon and was briefed over the radio to attack Tuguegarao, Northern Luzon, instead. They found a Japanese guerrilla air force of one Oscar and one Zeke near the field under heavy camouflage. Repeated strafing left both aircraft in flames.[59]

During May, Fifth Air Force kept up steady attacks on Formosan airfields and the railway system. The 3rd Fighter Squadron drew most of the Formosa missions while the 4th Squadron devoted most of its effort to close air support, but both squadrons suffered losses over the Isle of Hate.

The month began with the 4th Squadron flying a very productive sweep along the road and rail system. They destroyed seven locomotives, four boxcars, two trucks, and a bus, and damaged a single-engine fighter on the ground. However, 2nd Lieutenant Robert McNeill was lost when he crashed into the bus he was strafing.

On 5 May, the 3rd Squadron attacked Giran airdrome with fragmentation bombs while the 4th went after Matsuyama airdrome, hitting revetments, runways, and taxiways. The 3rd Squadron returned to Giran the next day, and both squadrons bombed the airfield complex at Okayama on the 11th, destroying barracks and airfield buildings in the face of intense anti-aircraft fire. Coming off the target Captain Louis Curdes and his wingman 1st Lieutenant Kenneth Ogden spotted a truck convoy and snuck up on it from behind, destroying five vehicles. As they swept past, a .50-caliber shell hit Ogden's Mustang in the cockpit and tore into his leg. Fighting unconsciousness and intense pain from his wound, Ogden struggled back to Gabu strip where he managed a safe landing.

The two squadrons went back to Formosa a week later for three days of airfield strikes, pounding Heito three days in a row. They covered the airfield barracks, hangars, and other buildings with over 30 tons of 500 lb. high explosives and 260 lb. fragmentation bombs.[60]

After a week of heavy close support work, the 3rd and 4th Squadrons returned to Formosa at the end of May as part of the continuing concerted effort against the Formosan railroad system.

On May 28, the 4th Squadron sent eight aircraft up the west coast of Formosa and another eight aircraft up the east coast. These sweeps destroyed two locomotives and three trucks and damaged 17 boxcars, and the next day's sorties destroyed two more locomotives and several rail cars.

The 3rd Squadron sent eight aircraft up to the west coast of Formosa on 30 May where they found and destroyed five locomotives, a pair of trucks, and a bus, and damaged a further ten boxcars but lost one pilot. 2nd Lieutenant Joe Bulack and his element leader had braved intense flak to destroy the five locomotives, and then had made a second pass to destroy the bus before turning and heading out to sea. The element leader saw Bulack make the turn, but when he looked around again a minute later, there was no sign of the wingman. He was never found.[61]

On a 31 May 1945 mission to Formosa the 4th Squadron lost two pilots. A sweep of the west coast had resulted in nine trucks and five locomotives destroyed and eight trucks and one locomotive damaged, but A Flight had nothing but hard luck. Captain John Bleecker led the flight, with Flying Officer Bernard Moncrief as his wingman. 1st Lieutenant Fergus Mead was the element leader with Lieutenant John Tillou as his wingman.

They had flown off the coast to the northern tip of Formosa and then headed over land and turned south, flying at an altitude of 200-300 feet, looking for targets of opportunity along the road and rail lines. Within minutes Mead's aircraft went into a spin and crashed, a victim of small arms fire.

Bleeker led the flight south but found no targets along the way, and when they were halfway down the island decided to call it a day and set course for home. Moncrief pulled into position off Bleeker's wing, and suddenly his cockpit filled with smoke and flames. He had flown right over a pom-pom gun which had apparently hit the Mustang's engine.

Moncrief jettisoned his canopy, pulled up to gain some altitude, and stood up in the cockpit to bail out, but his chute snagged. Fortunately at that moment the Mustang stalled and flipped to the right, flinging the pilot free. He pulled his rip cord, swung three times after the chute deployed, and hit the ground. Moncrief was captured and spent three difficult months on Formosa as a POW. When downed Moncrief had weighed 135 pounds; he was eighty-nine pounds when liberated.[62]

Sweeps during the first three days of June destroyed ten boxcars, five trucks, and one locomotive, and damaged a further 18 boxcars and one locomotive, but worthy targets were steadily fewer. Most often the squadrons simply flew cover missions. It was a frustrating time. While reading about fierce air battles over Okinawa and Japan, none of the Air Commandos had even seen an airborne Japanese since the 2 April mission to Hong Kong. Worse, during June army engineers completed the expansion of Gabu airstrip into an all-

Captain Rex Pealer, 4th Fighter Squadron, sitting on his P-51 at Gabu strip. (Courtesy Rex Pealer)

weather airfield to use as a staging field for advancing Fifth Air Force units to Okinawa. Pilots of the 3rd and 4th Fighter Squadrons had to sit by and watch as other fighter groups headed north to join the fighting. The war was passing them by. About the only boost to morale during the month was the opening of the "Casa Commando," a beach house a few miles away from Gabu where the pilots could get away for a day or two of rest and relaxation.

After two solid weeks of ground support work in early June 1945, the squadrons flew sweeps of Formosa on 17 and 20 June, destroying five trucks and one locomotive, and damaging 18 boxcars and one locomotive.

A mission on 26 June ended in disaster. The 4th Squadron had sent eight aircraft to Formosa on a fighter sweep, but the formation ran into severe weather and turned back. Captain John Bleeker, with 1st Lieutenant John Tillou and 2nd Lieutenant Raymond Wingo on his wing, headed off into the clouds. They were never seen again. One of the returning pilots reported seeing the flash of an explosion in the mountains along the route home, and it is most likely that Bleeker, Tillou, and Wingo flew into a mountainside. All three of the missing pilots were from the 4th Squadron's A Flight. Formosa missions had claimed five members of that flight in less than a month.[63]

Captain John Bleecker (above) and Lt. John Tillou (below) who were killed over Formosa on 26 June 1945 along with Lt. Ray Wingo, when they apparently flew into a mountain in bad weather. (Courtesy Rex Pealer)

In July 1945, with nothing moving along the roads or rail lines, the Air Commandos switched to bombing missions, attacking factories, warehouses, railroad stations, bridges, and tunnels. Flak over Formosa remained consistently heavy, but fortunately neither squadron lost any pilots on the last few missions to the island. The bombing operations were interspersed with cover missions. Each squadron would send three or four flights up to Formosa over the course of the day to protect bombers or to patrol over the rescue submarines waiting offshore. Given the dearth of targets they rarely went inland to strafe. With one or two exceptions, these cover missions were remarkable only for their boredom.

On 11 July, at 0700 hours, the 3rd Squadron sent off a flight of four Mustangs to cover a submarine and a rescue plane off the northwest coast of Formosa. They arrived over the submarine at 0820 hours, and set up an orbit. Two hours later the pilots were, according to the squadron history, "astonished beyond imagination" to see a Japanese airplane flying toward them. The element leader, 1st Lieutenant Herbert French, called out a bogey at three o'clock. Little more than a speck, the plane appeared to be coming from the China coast on its way to Formosa. The flight leader told French to take his wingman, 2nd Lieutenant George Mooney, and go after the Japanese airplane while he protected the submarine.

French and Mooney eagerly broke off and headed for the Japanese airplane, which soon saw the approaching P-51s and turned 180 degrees, diving from 10,000 feet to pick up more speed. The two Mustangs dropped their wing tanks, pushed the throttles forward, and began a long tail chase. About 75 miles and fifteen minutes later they caught up with the Japanese airplane, which they identified as a Kate. Since the enemy airplane was going at nearly 300 miles per hour, it is more likely that it was a Jill, a Nakajima B6N2 Carrier Attack Bomber, which was similar in plan and profile to the older Kate.

The pursuit was down to around 500 feet, with French to the left, and Mooney to the right, boxing in the enemy plane. In an evasive attempt the Japanese pilot broke right, flying into Mooney's sights. One burst from the Mustang's six guns hit the Jill in the engine and the right wing. Flaming, the enemy aircraft crashed into the sea. It would be the last Air Commando claim for a Japanese aircraft destroyed in the air or on the ground.[64]

4th Fighter Squadron pilots at an award ceremony after receiving Air Medals and Purple Hearts. L-R: Captain Rex Pealer, Lt. Robert Lacroix, Captain Robert Scalley, Captain Raymond Lahmeyer, Lt. Herbert Arnold, Lt. Robert Ankrom. (Courtesy Rex Pealer)

While the missions to Formosa brought more immediately-evident results, albeit at a far greater cost, the majority of the Air Commando fighter effort after moving to Laoag was devoted to the task of ground support. During May and June, the 3rd and 4th Fighter Squadrons flew a combined total of 1,546 bombing and strafing sorties and dropped 847 tons of bombs, almost all of which were in support of I Corps. May proved to be the best overall month in terms of bombing accuracy, with 94% of bombs on target. With constant practice the pilots became expert at delivering their ordnance in close proximity to American troop positions.[65]

I Corps' divisions continued their weary hammering against Japanese positions. American troops captured the town of Baguio on 26 April, but Japanese troops along the Villa Verde Trail and the Balete Pass continued to resist stubbornly. By 23 June, American paratroops landed at Appari on the north coast of Luzon and, pushing south, linked up with troops from I Corps on 26 June, securing the Cagayan Valley. The Shobu Group, with some 52,000 troops remaining, withdrew into the Cordillera Central into what became known as the Kiangan Pocket.[66]

All through May and June, V Fighter Command fighters kept up the pressure. They hammered Japanese forward troop concentrations and sought out supply areas behind the lines. The combined ground, air, and artillery attacks effectively destroyed the Japanese 2nd Tank Division and the 10th Infantry Division which were defending the Baguio, Villa Verde Trail, and the Balete Pass areas. Ground controllers and observers flying above the lines in L-5s would direct the fighters onto Japanese troop positions, pointing out the line of foxholes, pillboxes, or caves. The controllers would then bring the fighters in for strafing runs against these targets. Sometimes, after expending all their ammunition, the Mustangs would be called back to make dummy runs while American or Filipino guerrilla troops raced forward to take a position.

An example of this coordinated effort took place on 14 June 1945, when two flights from the 3rd Squadron participated in a combined attack on a Japanese hilltop position. After artillery preparation the ground controller called in the Mustang pilots who got two direct hits and several near misses on the pillbox. The P-51s came back in to strafe Japanese troops in trenches along the hill top. The ground controller then called one armed flight to hold off while he brought in the other flight for dummy runs over the heads of the advancing American troops seizing the enemy position. The sec-

Gabu airstrip at Laoag on the northwestern coast of Luzon. (Courtesy Ray Lahmeyer)

ond flight continued to circle overhead and kept an eye out for Japanese artillery that might threaten the Americans on the hill. An L-5 in the area spotted another fortified position and called in the Mustangs to strafe, which they did successfully. The forward air controller called it "the best example of ground-air-artillery coordination ever witnessed by the ground commander."[67]

The squadrons suffered only one loss in two months of ground support missions. On 5 June, Captain Charles Adams led the 3rd Squadron on a bombing mission. There was a layer of cloud over the target area, but Adams decided to proceed. The cloud layer was lower than he realized, and he was unable to pull out of his dive, crashing to his death.

Captain Thomas Williams took over command of the 3rd Squadron and Captain Donald Songer replaced him as Operations Officer. The 4th Squadron underwent a change of command on 18 June when Major Steve Wilkerson moved to become Group Air Inspector. Captain Ray Lahmeyer became squadron commander and Captain John Bleecker became the new operations officer. When Bleecker was lost over Formosa a week later, Lieutenant Robert Scalley replaced him.[68]

At the end of June, General MacArthur relieved Sixth Army and I Corps and withdrew them from combat in preparation for the invasion of Japan. Eighth Army and XIV Corps took over responsibility for elimination of the Shobu Group in its last stand area in the Cordillera Central. Although there was still much fighting left against the final Japanese pocket, General MacArthur declared an end to the Philippines campaign on 5 July.

The 3rd and 4th Fighter Squadrons continued their close support work for three more weeks, bombing Japanese troops in the Kiangan pocket area and searching out supply dumps. The desperate Japanese resorted to using trucks in daylight, and for the first time in several months, the Mustangs caught motor transport out in the open. On 23 July, ten Mustangs found 16 camouflaged trucks full of supplies on the highway from Baguio to the Kiangan valley, and in repeated strafing passes destroyed them. But the campaign was clearly nearing its end and all eyes were turned to the north.

The 3rd and 4th Fighter Squadrons flew their last combat missions on 25 July. During the day the two squadrons flew 44 sorties to bomb Japanese positions in the Mankayan area at the northern edge of the Kiangan pocket. The squadrons then stood down to prepare for their next move, to Okinawa. In their final three weeks of combat the two squadrons had flown 883 sorties and dropped 218 tons of bombs. In the Philippines campaign, the Air Commando fighter squadrons had flown 6,886 sorties with nearly 70% of these sorties in support of the ground forces, and had dropped 2,255 tons of bombs. During the last three months of the campaign, when the squadrons were operating from Gabu air strip, the 3rd and 4th Fighter Squadrons had the highest aircraft availability of all the fighter squadrons in V Fighter Command, a tremendous tribute to the skill and dedication of the ground crews.[69]

In the middle of July, Fifth Air Force alerted the 3rd Air Commando Group for a move to the island of Ie Shima, off the coast of Okinawa, in preparation for operations against Japan. The pilots took advantage of the break to rest. There was little in the way of flying apart from training sorties.

A few changes in command took place. Walker Mahurin, who had been promoted to Lieutenant Colonel, was appointed Deputy Commander of the 3rd Air Commando Group. Captain Thomas Williams, 3rd Squadron CO, replaced Mahurin as Group Operations Officer. Captain Donald Songer replaced Williams as Squadron Commander, and Captain Kenneth Heller moved up to become Operations Officer.

No one knew what role the Air Commandos would play in the coming invasion, but the pilots were hoping at long last to engage in some serious aerial combat. It was a source of continuing frustration that they had arrived in the theater too late to take part in the fierce air battles over Leyte, had missed the Okinawa campaign and, in seven months of combat, had managed to shoot down only nine Japanese aircraft.[70]

The 334th Airdrome Squadron set off for Ie Shima on 21 July, followed by the 335th and the 341st shortly thereafter. While the airdrome squadrons set to work preparing for the arrival of the air echelon, the pilots went into a transit camp and waited for the order to fly to Ie Shima. They were still waiting on 15 August 1945 when the war ended. The move to Ie Shima was an anti-climax.

The 4th Fighter Squadron flew north first, followed by the 3rd. They began flying patrol missions over southern Japan during the last week of August. A large group of new replacement pilots, fresh from the United States, arrived on Ie Shima soon after. Both old and new pilots were disappointed, the older ones for once again missing another chance for air combat, the goal of every fighter pilot; and the new ones for having had no chance at all.

Abandoned Zekes at the former Japanese Navy air base at Chitose, the 3rd Air Commandos final base of the war. (Courtesy Wilfred McCabe)

Far East Air Force assigned the 3rd Air Commando Group to occupation duties in Japan and on 20 September, they landed at Atsugi Airdrome, an Imperial Japanese Naval Air Force base outside of Tokyo. While at Atsugi the squadrons flew "show of force" patrols over central Japan.

Veteran leaders began rotating back to the States. With his long service overseas, Colonel Arvid Olson was one of the first senior officers to go, returning shortly after V-J Day. Bud Mahurin, on his second tour of combat, assumed command.

In October the Air Commandos moved to Chitose, on the northern island of Hokkaido, setting up shop at a former Imperial Navy training base. The remaining veterans organized an intensive training program for the new pilots and waited for their turn to go home. Hokkaido's winter snows were a novelty after the heat of Luzon and provided some diversion, but the main show was over. There were no more invasions planned, no more islands to seize. In March 1946, the entire 3rd Air Commando Group was inactivated and its fighter pilots assigned to the 49th Fighter Group.[71]

An idea born in the steaming jungles of Burma, had created the Air Commando concept. The vision came to life in the units that bore the name and fought and died in those same jungles. It ended on a snow-covered airfield in northern Japan. It would take another war, in another steaming Southeast Asian jungle, to bring them back.

From the jungles of the Pacific the 3rd Air Commandos went to the snows of Hokkaido, Japan. BARBARA ANN, a 4th Fighter Squadron Mustang at Chitose. (Courtesy Wilfred McCabe)

ENDNOTES

CHAPTER 1

1. Ehrman, J.: *Grand Strategy Volume V: August 1943-September 1944*, London, HMSO, 1957, pp. 124-31; Romanus, Charles and Sunderland, Riley: *Stillwell's Mission to China*, Washington, D.C., 1956, pp. 63-70, 320-27; Kirby, S. Woodburn: *The War Against Japan, Volume II*, London, HMSO, 1958, pp. 238-39, 492-93.
2. Kirby, S. Woodburn: *The War Against Japan, Volume III*, London, HMSO, 1961, pp 1-11, 36-38.
3. Sykes, Christopher: *Orde Wingate: A Biography*, Cleveland, World Publishing Company, 1959, pp. 324-26; Royale, Trevor: *Orde Wingate: Irregular Soldier,* London, Weidenfeld & Nicolson, 1995, pp. 233-35.
4. Arnold, H.H.: "The Aerial Invasion of Burma," *The National Geographic Magazine*, Volume LXXXVI, Number Two, August 1944, pp. 129-148;Thomas, Lowell: *Back to Mandalay*, New York, The Graystone Press, 1951, pp. 27-29.
5. Thomas, pp.52-98; Van Wagner, R.D.: *Any Place, Any Time, Any Where: The 1st Air Commandos in WWII*, Atglen, PA, Schiffer Publishing Ltd, 1998, pp. 21-41
6. For a detailed description of the second Chindit expedition, see Bidwell, Shelford: *The Chindit War: Stillwell, Wingate, and the Campaign in Burma:1944*, New York, Macmillian Publishing Company, Inc., 1979, and Chinnery, Philip D.: *March or Die: The Story of Wingate's Chindits*, England, Airlife Publishing Ltd., 1979.
7. General H.H. Arnold, Commanding General, Army Air Forces, to Admiral Lord Louis Mountbatten, Commander-in-Chief, South East Asia Command, 24 March 1944, in Air 8/1158, Office of the Chief of the Air Staff: "Air Commando Operations in South East Asia March-July 1944", Public Records Office, Kew, England; General H.H. Arnold, Commanding General, Army Air Forces, to General George C. Marshall, Chief of Staff, U.S.Army, 1 April 1944, in AC/AS Plans, 1st Air Commando Force and Combat Cargo Group Organization and Redeployment Correspondence and Memorandum, 1943-45. 145.81-170, in USAF Collection, USAFHRC.
8. Craven, W.F. and Cate, J.L.: *The Army Air Forces in World War II, Volume V: The Pacific: Matterhorn to Nagasaki*, Chicago, University of Chicago Press,1953,p. 334; Kirby, S. Woodburn: *The War Against Japan,Volume IV*, London, HMSO, 1965, Chapter I.

CHAPTER 2

1. Interview with 1st Air Commando fighter pilots, at fifty-second 1st Air Commando Group Reunion, 18-21 September 1996, personal possession.
2. Thomas, p. 78.
3. Colonel Philip Cochran to General H.H. Arnold, "History, Status, and Immediate Requirements of the First Air Commando Force," 21 January 1944, AC/AS, Plans, 1st Air Commando Force and Combat Cargo Groups organization and redeployment correspondence and memoranda, 1943-45, 145.81-170, in USAF Collection, USAFHRC; Bidwell, p. 169.
4. Thomas, pp.176-78; Interview with Jack Klarr, 20 May 1996, personal possession.
5. Olynyk, Frank*: Stars and Bars: A Tribute to the American Fighter Ace 1920-1973,* London, Grub Street, 1995, p. 566.
6. Interview with Air Commando fighter pilots, 18-21September 1996, personal possession.
7. "Unit History of the First Air Commando Force," Unit History, 1st Air Commando Group, GP-A-CMDO-1-HI, USAF Collection, USAFHRC.
8. AC/AS, Intelligence, *Chronological History of Project 9 (Cochran),* 17 August 1943-28 January 1944, 142.0411-9, USAF Collection, USAFHRC.
9. "Unit History of the First Air Commando Force."
10. *The Campaigns in the Far East, Volume IV, South East Asia*, (November 1943 to August 1945), Air 41/64, Public Records Office, Kew, pp. 134-35.
11. Ibid., p. 182.
12. Ibid.
13. Ibid.
14. Thomas, pp. 179-80; Interview with Walter Radovich, 18-21 September 1996, personal possession.
15. Ehrman, p. 153
16. Kirby, Volume III, pp. 58-65, 117-20, 128-29.
17. Ibid., pp. 73-78.
18. Ibid., pp. 169-70.
19. Ibid., p. 170; Royle, pp. 288-90.
20. Kirby, Volume III, pp. 172-75.
21. *The Campaigns in the Far East, Volume IV*, p. 143.
22. JICA/CBI, "Supplemental Report on First Air Commando Force (Group) in Burma," Report No. 1834, 15 April 1944, 810.6091A, USAF Collection, USAFHRC.
23. Ibid.
24. bid.; Olynyk, Frank: *Victory List No.4: AVG & USAAF (China-Burma-India Theater) Credits for the Destruction of Enemy Aircraft in Air-to-Air Combat World War 2,* 1986, p. 67; Letter from Osamu Tagaya to the author, 5 January 1997.
25. JCIA/CBI, Report No. 1834; Unit History, 1st Air Commando Group, *History of the 1st Air Commando Group*, September 1943-August 1945, GP-A-CMDO-1-HI, USAF Collection, USAFHRC.
26. Unit History, 1st Air Commando Group.
27. JCIA/CBI Report No. 1834.
28. Kirby, Volume III, pp. 179-81.
29. Bidwell, pp. 183-84.
30. Kirby, Volume III, pp. 90-91
31. Calvert, Michael: *Prisoners of Hope, Revised Edition*, London, Leo Cooper, 1996, pp. 52-53, 56-58.
32. Bidwell, p. 147.
33. Ibid.
34. Royle, pp. 310-12, 315-17.
35. Unit History, 1st Air Commando Group.
36. Kirby, Volume III, pp. 243-47.
37. Ibid., pp. 246-47, 283-84.
38. Ibid., pp. 185-86, 283-84.
39. JCIA/CBI, "Final Operations of the First Air Commando Group in Burma," Report No. 3137, 30 May 1944, 810.6091A, USAF Collection, USAFHRC.
40. Calvert, p.112.
41. JCIA/CBI, Report No. 3137.
42. Calvert, p. 131.
43. Ibid.
44. Ibid.,Pp. 131-33.
45. *The Campaigns in the Far East, Volume IV*, p. 69.
46. Ibid.; Osamu Tagaya to the author, 5 January 1997.
47. *Campaigns in the Far East, Volume IV*, pp. 69-72.
48. JCIA/CBI Report No. 1834.
49. Osamu Tagaya to the author, 5 January 1997.
50. Ibid.; Olynyk, Victory List No. 4, p. 67.
51. Interview with Hubert Krug, 18-21 September 1996, personal possession.
52. Osamu Tagaya to the author; Olynyk, Victory List No. 4, p. 67.
53. JCIA/CBI, Report No. 1834; interviews with 1st Air Commando pilots, 18-21 September 1996, personal possession.
54. Osamu Tagaya to the author.

55. Franks, Norman: *The Air Battle of Imphal, London*, William Kimber, 1985, p.40; the 1st Air Commando Association, "The Basha Blabber," Summer 1992; Osamu Tagaya to the author.
56. Interview with Olin B. Carter, 18-21 September 1996, personal possession.
57. "The Basha Blabber," Summer 1992.
58. Osamu Tagaya to the author.
59. *Campaigns in the Far East*, Volume IV, p. 79.
60. Krug interview.
61. Campaigns in the Far East, Volume IV, p.79; Krug interview.
62. JCIA/CBI, Report No. 1834.
63. JCIA/CBI, Report No. 1834, "Complete Report on Raid on Aungban," Unit History, 1st Air Commando Group.
64. Ibid.; *Campaigns in the Far East*, Volume IV, p. 75.
65. JCIA/CBI, Report No. 1834, "Complete Report on Raid on Aungban."
66. Ibid.
67. Ibid.; Osamu Tagaya to the author.
68. JCIA/CBI, Report No. 3137.
69. Franks, pp. 77-78; Osamu Tagaya to the author.
70. JCIA/CBI, Report No. 3137; Osamu Tagaya to the author; Izawa, Yasuho, "64th Flying Sentai, Part 3," Aero Album, Volume 5, Number 4, Winter 1972, p.12.
71. JCIA/CBI, Report No. 3137.
72. Interview with Jack Klarr, 20 May 1996, personal possession.
73. JCIA/CBI, Report No. 3137; Olynyk, Victory List No.4, p. 67.
74. *Campaigns in the Far East, Volume IV*, Appendix 22.
75. Ibid., Pp. 89-91.
76. Van Wagner, Major R.D,: *1st Air Commando Group: Any Place, Any Time, Any Where, Military History Series 86-1*, Air Command and Staff College, Maxwell AFB, 1986, pp. 91-92; Calvert, pp. 289-90; JCIA/CBI, Report No. 1834.
77. Unit History, 1st Air Commando Group; JCIA/CBI, Report No. 3137.
78. "The Basha Blabber, " April-May-June 1993.
79. Ibid.; Lieutenant Colonel Grant Mahony, to Commanding General USAAF, 27 April 1944, "Report on Rocket Installation on P-51 Type Aircraft," Unit History, 1st Air Commando Group.
80. Ibid.
81. Bidwell, pp. 206-8; Kirby, Volume III, pp. 280-82.
82. JCIA/CBI, Report No. 3137.
83. Van De Weighe Interview.
84. Unit History, 1st Air Commando Group.
85. Kirby, Volume III, pp. 408-8-9, 410-15.
86. Kirby, Volume III, pp. 444-45; Bidwell, p. 284.
87. Gordon, John W.: "Wingate," Keegan, John, ed.: *Churchill's Generals*, London, Warner Books, 1993, p. 296.
88. *Campaigns in the Far East, Volume IV*, pp. 184-185.

CHAPTER 3

1. William Burghardt, "History of the 5th and 6th Fighter Squadrons," pp. 1-2, personal possession; Unit History, 1st Air Commando Group, June-July 1944.
2. Maurer, Maurer, ed.: *Combat Squadrons of the Air Force, World War II*, Washington, D.C., U.S. Government Printing Office, 1982, p. 35; Maurer, Maurer, ed.: *Air Force Combat Units of World War II*, Washington, D.C., U.S. Government Printing Office, 1983, p. 19; Unit History, 1st Air Commando Group, September 1944.
3. Interview with Roland Lynn, 18-21 September 1996, personal possession.
4. Burghardt, p. 2; *Unit History, 6th Fighter Squadron (Commando), 1st Air Commando Group*, September 1944-August 1945, SQ-FI-CMDO-6-HI, USAF Collection, USAFHRC; Maurer, *Combat Squadrons*, p. 40.
5. Kirby, S. Woodburn: *The War Against Japan, Volume IV*, London, HMSO, 1965, pp. 26-29.
6. Eastern Air Command, "Weekly Intelligence Summary, No. 11," 10 November 1944, 820.607, USAF Collection, USAFHRC.
7. Ibid.
8. Roland Lynn interview; Olin B. Carter to the author, 24 October 1994, personal possession.
9. Eastern Air Command, "Weekly Intelligence Summary, No. 14," 1 December 1944.
10. Ibid.; Olin B. Carter to the author, 24 October 1994.
11. "Weekly Intelligence Summary, No. 14," 1 December 1944; Olynyk, Victory List No. 4, pp. 71-72; Roland Lynn interview.
12. Interview with Olin B. Carter, 18-21 September 1996; Interview with Air Commando Fighter Pilots, 18-21 September 1996, personal possession.
13. "The Basha Blabber," Summer 1992; Unit Histories, 5th and 6th Fighter Squadrons (Commando), October 1944; "Weekly Intelligence Summary, No. 14," 1 December 1944.
14. Burghardt; Unit History, 6th Fighter Squadron (Commando), October 1944.
15. Eastern Air Command, "Weekly Intelligence Summary, No. 12," 17 November 1944.
16. Ibid.
17. Ibid.
18. Ibid.
19. Allen, Louis: *Burma: The Longest War 1941-45*, London, Guild Publishing, 1984, pp. 386-88, 390-393.
20. Slim, Field Marshal Viscount William: *Defeat Into Victory*, London, Macmillan Publishers Ltd., 1986, pp. 380-82.
21. Eastern Air Command, "Weekly Intelligence Summary, No.16," 15 December 1944; *Campaigns in the Far East, Volume IV*, pp. 303-8.
22. *Campaigns in the Far East*, Volume IV, p. 356.
23. Unit History, 5th and 6th Fighter Squadrons (Commando), November 1944.
24. Unit History, 5th Fighter Squadron (Commando), November 1944.
25. Ibid.
26. Ibid.
27. Ibid.
28. Ibid.; Burghardt.
29. Unit History, 6th Fighter Squadron (Commando), December 1944.
30. Ibid.; Klarr interview; Air 24/1290, South East Asia Command, "Daily Operational Summaries," December 1944-January 1945, P.R.O.
31. Unit History, 6th Fighter Squadron (Commando), December 1944; "The Basha Blabber," January-February-March 1993.
32. Klarr interview; Olynyk, *Victory List No. 4*, pp. 71-72.
33. Unit History, 6th Fighter Squadron (Commando), December 1944; Eastern Air Command, "Weekly Intelligence Summary, No. 16-18," 15, 22-29 December 1944.
34. Unit History, 6th Fighter Squadron (Commando), December 1944.
35. Unit History, 6th Fighter Squadron (Commando), January 1945; Air 24/1290.
36. Eastern Air Command, "Weekly Intelligence Summary, No. 22," 26 January 1945.
37. Ibid.; Unit History, 5th Fighter Squadron (Commando), January 1945; Roland Lynn interview.
38. Unit History, 5th Fighter Squadron (Commando), January 1945; Eastern Air Command, "Weekly Intelligence Summary, No. 20-21," 12-19 January 1945.
39. Air 24/1290, "Daily Operational Summary No. 888," 17 January 1945.
40. Unit History, 5th Fighter Squadron (Commando), January 1945; Burghardt.
41. Air 24/1290, "Daily Operational Summary, No. 890," 19 January 1945.
42. Ibid.
43. Air 24/1290, "Daily Operational Summary, No. 893, 896, 897, 901, 902"; Eastern Air Command, "Weekly Intelligence Summary, No. 22," 26 January 1945.
44. Kirby, Volume IV, pp. 154-62.
45. Ibid., pp. 58-60.
46. Kirby, Volume IV, pp. 163-65; Allen, P.398.
47. Kirby, Volume IV, pp. 180-81; Eastern Air Command, "Weekly Intelligence Summary, No. 31," 30 March 1945, Section VI, "Joint Air-Ground Operations in Capture of Meiktila."
48. Kirby, Volume IV, pp. 180-81; "Future of Air Commandos," undated memo in WO 203/529 Air Commandos: *Planning Directives 1944*, June 1945, P.R.O.

49. Ibid.; Eastern Air Command, "Weekly Intelligence Summary, No. 31," 30 March 1945.
50. "Weekly Intelligence Summary, No. 31;" *Campaigns in the Far East, Volume IV*, p. 369; Probert, Henry*: The Forgotten Air Force: The Royal Air Force in the War Against Japan 1941-45*, London, Brassey's, 1995, p. 236.
51. Unit History, 6th Fighter Squadron (Commando), January 1945; 5th Fighter Squadron (Commando), February 1945.
52. "Weekly Intelligence Summary, No. 31."
53. Unit History, 5th and 6th Fighter Squadrons (Commando), February 1945.
54. Unit History, 1st Air Commando Group, "Missions in Support of IV Corps," 30 March 1945.
55. Kirby, Volume IV, p. 264.
56. "Missions in Support of IV Corps."
57. Ibid.
58. Frank Misfeldt, "The Basha Blabber, October-November-December 1992."
59. Ibid.
60. Interview with 1st Air Commando fighter pilots, personal possession.
61. "Missions in Support of IV Corps;" Unit History, 5th Fighter Squadron (Commando), February 1945.
62. "Missions in Support of IV Corps;" Unit History, 6th Fighter Squadron (Commando), February 1945.
63. "Missions in Support of IV Corps;" Unit History, 5th Fighter Squadron (Commando), February 1945; Eastern Air Command, "Weekly Intelligence Summary, No. 26," 23 February 1945; Izawa, p. 14.
64. Kirby, Volume IV, p. 267.
65. "Missions in Support of IV Corps;" Unit History, 5th Fighter Squadron (Commando), February 1945.
66. "Missions in Support of IV Corps;" Unit History, 6th Fighter Squadron (Commando), February 1945.
67. Izawa, p.14; Osamu Tagaya to the author, 4 October 1996, personal possession.
68. Roland Lynn interview; "The Basha Blabber, January-February-March 1993," p. 3.
69. "Missions in Support of IV Corps;" Osamu Tagaya to the author.
70. Ibid.
71. "Missions in Support of IV Corps;" Unit History, 5th Fighter Squadron (Commando), February 1945.
72. "Missions in Support of IV Corps."
73. Ibid.
74. "Joint Air-Ground Operations in Capture of Meiktila."
75. Kirby, Volume IV, pp. 270-71; *Official History of the Indian Armed Forces In the Second World War 1939-1945, The Reconquest of Burma, Volume II*, New Delhi, Orient Longmans, 1954, p. 295.
76. Kirby, Volume IV, p. 270; *Official History of the Indian Armed Forces*, pp. 296-300.; "Missions in Support of IV Corps."
77. *Official History of the Indian Armed Forces*, p.301.
78. "Missions in Support of IV Corps."
79. Slim, p. 452.
80. Unit History, 6th Fighter Squadron (Commando), February 1945.
81. Kirby, Volume IV, pp. 283-84; Allen, pp. 442-44.
82. "Missions in Support of IV Corps."
83. "Missions in Support of IV Corps;" Unit History, 5th and 6th Fighter Squadrons (Commando), March 1945.
84. *Campaigns in the Far East, Volume IV*, pp. 372-75.
85. Craven and Cate, Volume V, pp. 268-69; Probert, p. 248; Unit History, 5th Fighter Squadron (Commando), March 1945.
86. Kirby, Volume IV, pp. 297-98; Air 24/1291, "Daily Operational Summaries, February-March 1945;" *Campaigns in the Far East, Volume IV*, p. 376; Unit History, 5th and 6th Fighter Squadrons (Commando), March 1945.
87. Air 24/1291, "Daily Operational Summaries;" Unit History, 5th and 6th Fighter Squadrons (Commando), March 1945.
88. Ibid.
89. Kirby, Volume IV, pp. 309-13.
90. Ibid. pp. 321-31.
91. *Campaigns in the Far East, Volume IV,* pp. 376-78, 381-82; Unit History, 5th and 6th Fighter Squadron (Commando), April 1945.
92. "Missions in Support of IV Corps."
93. Kirby, Volume IV, pp. 384-93; Unit History, 5th and 6th Fighter Squadrons (Commando), April 1945.
94. Kirby, Volume IV, pp. 393-95; Unit History, 5th and 6th Fighter Squadrons (Commando), May 1945.
95. Probert, pp. 276-77.
96. Lieutenant Colonel K.K. Golledge, Asst. Actg. Gen., to Commanding General, Army Air Forces, 17 March 1945, "Reorganization of Air Commando & Combat Cargo Units," AC/AS, Plans, 1st Air Commando Force and Combat Cargo Groups organization and redeployment correspondence and memoranda, 1943-45, 145.81-170 in USAF Collection, USAFHRC.

CHAPTER 4

1. Taylor, Dr. Joe G.: *Air Supply in the Burma Campaigns, USAF Historical Studies No. 75,* USAF Historical Division, Research Studies Institute, Air University, 1957, pp. 1, 132; Air Chief Marshal Sir Keith Park, "Report on Air Operations June 1944-May 1945," London Gazette, 6 April 1951, No. 39196, p. 1970.
2. Park, "Report on Air Operations," p. 1970.
3. Unit History, 2nd Air Commando Group, History of the 2nd Air Commando Group, May 1944-November 1945, "Headquarters Organization and Administration," GP-A-CMDO-2-HI, in USAF Collection, USAFHRC.
4. General H.H. Arnold, Commanding General, Army Air Forces, to General George Marshall, Chief of Staff, 1 April 1944, in AC/AS, Plans, 1st Air Commando Force and Combat Cargo Groups organization and redeployment correspondence and memoranda, 1943-45, 145.80-170, in USAF Collection, USAFHRC.
5. Interview with W.R. Eason, personal possession; Unit History, 2nd Air Commando Group, May 1944.
6. Unit History, 1st and 2nd Fighter Squadrons (Commando), 2nd Air Commando Group, May 1944-November 1945, SQ-FI-CMDO-1/2-HI, in USAF Collection, USAFHRC, May 1944.
7. Ibid.
8. Unit History, 2nd Air Commando Group, June 1944; Craven and Cate, Volume V, pp. 208, 334.
9. Unit History, 2nd Air Commando Group, July 1944.
10. Unit History, 1st and 2nd Fighter Squadrons (Commando), July-August 1944; 2nd Air Commando Group, July-August 1944.
11. World War II Air Commandos Association*: World War II Air Commandos, Volume II*, pp. 7-8.
12. Unit History, 1st and 2nd Fighter Squadrons (Commando), January 1945.
13. Unit History, 2nd Fighter Squadron (Commando), February 1945; 2nd Air Commando Group, February 1945.
14. Kirby, Volume IV, pp. 181-82*; Campaigns in the Far East, Volume IV*, p. 368; Unit History, 2nd Air Commando Group, February 1945.
15. Interview with Kevin Mallen, 8 November 1945, in possession of the author.
16. Air 24/1291, "Daily Operational Summaries, February-March 1945."
17. Ibid.
18. *World War II Air Commandos, Volume II*, p. 19.
19. Air 24/1311, Air Command, South East Asia, Intelligence, "Weekly Intelligence Summary, No. 66," 18th February 1945, No. 67, 25th February 1945, P.R.O.; Air 24/1291.
20. *World War II Air Commandos, Volume II*, pp. 21-22.
21. Unit History, 1st and 2nd Fighter Squadrons (Commando), February 1945.
22. Air 24/1291.
23. Major General George Stratemeyer, to A.O.C. 224 Group RAF et al., 1 March 1945, in Unit History, 2nd Air Commando Group, March 1945.
24. Kirby, Volume IV, Appendix 17; *Campaigns in the Far East, Volume IV*, Appendix 30.
25. Izawa, p. 14; Eastern Air Command, "Weekly Intelligence Summary, No. 23," 2 February 1945, No. 24, 9 February 1945, No. 25, 16 February 1945.

26. Ibid.; Air 24/1312, Weekly Intelligence Summary, No. 69, 11 March 1945.
27. Ibid.
28. Slim, pp. 397, 438.
29. Interrogation of Major General Morimoto, Interrogation of Japanese Army Air Force Officers on why the Japanese Army Air Force was defeated, WO 106/5845, P.R.O.
30. Interview with W.R. Eason, in personal possession of the author; Unit History, 1st and 2nd Fighter Squadrons (Commando), March 1945; 2nd Air Commando Group, March 1945.
31. Ibid.; Izawa, p. 14.
32. Eastern Air Command, Weekly Intelligence Summary, No. 25, 16 February 1945, No. 28, 9 March 1945;
33. Interview with Kevin Mallen.
34. Ibid.; Unit History, 2nd Air Commando Group, March 1945.
35. Interview with W.R. Eason; "Narrative of Account of Strike Against Don Muang," in Unit History, 2nd Air Commando Group.
36. Ibid.
37. Interview with W. R. Eason; Letter from William Gadow to the author, 3 September 1985; Letters from W.R. Eason to the author, 20 August 1985 and 15 April 1991; Letter from Hadley Dixon to the author, 14 August 1985.
38. Hadley Dixon to the author; Combat reports of Lieutenant Colonel Levi Chase and Lieutenant Hadley Dixon, and "Enemy Game Bag," in Unit History, 2nd Air Commando Group.
39. W.R. Eason to the author, 6 August 1991, personal possession.
40. Unit History, 1st Fighter Squadron (Commando), March 1945; W.R. Eason to the author, 6 August 1991; World War II Air Commando Association Newsletter December 1991.
41. Bob Spann to the author, 9 August 1991, personal possession. Combat report of Lieutenant Bob Spann, in Unit History, 2nd Air Commando Group.
42. Spann to the author, 9 August 1991.
43. "Enemy Game Bag," various combat reports, in Unit History, 2nd Air Commando Group.
44. Eason to the author, 6 August 1991; combat reports in Unit History, 2nd Air Commando Group.
45. Eason to the author, 20 August 1985, August 6, 1991; Mallen interview.
46. "Enemy Game Bag," Unit History, 2nd Air Commando Group, March 1945; Eastern Air Command, Weekly Intelligence Summary, No. 30, 23 March 1945, No. 31, 30 March 1945.
47. 2nd Air Commando Group, History of Operations,1945, copy in possession of the author.
48. Interview with W.R. Eason; "Enemy Game Bag."
49. Combat Report from Captain Edward Atha, "Enemy Game Bag."
50. Unit History, 1st Fighter Squadron (Commando), March 1945.
51. Unit History, 1st and 2nd Fighter Squadrons (Commando), March 1945.
52. Ibid.; Eason to the author, 20 August 1985.
53. Hata, Ikuhiko, and Izawa, Yasuho:(*Japanese Army Fighter Units and Aces Biographies, New Revised Edition*), Tokyo 1984, pp. 180-182; Kasuya, Yoshio: *Kato Hayabusa Sentotai No Saigo (Last Days of the Kato Hayabusa Fighter Unit*), Tokyo 1970, p. 259; Combat Reports of Lieutenant Colonel Levi Chase, Lieutenant Bob Spann, Lieutenant Harold Hettema; "Enemy Game Bag."
54. *World War II Air Commandos, Volume II*, p. 25; Air 24/1316, "Weekly Intelligence Summary, No. 80," 27 May 1945.
55. *World War II Air Commandos, Volume II*, p. 25-26.
56. Ibid. p. 27.
57. Ibid. p. 25; Interview with W.R. Eason.
58. "Weekly Intelligence Summary, No. 80," 27 May 1945.
59. *World War II Air Commandos, Volume II*, p. 26.
60. Unit History, 2nd Fighter Squadron (Commando), March 1945; 2nd Air Commando Group, History of Operations.
61. Air 24/1312, Review of Enemy Air Activity During March 1945, P.R.O.; Eastern Air Command, "Weekly Intelligence Summary, No. 30," 23 March 1945, No. 31, 30 March 1945.
62. Air 24/1313, Review of Enemy Air Activity During April 1945, P.R.O.; Air 25/457, "Estimate Of Japanese Air Activity And Bases From Which It Might Be Supported," 16 April 1945; Izawa, P.14.
63. Unit History, 1st and 2nd Fighter Squadrons (Commando), April 1945.
64. Ibid.; Unit History, 2nd Air Commando Group, April 1945; Eastern Air Command, "Weekly Intelligence Summary, No. 32," 6 April 1945, No. 33, 13 April 1945; Eason interview.
65. *World War II Air Commandos, Volume II*, p. 32.
66. Ibid.; Unit History, 1st and 2nd Fighter Squadrons (Commando), April 1945; Eason to the author, 6 August 1991.
67. Unit History, 2nd Fighter Squadron (Commando), April 1945; Eason to the author, 6 August 1991.
68. *World War II Air Commandos, Volume II*, pp. 31-33.
69. Unit History, 2nd Air Commando Group, April 1945.
70.. *World War II Air Commandos, Volume II*, p. 15.
71. Unit History, 1st Fighter Squadron (Commando), April 1945; W.R. Eason to the author, 15 August 1993, personal possession.
72. Unit History, 1st and 2nd Fighter Squadrons (Commando), April 1945; 2nd Air Commando Group, April 1945; *Campaigns in the Far East, Volume IV*, pp. 383-84.
73. World War II Air Commandos Association, *World War II Air Commandos: Photo Supplement to Volumes I and II*, p. 27.
74. *World War II Air Commandos, Volume II*, p. 30.
75. Ibid.; Unit History, 1st Fighter Squadron (Commando), April 1945.
76. Air 24/1292, "Daily Operational Summaries;" Eastern Air Command, "Weekly Intelligence Summaries, No. 36," 4 May 1945; Unit History, 1st Fighter Squadron (Commando), April 1945.
77. Unit History, 2nd Fighter Squadron (Commando), April 1945; 2nd Air Commando Group, April 1945.
78. Kirby, Volume IV, p. 394; Unit History, 2nd Air Commando Group, May 1945.
79. Kirby, Volume IV, pp. 395-97.
80. World War II Air Commandos, Volume II, p. 34.
81. Unit History, 1st and 2nd Fighter Squadrons (Commando), May-June 1945; 2nd Air Commando Group, May-June 1945.

CHAPTER 5

1. Unit History, 3rd and 4th Fighter Squadrons (Commando), 3rd Air Commando Group, May 1944-January 1946, SQ-FI-CMDO-3/4-HI, USAF Collection, USAFHRC.
2. Ibid.; Unit History, 3rd Air Commando Group, May 1944-January 1945, GP-A-CMDO-3-HI, USAF Collection, USAFHRC.
3. Unit History, 3rd and 4th Fighter Squadrons (Commando), June-July 1944; World War II Air Commandos Association: *History of the World War II Air Commandos*, Dallas, Taylor Publishing Company, 1989, pp. 91-92, 94-95, 98.
4. Unit History, 3rd and 4th Fighter Squadrons (Commando), August-September 1944.
5. Craven and Cate, Volume V, pp. 281-84, 341-42; Unit History, 3rd and 4th Fighter Squadrons (Commando), 3rd Air Commando Group, October-December 1944; *History of the World War II Air Commandos*, p. 95
6. Ibid.
7. Craven and Cate, Volume V, pp. 373-74, 83-86.
8. Lieutenant Colonel Donald W. Maggert (Ret'd), "The Air Commandos," World War II Air Commando Association Newsletter, November 1994.
9. Smith, Robert Ross: *United States Army in World War II: The War in the Pacific: Triumph in the Philippines*, Washington, D.C., Center of Military History, 1984, pp. 29-30.
10. Ibid. pp. 90-91.
11. Ibid. p. 94.
12. Craven and Cate, Volume V, pp. 405, 416-18; Unit History, History of V Fighter Command, Chapter 5 (January-March 1945), 731.01, USAF Collection, USAFHRC, pp. 4-6.
13. Unit History, "History of the 3rd Air Commando Group Since Arrival in this Theater," 3rd Air Commando Group, undated; 3rd and 4th Fighter Squadrons (Commando), December 1944-January 1945; *History of the World War II Air Commandos*, p. 98.
14. Ibid.
15. Unit History, 3rd Fighter Squadron (Commando), January 1945.
16. Unit History, V Fighter Command, A-2 Summary, No. 14, 14 Janu-

ary, 1945, 730.607, USAF Collection, USAFHRC.
17. V Fighter Command, A-2 Summary, No. 15, 15 January 1945; Unit History, 3rd Fighter Squadron (Commando), January 1945.
18. V Fighter Command, A-2 Summary, No. 17, 17 January 1945; Unit History, 3rd Fighter Squadron (Commando), January 1945.
19. V Fighter Command, A-2 Summary, No. 16, 16 January 1945; Unit History, 3rd Fighter Squadron (Commando), January 1945.
20. V Fighter Command, A-2 Summary, No. 19, 19 January 1945; Interview with Ray Lahmeyer, 14 October 1995, personal possession.
21. History of V Fighter Command, Chapter 5, pp. 4-20; Unit History, 3rd Air Commando Group, January 1945.
22. Unit History, 3rd and 4th Fighter Squadrons (Commando), January 1945; Interview with Vincent Clark, 11 March 1996, personal possession.
23. Smith, Chapters X, XI.
24. Smith, p. 235.
25. History of V Fighter Command, Chapter 5, p. 12; Unit History, 4th Fighter Squadron (Commando), January 1945.
26. Smith, pp. 94-101, 450-52.
27. Ibid. p. 469.
28. Ibid. p. 498.
29. Ibid. p. 497.
30. Ibid. pp. 463-65.
31. History of V Fighter Command, Chapter 5, pp. 29-30; Taylor, Joe Gray: "American Experience in the Southwest Pacific," Cooling, Benjamin Franklin, ed.: *Case Studies in the Development of Close Air Support*, Washington, D.C., Office of Air Force History, 1990, pp. 325-27; *History of the World War II Air Commandos*, p. 107.
32. Interview with Jacques Young, 14 October 1995, personal possession.
33. Ibid.
34. Smith, pp. 459-61, 471, 491-93.
35. V Fighter Command, *Weekly Intelligence Review*, 10/11, 20/21 March 1945, 730.607, USAF Collection, USAFHRC; Unit History, 3rd and 4th Fighter Squadrons (Commando), March 1945.
36. "History of the 3rd Air Commando Group Since Arrival in this Theater;" Unit History, 3rd Fighter Squadron (Commando), March 1945; 3rd Air Commando Group, March 1945.
37. History of V Fighter Command, Chapter 5, V Fighter Command Statistics for March 1945.
38. Lahmeyer interview.
39. Craven and Cate, Volume V, pp. 470-71, 479.
40. Ibid. pp. 470-71.
41. History of V Fighter Command, Chapter 5, p. 51; Maggert; Unit History, 4th Fighter Squadron (Commando), May 1945.
42. Unit History, 3rd and 4th Fighter Squadrons (Commando), February 1945.
43. Unit History, 3rd and 4th Fighter Squadrons (Commando), February 1945; V Fighter Command, A-2 Summary, 11 February 1945.
44. Lacroix, Robert: "A Yank for Good Measure," *World War II Air Commandos, Volume II*, p. 107.
45. Ibid.; *History of World War II Air Commandos*, p. 100; Unit History, 4th Fighter Squadron (Commando), February 1945.
46. Unit History, 4th Fighter Squadron (Commando), February 1945.
47. Bower, Elder: "Formosa on the American Plan," *World War II Air Commandos, Volume II*, pp. 103-104.
48. Unit History, 4th Fighter Squadron (Commando), February 1945.
49. Unit History, 3rd Fighter Squadron (Commando), February 1945; V Fighter Command, *Weekly Intelligence Review*, 25/26 February 1945.
50. Unit History, 3rd and 4th Fighter Squadrons (Commando), March-April 1945; V Fighter Command, *Weekly Intelligence Review*, March-April 1945.
51. Unit History, 3rd Air Commando Group, March 1945.
52. Mahurin, Walker: *Honest John*, New York, G.P. Putnam's Sons, 1962, p. 160.
53. Unit History, 3rd Fighter Squadron (Commando), April 1945; 3rd Air Commando Group; Interview with Joe Singletary, 9 September, 14 October 1995, personal possession.
54. Unit History, 308th Bombardment Wing (H), 1 January- 28 May 1945, USAF Collection, USAFHRC, pp. 37-38.
55. *History of the World War II Air Commandos*, pp.114-19; Unit History, 3rd Air Commando Group, April 1945.
56. Unit History, 3rd and 4th Fighter Squadrons (Commando), April 1945.
57. Unit History, 3rd Fighter Squadron (Commando), April 1945.
58. Craven and Cate, Volume V, pp. 479-80.
59. V Fighter Command, *Weekly Intelligence Review*, April 1945.
60. V Fighter Command, *Weekly Intelligence Review*, May 1945; Unit History, 3rd and 4th Fighter Squadrons (Commando), May 1945.
61. Unit History, 3rd and 4th Fighter Squadrons (Commando), May 1945.
62. Unit History, 4th Fighter Squadron (Commando), May 1945; *World War II Air Commandos, Volume II*, pp. 105-6.
63. Unit History, 4th Fighter Squadron (Commando), June 1945.
64. Unit History, 3rd Fighter Squadron (Commando), June 1945.
65. History of V Fighter Command, Chapter 6, 1 April- 2 September 1945, V Fighter Command Statistics for May, June 1945.
66. Smith, pp. 504-37, 558-67.
67. Unit History, 3rd Fighter Squadron (Commando), June 1945; 3rd Air Commando Group, June 1945.
68. Unit History, 3rd and 4th Fighter Squadrons (Commando), June 1945; Lahmeyer interview.
69. History of V Fighter Command, Chapter 6; Unit History, 3rd and 4th Fighter Squadrons (Commando), July 1945.
70. Unit History, 3rd Air Commando Group, July-August 1945.
71. Unit History, 3rd Air Commando Group, September 1945-March 1946.

AIR COMMANDO ALBUM

A well-known photo of Major Robert Petit flying his P-51A, MRS. VIRGINIA, with 2nd Lt. A.R. Van De Weghe flying Colonel Cochran's P-51A behind. While he was on Guadalcanal Petit flew a P-38 named MISS VIRGINIA, named after his then girlfriend. On his return to the U.S. he and his girlfriend were married, and when he returned to combat his airplane reflected the change in their relationship! (Courtesy Thomas Y'Blood, Office of Air Force History)

Lieutenant Colonel Mahony and other Fighter Section pilots leaving the operations basha after the mission to Anisakan, 8 March 1944. (Courtesy A.R. Van De Weghe)

In mid-April the Fighter Section received a batch of P-51Bs as replacements for the P-51As lost in combat. The nearer P-51B was named JUNGLE JOLLY. (Courtesy A.R. Van De Weghe)

P-51B JUNGLE JOLLY following a landing accident at Asansol. (Courtesy William Burghardt).

Captain Olin Carter, commander of the 6th Fighter Squadron, and Albert Piester, his crew chief, with Carter's Thunderbolt LITTLE KITTEN II, in which he destroyed two Oscars and a Dinah on the ground during the 18 and 20 October missions to Rangoon. (Courtesy Olin Carter)

1st Lieutenant "Moon" Mullins, 5th Fighter Squadron, who damaged an Oscar in the air battle over Mingaladon on 20 October. Taken after the October raids when the 5th and 6th Fighter Squadrons were painting theater and squadron markings on their aircraft. The 5th Fighter Squadron painted plane numbers under the cockpit while the 6th Fighter Squadron painted their numbers in the blue band on the tail. Mullins' Thunderbolt was number 19. (Courtesy 1st Air Commando Association)

A 1st Air Commando Group B-25 that the 5th and 6th Fighter Squadrons sometimes used as a squadron "hack." (Courtesy 1st Air Commando Association)

Loading 500 lb. bombs on a 1st Squadron Mustang before the first combat mission on 14 February 1945. (Courtesy World War II Air Commandos Association)

The 1st Fighter Squadron's senior Line and Flight Chiefs. These men, who had years of experience on fighter aircraft, and the individual crew chiefs and armorers, were exceptionally dedicated and compiled an excellent record for serviceability. Rear Row (L-R): Master Sergeant Wilson Wendt, Technical Sergeant Paul Milhoan, Technical Sergeant Crites, Technical Sergeant Ernest Edens; *Front Row* (L-R): Technical Sergeant Rumsey Evans, Technical Sergeant William O'Keefe, Technical Sergeant George Sapp, Master Sergeant David Stiles. M/Sgt Wendt had just been awarded a Legion of Merit in recognition of his contribution to the success of the squadron. (W W II Air Commandos Association)

Pilots chose a wide variety of names for their aircraft. Lieutenant William Wilson chose to name his Mustang NOONER. (Courtesy World War II Air Commandos Association)

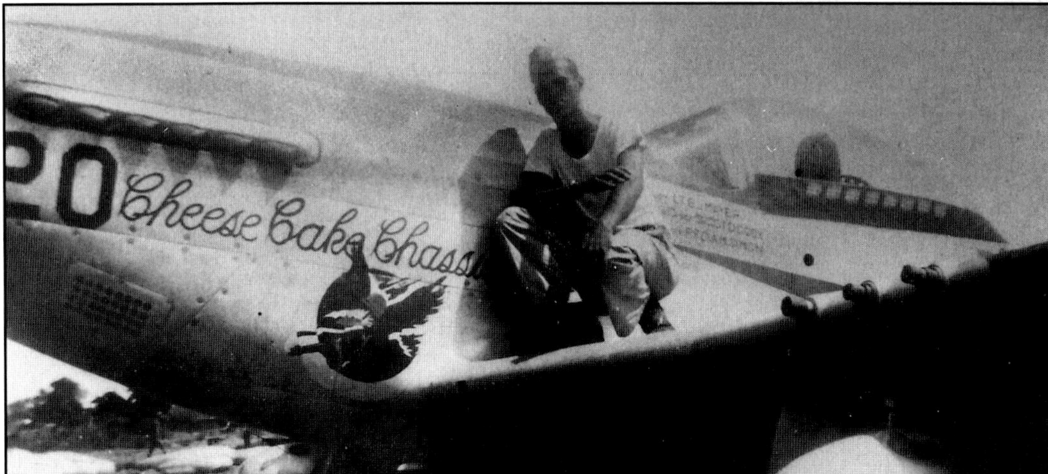

The 2nd Fighter Squadron adopted an emblem of a diving eagle with a dagger in its beak and a Tommy gun in its claws. Several pilots painted the emblem on their airplanes. Lieutenant Bonnie Mayer named his plane CHEESE CAKE CHASSIE. (Courtesy B.J. Maye)

The 1st Fighter Squadron in early April 1945. Back Row (L-R): Harold Hettema, John Maher, McGinnis Clark, William Holman, James Mason, Hadley Dixon, Benjamin Lundberg, Richard Fishburn, John McClennahan, William Nash; Middle Row (L-R): Don Branyan (Engineering Officer), Bert Lutton, Malcolm Mackenzie, Herman Lyons, Robert Cason, Dale Grastorf, John Hannah, Frank Hefner, Edwin Harkins; Front Row (L-R):George Dent (Adjutant), W.R. Eason, William Marshall, William Buxton (C.O.), Ed Booth (Flight Surgeon), William Gadow, Roger Morrison. (Courtesy World War II Air Commandos Association)

A pilot and crew chief in conversation shortly before takeoff for Thailand. Note the sandwiches next to the gun sight. Other pilots took candy bars and thermoses of coffee or canteens. (Courtesy World War II Air Commandos Association)

Lt. McMullen, 4th Fighter Squadron, stands on the wing of PILOT'S HEAVEN, equipped with long-range tanks for missions to Formosa or the China coast. (Courtesy Ray Van Order)

Lt. Herbert "Hap" Arnold, right, with his crew in front of their P-51D Mustang, HAP HAP HAPPY, at Mangaldan, March 1945. (Courtesy Rex Pealer)

Some of the 4th Fighter Squadron's ground crew with GYPSY at Mangaldan. Bottom (L-R) Mauro, Gill, Van Order; Middle (L-R) Stager, Kerl, Starbeck, Withers, Kinney; Top: (L-R) Hand, Lee, Banano, Goodwin. (Courtesy Ray Van Order)

Compared to their Luzon digs, pilots lived in relative splendor in Japan as seen in this view of the Chitose officer's dining room. Note the P-51 mural.

A replacement pilot pranged Colonel Mahurin's Mustang near Chitose. (Courtesy USAF Museum)

INDEX OF INDIVIDUALS